11/10

Dear Josephine,

Blessings and peace!

Fr. Robert B. Repenning

By My Side: The Tikrit Diaries
by Robert B. Repenning

Printed in the United States of America

Revised edition 2009

ISBN 978-0-557-22570-5

For my uncle, Marion "Michael" Wyatt
"You will never be alone."

By My Side: The Tikrit Diaries

Preface

Not too long ago, I was at a restaurant. I had just stepped outside, and simultaneously, an 18-wheeler truck put on its Jake Brake, no more than thirty feet away from me. My heart practically exploded right there. Bullet moment. The fuse was lit and two thoughts raced into my skull; the chopper was here and/or I was being shot at by a .50 cal machine gun. Instantaneously, rationality was gone, I was rendered breathless, and rationality returned. My Iraq was perfectly crystallized in that moment.

I say my Iraq because, as some unsung philosopher of this war has said, and is often repeated, everyone has his or her own Iraq. My Iraq was a psychological funhouse in which regular people were forced to endure history, lunacy, a taunting specter of military expertise and an apparition of purpose, all while languishing in infernal heat, the "cradle of civilization" repeatedly facing an enemy that was haphazard, barbaric, and markedly effeminate.

For most of 2005, I whiled and worked away the days in a land of hopeless jeopardy, in the midst of conflicts, serving as an Army Chaplain. Inspired by Henry Rollins and his book "Smile, You're Traveling," I journaled the experience. I wish it were less argumentative, more pious, a tad more inspiring, and something that could paint me in an ideal flattering light. Instead, though, I was immersed in the discipline of writing something practically everyday. In addition to the writing, I chose to write in a public arena, on a web log. If you are not familiar with the term, a web log or a blog is an on-line journal that people can write on and others can read and comment on.

The blog was my forum to not only journal but to engage others; I told stories, shared experiences, raged against the machine, offered some spiritual meditations and let a very politically heated issue, the war, have a human face. My face. This ensured that my journal was not a purely solipsistic exercise that would only be read and forgotten by me. It became something bigger than me. The blog was written in real time, on location, without the luxury of much reflection.

This, what you hold in your hands right now, is the print copy of the blog that I would post each day on the Internet. Each day, I would go to one of the MWR (Morale Welfare Recreation) Facilities wherever I was that day. Sometimes they were only a room or a small building and sometimes they occupied an entire Palace. Depending on the size there might be a gym or a phone center or a computer center. Many times, I would be writing in room with about fifty or so other soldiers sitting at our respective computers for a set time limit typing furiously away. I'd fire off some e-mail and then on to the blog.

I would sit at the computer for twenty minutes or so and just write as much as I could. My energy level, the days events, my state of mind, the news of the day, or something that grabbed my attention that day, or just to say "all is well" (which was my delicate coded way of quoting Monty Python: "I'm not dead yet") all influenced what I would choose to write about. I also needed to juggle the time constraint, operational security (OPSEC), and the emotional well being of loved ones while composing the daily entry.

In the interest of fidelity to that which was already written in the blog, I have attempted to maintain as much consistency as possible between the electronic text and the printed text. I also included the songs that I was either thinking about while writing the entries or that I was listening to while writing the entries. I definitely encourage you to purchase the songs if you don't have them and enjoy the suggested soundtrack.

I have omitted some material, where permissions were not possible, or where my mental diversions even were confusing to me, or when my politics felt a bit too divisive. Also, as I was writing, the entries are filled with digressions and parenthetical sub-references, as well as many where my love of puns, humor, and wordplay just violate the standards of proper English usage to an extreme so I tweaked some entries, corrected misspellings and tried to straighten up instances of poor syntax. Finally, there are few minor additions not originally presented in the blog, which appear in this text italicized.

Before beginning, I wish to thank, in a special way a very brave American, my Mom. I also thank my family and friends who held me up with their prayers and thoughts and for all the love and outpouring of support they gave me. And last but certainly not least, I am grateful to God for His abiding presence "by my side."

Robert B. Repenning
Fishkill, New York
December 4, 2009

1

FORT DRUM TO KUWAIT

4 SEP 04 15:55 Home Sweet Home

The 4th of September. Yesterday was graduation from the Chaplain Officer Basic Course (CHOBC) down at Fort Jackson, South Carolina. Six years ago I started there, took a six year break and now I have finally finished. Wow! There are still some loose ends to tie regarding paperwork before I know the next step in the deployment process. As news comes in, I will provide updates. Also, glad to see this is working, and to hear from some familiar faces. Within the next few days I will update the contact information regarding e-mail, so if one has a message they don't wish to post for everyone to read they can leave the message with me. All my best to everyone! I hope you all are doing well, and that you had a great summer. Bye for now, Fr. Rob

9 SEP 04 14:41 Federally recognized!

Yesterday, I received notification that I am federally recognized as a Chaplain in the U.S. Army National Guard. Prior to that, my official title was a Chaplain Candidate. I am still waiting for a report date but am keeping busy with chores at home, and hanging out with my cats Cee Cee, Smokey, and Sportie. Bye for now, Fr. Robert.

29 SEP 04 19:07 The Longest Farewell in the History of Farewells

Hola! Well the orders have arrived and I report to Fort Drum this Saturday, thus bringing to a conclusion one of the longest farewells in the history of farewells. With a certain degree of nervousness I approach this, but I am confident that all the training will now fall into place. This blog will be updated and in the next few weeks I will be adding a couple of links. A direct link to my e-mail will be added for the brave navigators of this virtual world. Also, I will be adding a photo gallery to provide a more multi-dimensional experience. Bye for now, Fr. Rob

15 OCT 04 11:16 Beating the Drum (I love the pun)

So, I am training and things are going well. Am meeting most of the folks I will be working and living with for the next year. A week ago, my arms played pincushions to the various and sundry inoculations and whatnots necessary for foreign living. Training is neat, too, learning new things and reviewing previously learned skills i.e. using a compass and azimuth and a map (imagine that a man needing a map, ha!). In a few days, I say bye bye to my green camouflage uniforms and begin wearing my desert camouflage uniforms (DCUs). I think beige is a much more palatable color for the fall than the greens anyway. Oh, and I almost forgot -the food! All you veterans and prior service and marines (cause one is never a former Marine) the food is actually pretty good. Granted I had Sukiyaki three times this week, I have to admit it is pretty good. MREs (don't even ask me what that stands for, but that's the Army Rations) are really pretty neat, too. I have a weakness for any food that you can eat cold, warm or hot. Sometimes they include a powdered strawberry shake, which needs only water to be added and contains about as many calories as a Girl Scout cookie (about 2 million calories, ha).

Finally, last Saturday night, I said my first official Mass as an Army Chaplain. The congregation was a grand total of one (so we just slid under that "Where two or three are gathered" bit. Sunday morning 11:00, Mass is scheduled to begin nobody is there. 11:05 nobody. 11:10 nobody. 11:15

now I'm starting to take it personal. 11:20 I put the collection basket away. 11:25 still nobody so I close up shop, so to speak. I should add that most people were on weekend leave. However, that evening, 19:00 or 7:00pm for regular folks, I said Mass for a unit scheduled to deploy, the homily I wrote finally was heard by more than one person! It was a great Mass, about twenty folks of a variety of rank who interestingly enough brought (because its a training environment) their rifles with them. Truly a new and interesting experience. Well, there you have it, a few days in the life.

Hope you all are well. Please be assured of my prayers.

Just a side thought, but as you pray for our soldiers and their families, I'd ask that you also pray for the enemies of our nation and specifically that they may be touched by God and that they may undergo a conversion of the heart and embrace the love of God and neighbor. As a Catholic I believe that no one is beyond redemption. Wouldn't it be great that our enemies would lay down their weapons and adopt peace? It might sound beyond comprehension, but miracles can happen, all we have to do is have faith, be open to the limitless possibilities of God's power, and put aside the cynicism of the world. Polly Annish? No. I'm just being a realist; perhaps we also might need to liberate God from the limits we impose on him. With God there is nothing impossible.

Incidentally, one of my roommates calls me Chappy. Yes, you heard me correctly. I am 31 years old and I have two roommates. Having said that. Bye for now, Chappy

16 OCT 04 17:42 Absentee ballot

Well yesterday was Election Day for me. So many choices. Luckily we don't live in Florida. Voting here is simple. My public service message for all you eligible voters is this: Do the right thing. Make sure on Election Day you vote. This is not a time for slackers. As many of you know I am a political beast but if you want me to tell you who to vote for, you're barking up the wrong tree. What a strange expression. Barking up the wrong tree. Bark/tree. Wouldn't it be the wrong bark?

This evening, I said Mass for some soldiers ho are heading to Baghdad within the next few months. Granted it's a little anonymous, but I'd ask that you include them in your prayers. God will know which ones you mean. If you have been in tune with the news you may know, Baghdad has been getting hit with homicide bombings and these folks and their families are understandably filled with consternation. They can use all the prayers they can get. God knows they'll need them so that they can keep their morale up, go and do their mission and get back home safely.

Me? I am doing well. Life is good. Had a chance to get home, and am blessed with another opportunity soon for a day or two. I have my classes to go to, and I am learning a lot. As you can see I am also a little punchy which means one thing. This little soldier's pajamas are calling (quietly so as to not alert the enemy and their pajamas). Good night, Chappy

27 OCT 04 19:34 Waiting

Still waiting...Nothing much to say than that. Today I completed my training. Learned how to use the radio today. No, not the FM radio. Bye for now, Chappy

30 OCT 04 20:25 Short of stature

Well dear friends, the wait is far from over. The word for us is no word except wait. In the meanwhile, things have been interesting. I received my validation, meaning I am ready and trained for deployment. If you heard anything about anthrax shots being put on hold for the time being, know that it has directly affected me. Just the other day I was going to get one of my anthrax shots and behold it has been delayed. Those of us who have the shots sure appreciate the reprieve. Imagine the feeling of a warm golf ball in the center of you arm for about a week and that comes close to how it feels.

Now you might ask, what is this about short of stature? I am referring to the Gospel for this Sunday, silly. Back in college, this Gospel was the ammunition I needed to get back at my best friend, Joe (Happy Birthday belated) who was teasing me one day. Coincidentally, just before dinner we had been at Mass and the story of Zacchaeus was proclaimed. Now if you can imagine this, Joe was/is shorter than me. I forgot what Joe said to me at dinner, but I immediately flashed a sensitive German face at him and addressed him as Zacchaeus.

Little did I know that I was secretly giving Joe a compliment. Our man Zacchaeus is most definitely a role model for us, whereas, the crowd grumbles at Jesus talking and dining with a sinner. Zacchaeus shows us how we should really act in the presence of Jesus. He climbs the tree, doing what he can to see Jesus. Hopefully, the sycamore trees were not as tall as on Clinton Street (which now that the leaves have fallen, will return to my favor as my favorite trees in the Northeast), but he makes the effort to see Jesus. Which leaves (no pun intended) us with the question we should ask, "Are we grumblers, or tree climbers?" If you are like me you probably are a grumbler from time to time. Maybe Zacchaeus was too. But we are called to be tree climbers.

Monday is All Saints Day, the perfect time to ask our saints for help. As we honor their achievements, we might want to ask them to assist us with their prayers to rise above the din of grumblers, to recall we too are like Zacchaeus (not finished products or saints yet) and to strive to be transformed. GOD DESIRES US TO BE SAINTS! He desires to dine with us and to be with us, and for us to enjoy being in His presence, enjoying his hospitality, not just for one meal or a few meals but for all eternity in the heavenly banquet. Remember as you pray for the people you love also pray for our enemies. By the way, thanks for your prayers and love and goodwill, it keeps me sane. May God be with us all.

30 OCT 04 20:49 World Series

For the record, congratulations to Boston. They finally broke the Bambino's curse. And they also managed not to burn down their city celebrating. I know somewhere Fr. Des and Bob Shea are smiling. Which reminds me of the time, while visiting classes at St. Mary's when I, not intentionally, mocked Bob's son for being a Red Sox fan in front of his entire class. Mea culpa and good night. Fr. Rob

2 NOV 04 11:41 Election Day Part Deux

Congratulations to my grandmother (Oma). Just the other day she filled out her absentee ballot and participated in her first ever election, since becoming American 52 years ago. This is a good proof that you are never too old to be concerned about this country and to let your voice be heard.

4 NOV 04 20:35 November Rain

Well the day started beautifully with a gorgeous sunrise and the sky big and blue and sparkling. It should be noted; today was the first day that the car windows were frosted over and in need of scraping. Later in the morning, some grey clouds snuck into the area and they invited some friends and in turn the whole mess of them invited more friends and some brought rain, and the ones that didn't bring rain felt they now had to give rain too and pretty soon there was more rain than anyone knew what to do with. And so now it is cold and rainy and the perfect night to get into pajamas, get into bed and curl up with a good book.

For the most part, life up here is good. I certainly miss being home, but at least I am still in the state. Ciao.

6 NOV 04 09:46 Friends

Thank you to all my friends. I just want you to know I am thinking about you and missing you, too.

8 NOV 04 14:15 Yesterday

Well it was very cool this weekend to have visitors. Richard Smith, Elizabeth Smith and Mom braved the four hours of highways and byways and ventured into the northern country bringing with them a fresh supply of sunshine and rainbows. They also boosted the attendance at one of my Masses by 300%.

In regards to the Gospel, Resurrection is the key. The Sadducees proposed a ridiculous little scenario with the intent of mocking the concept of resurrection. Recall their sect of Judaism did not believe in resurrection (As far as I understand Judaism has various views concerning resurrection.) From what I understand, life after death in mainstream Judaism does not have to literally mean resurrection. So for instance, in Judaism memory is a way in which one can live on after death. Therefore, having children to carry on one's name and memory is a way in which a person and their legacy can live on. (Think how radical celibacy would be/is from a Jewish perspective. I did a paper on this in the seminary.)

Memorials are another way in which those who have died can live on. (Think the Holocaust Museums and some of the varied remembrances that are offered for the victims of that horrific tragedy.) Well Jesus does work within a traditional Judaic understanding of life after death at the Last Supper when he mandates that to "do this in memory of me." But Jesus doesn't just stop there, obviously, but recall how the disciples know they have seen the risen Lord after Easter. Yes, they recognize him in the breaking of the bread. That memory brings them into a new and unexplored territory, into the Resurrection.

I confess, I sometimes make fun of the extremist Muslim perspective of resurrection, which seems obsessed with genital activity (72 virgins?). Quite a few laughs can be generated about the rewards in Paradise for one who wages jihad, however, I feel a little guilty. The concept of resurrection has been corrupted and twisted by some religious leaders to coerce them into a cause they may otherwise have not joined. But, there is a belief in resurrection, nonetheless. They are willing to throw their lives away, virtually, for this view.

What are my fellow Catholics willing to do, in light of the resurrection? Hopefully, we will never waste our lives like the homicide bomber, but rather at least be willing to give our lives in service of our brothers and sisters. Giving of our lives doesn't mean we have to die.

Giving of our lives does mean that we remember right order in living. God is first. Others (or our neighbors) are next. And then, ourselves. The caution has to be made that if we say, "Well brother or sister you have to wait till I first deal with God," we are missing the boat. God desires to be first in our life. But we shouldn't use Him as an excuse for not helping or treating our brother/sister as they ought to be treated. A perfect example is in Church, when we get annoyed with someone who may be a distraction, how often do we get angry and direct ill will toward them because they are interrupting our prayer? C'mon I feel the same way at times, but it doesn't make it right. Well I guess I may have bit off more than I can chew here, but food for thought nonetheless. Bye for now.

12 NOV 04 10:28 PT, the weather and Burt Bacharach (bad humor)

Here I am in scenic Upstate New York, where they stuff the Sunday Comics in each issue of the Sunday New York Times.

"Well Heck Vern, no sense these folks not gittin no funnies. How can they be stayin' up date on the war and all without Beatle Bailey. Heck all that Times got is words 'n more of 'em."

Well with great sadness we saw LT Simeon, our Physical Training taskmaster, and one of my roommates, leave yesterday for the sandbox. If you ask me his MOS (Military Occupational Specialty) was torture. Each morning he was in charge of our physical training and he had no problems coming up with new methods to bring pain to our muscles. Ergo the torture comment. One of his specialties is what I called Officer Assisted Suicide and what he dubbed, the more humane sounding, Partner Assisted PT. This entailed wheelbarrow pushups, crunches, sit-ups and other ways to make you wish you didn't get up early.

Captain Bowden, the Texas Longhorn Hating Okie who lives in Missouri is our new torture master. This morning I received an epiphany as he fatigued our muscles with his brutal form of PT, Physical training is a method of focusing our negative attention on our enemies. Thanks to them, we have to get up early and run 2 miles. HMMM, I wonder if the terrorists feel this way about their training?

The weather here is awful. It changes more than J Lo's or

Britney Spears' marital status. And speaking of Brit, how is that she has a greatest hits album? Furthermore, her greatest hits album was just released the same day as Neil Young. Supposedly she has more than Neil.

Also, speaking of changes, we hope that in the absence of the homicidal Norman Fell (Mr. Roper of Three's Company fame (kudos to Dennis Miller for his noting the similarities)) look-alike peace in Israel and Palestine may now be possible. Arafat was so good at being a roadblock to peace he was more like a toll collector for the Tappan Zee Bridge than a politician. If he hadn't been a terrorist, he would have fit in well with the political cholesterol in Albany. Regardless of one's political affiliation that troika is about as useless as a Britney greatest hits album.

And finally, there is no finer revenge on your PT leader than playing "(They Long to Be) Close to You" for him as we drive to PT, with that so cheesy its classic trumpet part, especially in the early morning. That is torture, Roberto style.

With all that said, a note of seriousness, please keep our Marines and soldiers in your prayers (especially those in Fallujah) and please keep their families in your prayers too. The news loves to give a one-sided view of whatever we do and will show our death toll and ignore the fact that insurgents are dying and thus will not be able to harm either our soldiers or civilians ever again. One of the great frustrations for a soldier is dealing with more than one enemy, the insurgents and the media. The media love to glorify failure and setbacks and the human loss of this conflict. But in their attempt to report the news they also, whether inadvertently or purposefully, affect our morale.

17 NOV 04 14:47 Alibi

Well the tempo is increasing...things are now

moving...packing things...getting my gear in order...ordering altar wine for a year in theater...(strictly for Mass purposes, no private stash allowed)...firing off memos...getting the show ready for the road...in the other words things are getting exciting. That's the alibi...if you have a web log you have to make time to write, I know that, but it's been crazy. On the off hours, let the hair down watching Dallas (not football) and hearing and witnessing the insane diatribes of an Oklahoma fan (my roommate, CPT Bowden) among a nation of Texas fans (football, college). As most of you know football is for the birds, everyone knows the more manly sport is karaoke. I have my own ways to counteract his football mania, last night I paid tribute to the late Russell Jones (O.D.B. Rest in Peace).

Well next week, I will be going home for a few days to celebrate Thanksgiving. This year, I will choose to rebel against my usual rebelliousness and actually have some turkey. If things get totally out of hand I may even partake of the sauce of cranberry, which has never really been on my fondness list. Tomorrow is the Army Physical Training Test, only a diagnostic test but a test nonetheless. The routine is a two mile timed run, two minutes of push ups (or is it pushes up?) and two minutes of sit ups (sits up?). The numbers to pass this time around are 39 push-ups 45 sit-ups and 17 minutes for the run. That's passing. I will once again push it out and see about raising the bar. That means no barley/oats and karaoke for this cat tonight (ah the sacrifices one must make) and also it means that I will strive for more than 60%! I will pass. Tomorrow I will aim to improve my score.

One additional note is a bit of somewhat sad news. I heard that one of my St. Mary's parishioners; Jeanette died this past weekend, at the age of 97. On her last birthday, I remember Monsignor Bellew pointing out Jeanette and announcing her birthday and that she was one of our oldest parishioners. Our faith informs the sadness with the reality that she now has encountered our Risen Lord. I learned the lesson of joy from Jeanette; she always had a smile on her face, which beautifully sums up one of our callings in this life. In Jeanette's case that joy was present, even in her quiet manner.

As folks know I can be a bit outspoken but I so admire and aspire to the ability to communicate a message in a peaceful calm manner. My grandfather, Opa, was practically a Zen master in this regard. His peace was so tangible that you could sit in a room with him and not say a word for thirty minutes or more and still feel this joyful peace. That is the sign of abiding love. A love that animates a person and other people and is a presence in and of itself. So to conclude my remarks, kudos to Jeanette for a job well done! Did these words describe someone in your life? If they are alive as we approach Thanksgiving, please tell them thank you and tell them why, and if this significant person has died make sure you still express your gratitude and also say a prayer for them. They are gifts and gifts need to be acknowledged. If these words didn't remind you of anyone, hang in there, help is on the way, just keep your eyes open and your heart open too. Bye for now.

20 NOV 04 09:11 Physical Training

That PT test the other day was not too good. Push ups 44. Good. Sit ups 55. The run 17:42. Need to shave a minute off that. Speaking of shaving, I need to shave some poundage off my Adonis-like 230 lbs.

25 NOV 04 22:59 Happy Thanksgiving!

How wonderful it is to have a holiday like Thanksgiving. How wonderful it is to feel thankful. My heart is filled with gratitude, to God, for all the blessings in my life. This Thanksgiving, the blessings I am most grateful for are my family and my friends. Thanks to all of you from my very appreciative heart.

3 DEC 04 12:56   Snow blind

Greetings and salutations! It is a beautiful and picturesque day as we at Ft. Drum welcome the first significant snow fall of the season. A gracious blanket of snow is covering our training environment outdoors, while inside the first batch of decorations are being put up. Many thanks to our decoration donors; you have brightened our otherwise drab surroundings. I moved the other day for the third time since I arrived to the bachelor officers' quarters. I don't have a room mate now, but I do have a few of the trappings of the good life. Granted I don't have my own bathroom, but at least now I can watch FOX News while I get dressed and before I go to sleep.

Hope everyone is doing well, especially all my friends at St. Mary's School and the St. Mary's Teen Group (thank you for the cards you have brightened my days and my soldiers', too.) Bye for now. Chappy

4 DEC 04 09:54   How about some good news about Iraq?

Like the old expression goes, "Tell me when I do something right." From time to time, I would feel the dispiriting effects of a media more bent on influencing opinions by manipulating facts, as opposed to reporting the facts. I would then post articles that sought to present the other side of the story. While the fact is that Operation Iraqi Freedom has not been a completely positive experience overall, the often chooses to avoid presenting stories that might offer Americans a balanced viewpoint.

This week, we continue our preparation for the Lord's birth. We will commemorate the past event at Christmas. We also look to that future event, the glorious return of Jesus. We also are made aware of the Lord's presence in our world in this present moment. Now is an important moment. As we go through the week, let's look at the moment we call now. We should ask where is Jesus, and look closely, and if we are at a loss for the answer recall the Lord's own statement, "What you do for the least of my people that you do unto me."

I know some of the people I look at as the least of His people. I am ashamed to say, my treatment of them is hardly befitting the treatment of Jesus. Jesus doesn't qualify, "Hey, I only mean the nice people, the responsible people, the well mannered, the people who smell good or look good or who are well off, yada yada yada (I suppose Jesus knows what Seinfeld is). He plainly said, "What you do for the least of my people that you do unto me."

It's all fine and good to prepare for Christmas. But it doesn't mean a hill of beans (a lot of beans in our Dining Facility (D-FAC) here at Ft. Drum) if we don't welcome Christ when He is showing up every day. He is there and present in all the people we meet each day. He is present in EVERY single one of the people we encounter each day, whether they realize it or not. Just because they don't act like Christ, sometimes, shouldn't change the way they are to treat them. Think about it. It is, though, a rather disconcerting thought. It should make us feel a little uncomfortable. It should illustrate that we are not finished products. God still has some work for us to do with Him. Lets approach that task with the same joy we will approach Christmas, eagerly and joyously.

9 DEC 04 16:32 St. Mary's Teen Group (and their big hearts!)

Well the teen group made my day today. I received a most excellent gift of home made ornaments for the Christmas Tree made by St. Mary's Teen Group, as well as some candy and candy canes and a great card. I'd like to thank them for the kind thought and the love and care that went into making the ornaments. SGT Swain is decorating the tree as we speak with the decorations. The tree is just like the ones at St. Mary's Church, simple white lights (on loan from my MOM), there is silver tinsel courtesy of Mrs. Maggiacomo and her Kindergarten class (as well as some holiday decorations, including Hanukkah decorations (Happy Hanukkah to all who are celebrating)), a Santa tree topper from an anonymous donor, and nice red white and blue with a flag motif courtesy of Susan and a whole lot of holiday spirit and cheer from my friends at Saint Mary's School. Cards were made by most of the classes, delivered to the soldiers but there were also a number addressed specifically to me. Needless to say, the sentiments of joy and kindness and love are inspiring.

In other news, my departure date is fairly certain. For security concerns the date has to remain hush hush on the cue tea until I embark on the journey. However, fear not I will be playing through the Dutchess, Putnam, Orange and Rockland area for 10 days at X-Mas time. For all you purists out there clenching your jaw like my cat does when I scratch her head, X-Mas is short hand for Christmas. XP in Greek the Kai Ro (pardon the spelling but I'm short on time here) are the first letters of Christ. The very same XP is all over our Church's reminding us of Christ. So to make a short story even longer, with that in mind, chuckle the next time you see X-Mas, the joke is on those who try to squeeze Jesus out of the season.

Well karaoke was last night, tonight Charlie Company hits the bowling alley and since I didn't injure myself last night singing last night ("Mack the Knife" by Bobby Darin, "Like A Prayer" by Madonna in the style of Metallica, and "Just a Gigolo" by David Lee Roth) I figure I'll kick out the jams and rock steady with Charlie Company and do some serious bowling.

To all music buffs check out "Seagull" if you want to hear a great song it's on the first Bad Company album. I'm listening to that, the new U2 album with the hottest song in recent memory, filled with originality and musical genius called "Love and Peace or Else" and Frampton Comes Alive II (John you rock!!!!!!!!) found that little gem in Watertown's requisite used Compact disc store, and Styx LIVE, especially "Show Me The Way" which just kicks butt, even if Tommy Shaw and gang snickered when I mentioned it to them this past June. Well, I best get going now. You all take care now, y'hear. Chappy

11 DEC 04 10:36 More Kudos

Many thanks to some gracious persons. The Smith Family inaugurated our new Battalion Reading Library and they were quickly followed by a nice selection of books by the Duke Family, as well. The Smith's also hooked me up with an Advent Wreath (which incidentally was, to best of my knowledge, sold by last year's Mother's Guild). Currently, we have most of our books loaded up and en route to the sandbox, but there are still a few books that we haven't packed up yet.

Also, I forgot to mention that I won a prize for karaoke the other night consisting of: a bucket of popcorn, KILL BILL Volume 2 and a $10 Gift Certificate.

The word of the day today for yesterday is/was joy. Talking about joy, guess what color Chappy wore at Mass yesterday? Give up? Purple. Praise the Lord there are no rose vestments up here at Fort Drum. So, I did not belly ache about wearing pink nor did I crack my usual joke about getting in touch with my feminine side. Anyway. Keep joy alive in your heart; joy means more than happiness.

18 DEC 04 10:33 S'more Kudos

More thanks to some cheering holiday spirits and a correction. First the thanks. This week I received some more decorations for our Christmas tree and a couple of nice homey decorations. Many thanks to the Fratto family. A big hit here is Santa who does the hip rotation whilst the tune Jingle Bell Rock is performed. The Commander took a liking to the cinnamon candle. And scattered about the office are a few bits of holiday cheer, Santas and angels. Also, this week we got a big box of delicious cookies and candies from the folks at MTM Pharmacy. The cookies were a big hit, and nary a crumb remains. It should be noted, however, that I was teased like a Cher's hair for a while about getting cookies (it's a military thing). And an amendment to the wreath mention a couple of entries ago. The Smiths have informed me that that particular wreath was acquired through different means than the Mother's Guild. A big congrats though to Josephine for making memorable wreaths last year. More later.

20 DEC 04 09:53 Negative Attitude

Watertown, NY. Current temperature: 15 degrees below zero, Fahrenheit. Yowzers! It is so cold right now, you can't even feel cold. Its a beyond cold feeling. Even the goose pimples say, "Later for this. Good luck with that." And they hide like the cowards they are. Yeah it's cold. Lake effect, they say. I just say real freezing cold!

24 DEC 04 11:51 Christmas Eve

Greetings to all! Merry Christmas! What a blessing to be home for Christmas! Yesterday morning, I left Fort Drum with one of my new friends, my roommate and PT torturer CPT Bowden, also known as Justin, to begin our leave. Took a different route but the torrential rain was a bit much. New York, though, is one beautiful state. (Took Route 32 down to Route 17, once near New City we stopped in picked up my Mom and headed out to Newark Airport to pick up Justin's wife Shannon and their boy Ethan). While coming down form Fort Drum we must have listened to "Aerosmith Live Bootleg!" about ten times straight. Wow, those cats were wasted!

Well now I am back in New City, my hair is grown out to about 3/4 inch and I am starting to feel like a hippie. Mom is delighted that I could be home for the holidays, as are the cats. Cee Cee, however, is a little miffed because she now has to share her room (which is mine!!!) with me.

Dr. Paul Wolfowitz visited us last week. He is the Deputy Secretary of Defense, and it was great that he could come visit us. He gave us some words of encouragement and some updates on the situation in Iraq. For a government official, I was struck by his seeming sincerity. His manner was less a bureaucratic functionary as opposed to a man capable of warmth and compassion. Although, it was an official visit it was not a stuffy affair, and his candor was well received. It was nice also, that he placed our present mission in the greater historical context of our Division.

After Dr. Wolfowitz spoke with us, I went over to the Post Chapel and assisted with Confessions. It was there that I thought how blessedly blessed Advent and preparation for Christmas can be if we allow it to be blessed and allow some room to breath in the schedule. We all definitely have room for improvement in not getting so frazzled before the holidays.

Well, hopefully the next ten days won't go so quickly. It will be good to be home, and hopefully have time to see some friends. I miss you all tremendously, especially my St. Mary's family. I miss you all, and please be assured of my prayers and best wishes and love.

So to all of you, may God's blessings be upon you, may this Holiday be one of gratitude and joy, and may the coming New Year one be a year of fulfillment and peace. Please keep me in your prayers and please keep my soldiers and all the men and women who serve our country in your prayers. I would also ask for your prayers for the soldiers and their families who can't be together this holiday season, they need our prayers so much.

As Monsignor Gillen (my Pastor back at St. Augustine's when I was a kid) says, "Have a Mary's Christmas!

28 DEC 04 16:47   E-mail to Herb

Dear Herb,

Merry Christmas, Happy New Year!!! Thank you for your excellent e-mail. I am home for a few days, which is cool considering it's the holidays plus it's also my Mom's birthday. I am rapidly approaching my departure date, and after this vacation, until the 2nd, I am looking forward to this limbo to finally conclude. I am looking forward to finally getting things moving, and to head on over. More than half of my unit is now over there and most of them I haven't even met because they were at different training places in Jersey and Louisiana.

I am with some real cool people. They are Signal soldiers, and they are the communications people over there. Almost all of them are Jerseyites, with a couple of Missourians, Californians, and three New Yorkers (myself included) to round out bunch. There are also a few isolated Kansans and Minnesotans included for garnishment. I have been quite busy but also I have been having a lot of fun, National Guard people know how to yuck it up, have fun, and get the job done all the same. Over yonder, I will be basically taking my familiar gig with me, trying to add as much joy as I can to a fairly discouraging scene.

We all have a good attitude about things, and we know we will get the job done, but we also have a lot on our minds with the loved ones we leave behind. I am looking at it as if I were on tour with a band. If Mick Jagger, at his age, can go away from home for 18 months at a time I am sure I can manage ten months to a year. The culture shock is another factor we will be dealing with, but God knows we bring enough reminders of home with us that we should be set.

I have found that I am preaching longer. More instructive with a hint of Dennis Miller in it to keep it interesting (no cussing though and a poorer vocabulary). I find it neat, teaching adults some of the basics and lament what priests are talking about in Church that things like what the wreath or advent candles or the crucifix or even scripture aren't even dealt with. When I was a kid my guys rocked and taught us so much and we felt like we had a clue what was going on. Those priests were killer. Anyway, I am enjoying sharing things about the faith and hopefully getting people interested in it again for better reasons than we are going to war.

And about that war. Please assure Emily that Father Robert will be as safe as he can be. Assure her that I will be smart and listen to what MY teachers have taught me, and listen to MY superiors and those who know what they are talking about have told me and are telling me to do. Tell her that I am going to pretend that I am 8 years old again, and listen to what is expected of me and to do what I am told, and I will do things like look both ways when I cross the street and stuff like that. I also am blessed to have an Assistant who is like my bodyguard, secretary, military *expert, driver, confidante, altar server/sacristan, and friend all rolled up and stuffed into a Sergeant suit. He is approaching his twentieth year and knows his stuff really well. Also, God will take care of me, and give me what I need to complete my Army mission and come home safely. In other words, tell her that I am glad she is worried but I hope she will worry less. Although, her prayers would greatly be appreciated.*

Well, now that I've talked your eyes off, I better go. Please keep in touch and send everyone my best.

In Christ,
Robert

1 JAN 05 19:15 New Year's Day

Instead of "New Year's Day" I'll try "Sometimes You Can't Make It On Your Own" by U2

HAPPY BIRTHDAY 2005!!! HAPPY NEW YEAR EVERYONE!!! In my "Bah humbug days", I used to look with disdain on the concept of New Year's resolutions. As a realist, I look at resolutions as a hopeless endeavor. Certainly, in a few weeks the resolutions we made will weaken and crumble and fade into the mists of a mindless tradition. But that seems so pessimistic. This year, I will break with my old ways and make a New Year's resolution, and I encourage you to do the same. Resolutions can be successful. Case and point, six years ago this week, Mom quit smoking, cold turkey, after our trip to Rome. She says that Pope John Paul II inspired her to finally kick the habit. It was a resolution she made yet she refrained from assigning it the title "resolution". Resolution sounds harsh. So why not assign it a different name, or throw out the label all together and give it no name.

I am dedicating the year 2005 to being a man of hope. As I was baptizing a week old baby (MAJ Rumley's son,

Garrett) yesterday, I couldn't help marvel at the blessing for the Baptismal water (which must be on line somewhere, which if I find I will post it), which in simple language traces the use of water as a symbol through out Sacred Scripture. The blessing brought to mind how this water that I was pouring over Garrett's head I considered how this very element had taken the lives of thousands of human beings in another part of the world. In this simple ceremony, I could feel the bright light of hope that this child means to his family. I could also see the need of hope for those mourning this horrible tragedy in southern Asia.

The great Burt Bacharach and Hal David wrote, "what the world needs now is love sweet love." Who am I to deny their philosophical viewpoint? I am a mere mortal, however, I think that we forget the package of Faith, Hope and Love. A lot of love is flowing right now to those who are suffering in the form of financial and material assistance. We need to also let the faith flow and not be cajoled into thinking that God is indifferent or absent. And likewise we need to allow hope to flow. Often, hope is in short supply, but isn't it hope which we see in the person of Jesus the infant? Isn't it the hope of the infant Christ which draws the Magi to his stable? Isn't it hope which the Nazorean brings to all those he touched in his ministry? Isn't it hope, which has been given to us by our Savior as He conquered death?

Hope goes a long way. I may be a realist, but I would be denying reality if I didn't hope. James Young (JY, from STYX to those in the know zone) said, in June, that I was going to a bad place to bring some good. Actually, I am not alone, I got some heavy-duty backup armed to the teeth with goodwill and a desire to bring peace and justice to a land thirsting for it. If that isn't hope I don't know what is. But I do know that hope must confront the world. Hope must face things that seem un-doable and allow the doable to happen. Hope is essential for us to be who we are called to be.

"Hang in their kid," as Monsignor James Sullivan used to often tell me, back in my high school and college days. That's my motto for this year. Nourished by that divine gift of Hope. That little baby has some great gifts for us. One of them is hope. If we need it right now, share it. Like all the gifts God gives us, if we give we receive. The world needs hope now. I am forsaking more of my curmudgeon self, I'm placing my bets and taking the risk. I will allow hope to flow through my person, as much as I am possible, and along the way I'll share some of my results. I am only guessing, but I think I will be pleasantly surprised by this resolution. God bless all of you, and God bless this year of 2005!!!

4 JAN 05 17:11 Epiphany - Fitness for Royalty
"Give A Little Bit" by Supertramp

Random thoughts from a tangential mind. Gold, frankincense, and myrrh. The Magi brought the infant Jesus these gifts. After all the gift giving, what have we given Him? We celebrate his birthday, but did we give Him any gifts? Well don't you think we should? And shouldn't we give Him a little more than everyone else? For 2005, perhaps we should give Him something similar to the Magi: gold, frankincense (not Frankenstein) and myrrh.

Gold: A little of our material wealth. This is a perfect time to send a few slices of cheddar (slang for money) to the least of our brothers and sisters in South Asia. (What we do for them we do for Him). Frankincense: Prayer to our God. A little added prayer, and giving a little more love back to Him. And Myrrh (what is that? stuff they used to put on dead bodies): Giving of ourselves selflessly. Or like Sister Bernard used to call it in the old days, "dying to oneself." That one is easier than it seems. Just look around you and if you see that real pain in the neck person that makes you wish you could wrap your fingers around their neck and wring out the excess fluid from their cranial column,

BINGO, you found the right candidate to try this one out on. Instead of giving them what you think they deserve, try giving them what that cute infant Jesus would deserve. (The ole what we do for them we do for Him bit again). Sometimes it can be a real pain to love Him, but who said He said it would be a rose garden?

9 JAN 05 Goodbye

I said bye to Mom. She and Anthony and Carol had spent a few days at Fort Drum. It was hard. The moment the car pulled away I felt such pain. I went into my room, crying and heaving and I just wrote these words down:

There's little that I have left
and man it's all gone
now it's just me, a few bags of stuff,
my heart and uncertainty.

I don't know where I am going,
I know in theory but that's it,
now it's into the unknown,
into the heart of the storm,

today it's a day of goodbyes
the promise of tomorrows

a day of hope
and the leap of faith

possibility awaits
but right now I just feel the hurt.

Tears will water
seeds will grow
hope springs eternal.

12 JAN 05 13:39 Winter
"Miss You" by The Rolling Stones

In protest to the ungodly rage of the lake-effect weather (all you meteorological aficionados should know about lake-effect (brrrr) that brutalizes the Watertown area I am moving to a more temperate climate. Ha, if only life could be that simple. I am moving, though, to warmer climate, but it is more of a command performance affair.

In my absence, please be assured of my prayers and frequent thoughts. I look forward to seeing you all sometime soon, when I can get a couple days off and come home safely. As per most advice, I will utilize the waterfowl methods of armed combat, whenever necessary, and I have complete trust in my faithful Chaplain Assistant, SGT Swain (Jerry), who contrary to his own desire has yet to put a bell around my neck. He claims I am elusive, he doesn't realize I have been testing him). Apparently, he is not fond of folks wishing to do me harm, and has promised a commensurate and proportionate response should he be forced to do so.

Know that I won't be missing you too much because I am carrying as many of you as I can in my heart (I should be able to fit you all, however, in my coronary cavity if there is any truth to all of your kind sentiments). With love, Chappy

14 JAN 05 12:57   And away we went

"We do not want our children to become a nation of spectators. Rather, we want each of them to be a participant in the vigorous life."

- John Fitzgerald Kennedy

Just a few days before I spent some time with Mom and the Quaids and everything seemed so normal. A few days later and it was off to war.

We left from NY at about 21:00 12 JAN 05. The military – a real fly by night operation. Contrary to popular belief, 13 JAN was shortest day of the year. Most of it was spent in the air. We had a layover in Shannon, Ireland for a couple of hours, where I did some shopping and was stupid and ordered coffee (duh, after living with Monsignor Bellew for three years you think I would have learned tea is the way in Ireland (he still makes the best tea ever aside from Mom's of course). Near done reading the book I bought in Ireland called Fat Land (not to be confused with Tommy Land), which is sort of an appendix to Fast Food Nation (which I consider to be near-sacred text even if I did break down and eat junk food again). Just a word to the wise, check out the damage soda does to kids. Holy Cow! This book opens wide the horror of what we are allowing our children to eat and what it does to them. Forgive me for preaching, but it is scary stuff.

Anyways, went to pest or was it Buddha (sadly no shopping, but it was nice to have some goulash like Oma used to make right there alongside the potatoes (is this right or just a subconscious homage to Dan Quayle?) just like she used to make too) for a bit and then onward (to victory). *This oblique reference as it appeared was meant to convey to the punsters that I had landed in Budapest.*

Somewhere along the way though the day was radically reduced and daylight was as fleeting as a Christmas card from me (sorry I didn't send one (I had about as much holiday spirit to spare as the Grinch pre-metanoia). Well I must get going.

Chow.

14 JAN 05 13:15 Half A World Away Day 1ish
"Beautiful Day" by U2

Greetings from Kuwait! Well after a multitude of hours too numerous to be just one day I have arrived. After a most excellent breakfast (no I am not being sarcastic, the food rocks!) and a brief reunion with some of the brothers (folks who had arrived prior to us and who were gracious enough to drag their weary bones up and welcome us) I hit the cot and apprehended a couple of elusive winks. Aside from being jet-lagged, culture shocked, homesick, and feeling physically beat down (yes I over pack even for war) this looks to be a very enjoyable and rewarding experience.

The desert is everything like I expected it to be and less. It is flat here. The sky is bluish. And I have seen more sun in the past two hours than I did collectively in several months in Watertown. Thank God it is also warmer here, although at nights are quite cold. I am getting acquainted with life here and will probably be a little irregular blogging until I adapt to the new environs and the battle rhythm, so please be patient.

Oh, by the way I saw my first Middle Eastern wildlife this morning in the visage of sparrows. For you astronomy fans I also saw the Big Dipper (which is upside down when I look north). And in case you are wondering, it is about eight hours ahead here, so morning for me is last night for you. Confused? Good, I will not be alone then (or is it now?). Bye for now, Don Padre

24 JAN 05 22:31 Blizzard!!!
"Kashmir" by Led Zeppelin

Well, imagine my surprise after three days in the desert training, to return to "civilization" and hear that New York was hit by a huge snowstorm. You guys made the "Stars and Stripes" (one of our journalistic information organs).

Actually, the Northeast and a scant mention of the greatest state this side of Oklahoma. As Bill Clinton used to say, "I feel your pain." Just spending some time on the popsicle farm in Watertown instilled in me a deep dislike for the cold that even grips me here. Believe it or not it is chilly here, but hardly 5 degrees or 0 degrees or that amazing 20 degrees below zero that hit Watertown this week.

I mentioned training, which for the soldier is second only to combat itself in importance. We have had a few excellent opportunities here to hone our skills and further excel in the warrior ethos. The training has been invigorating, although taxing, but quite enjoyable. Granted it is not my style to go three days without a shower or a change of clothes, but it sure is fun to have an M-16 rattle off shots a mere foot from one's head, driving on a bumpy dune road, awake since four thirty that morning. Wow! Those things are loud, like good ole rock n roll the way I like it. There are positives and negatives, but being with a team that is into it and pumped up with positive vibes makes it worth it. My soldiers are awesome! I am really privileged to work with some really topnotch quality folks; it sure makes this whole deployment thing bearable.

Some other things help, too. For instance, this whole desert thing, man alive, it sure is neat. Take yesterday, by sunrise I was already up two hours (and for those of you who know my morning demeanor this is tantamount to me walking on water or healing a leper, early morning is just not my time of day usually). But anyway, I had the privilege to see the moonset, the sunrise, and later in the day the sunset. Wowzers. Seeing all that in the desert is amazing and exactly what I dreamed it would be like. Except, I figured it would be a little warmer.

Since I first heard the opening riffs of Led Zeppelin's "Kashmir" I have yearned to one day find myself in the desert, in that sacred spare space of mystical intrigue. A place where time seemingly stands still. The real hope is to one day tread across the sands of the Sahara and see this neat music festival that is either in Marrakesh or Timbuktu (not Indiana) of which there is a DVD documenting one such festival attended by Led Zeppelin's Robert Plant. Morocco would be cool to see, as would Western Sahara, Mauritania, and Libya.

Libya? Yes, Libya. Although, old boy Colonel Qaddafi still holds power there, I have heard that he has been renovating some of the ancient monasteries for many years now in the hopes that when the trade embargo was lifted, he could attract some tourists. Libya is as far as I know where Hippo (not the animal, but Augustine of Hippo, Hippo) can be found. All you Hannibal fans (no not Lekter) (...and a nice Chianti...pftpftpft) will recall that Carthage is over yonder as well as the site of some significant ancient and modern battles.

Today, I was able to see a few neat things in the midst of training. Like, while lying prone near my vehicle my face close to the sandy ground I noticed little tiny grass just below the surface, almost resembling pigmy scallions. I tasted one blade of the grass and found it to be as unremarkable in taste as it was remarkable to find in what is usually called a wasteland. I saw also, in a not so convenient time a whole (I don't know what you would call it other than a) flock of butterflies just fluttering away off to where ever they were going. I also got to see a whole bunch of camels. Saw a lot of camels, sadly, none up close.

But all that pales in comparison to the nighttime. It is truly an awe inspiring and spiritual feeling to stare up at the stars and find that they are there and that light pollution is at a minimum. The only hindrance to an even more startling (ha!) exhibition of the celestial gape is the desert moon. With the slight bent in perspective courtesy of the axis of evil, er no I mean the Earth's axis the moon for me is more rabbit centered than the Jackie Gleason face in the moon type of thing. (If you are lost in what I am saying, try finding the rabbit in the moon, and to do so you need to tilt your head in the opposite direction of the face in the moon). The moon right now looks like a brilliant pearl with the etching of a rabbit in it.

And the other day, in my first real Humvee drive, I drove through one of the worst rainstorms (no kidding, RAIN!) this area has seen in about two years (at least that's what we were told by some folks in the know zone). Much to the dismay of SGT Swain, CPT Bowden and SPC Giles I hit as many bumps as possible obscuring SGT Swain's view of the windshield (his wiper wasn't working) with the splash of muddy water and or thick mud, as well as kicking up plenty of mud through the small hole in the floor of the vehicle which seemed to soak his pant legs and also get some mud on them. (No one ever accused me of having a normal sense of humor.) But needless to say we all, really, did have fun. "Solidarity, brothers."

Just a final thought. Things for the most part are upbeat. Granted there are things like early morning wake-ups (not tomorrow though) and cold showers (this afternoon, unfortunately) and Porto sans (those little mobile bathrooms, which are the most awful thing since the outside, thank God however for this magical blue fluid which quells the odor, for the most part, and adds some semblance of dignity top the whole waste removal process) and having to get up in the middle of the night to relieve oneself (and if your not, you're not drinking enough water). But for the most part, it is good. I'm working with good people, smart people, dedicated people who have handed themselves over for the next year sacrificing time with their families and loved ones to serve a greater purpose, liberty.

Funny, as now I have entered the liberty business, I am now meditating on the freedom I have taken for granted. I see I have taken a lot for granted in my life. Each day, one or two of those things come to mind, and I think how I really miss them. Sometimes it's significant, like people I love and care about, my family and friends. Other times it's the mundane things, like butter or the sound of kids playing at a playground. Both of which I felt the absence of, yesterday.

If I had something to ring bells about today it is this; Appreciate it all, because we are the lucky folks in the world. We are the lucky ones. It's a fact. It would be a shame to go through this entire life and just be oblivious to that fact. We have been given so much, but have we said thank you.

So for Kuwait and the wait (and what a wait its been here cause there's a line for everything here) I say to the good Lord THANK YOU and thanks to all of you readers out there. Hope you are enjoying this as much as I am writing it. Bye for now. R

P.S. If you want to read a pretty cool book, I just started "Danny Boy" by one of those rowdy McCourt brothers, not the Angela's Ashes guy or maybe, I'm too tired right now to remember. It is an amazing little exposition on the popular song. A really neat little book though. All right, good night.

27 JAN 05 13:18 Trying to Throw Ones Arms Around the World
"Freedom '90" by George Michael

So far, so good? For the most part things are going well here. A lot of administrative work the past few days, getting all sorts of things in order. The amount of planning involved in preparing religious support is pretty impressive. My typing chops are definitely improving. If you've been reading or hearing the news, things have been grim, especially with yesterday's helicopter crash. It's weird to be in the midst of all this and hear about things going on from both the outside and the inside. A lot of you are praying for me and I am thankful, but please keep the other soldiers in your prayers. Some of them are carrying heavy crosses and have had to let go of so much to be here and to put in their time. There are a lot of people suffering to in CONUS (continental U.S. (alright Hawaii and Alaska too)) because of these tragedies and because they miss their loved ones. My heart goes out to all of these folks.

It's also weird that the weather I was complaining about (not on this blog, but when I called Mom) was the very same type of weather that contributed to that helicopter crash. If you can imagine, some days are just this dusty haze that makes you want to cough just looking at it. The other day, the sun was out but the best description I could provide is that it looked like a communion wafer. In fact, a few people said the conditions were perfect save for the wind for a sandstorm. Last entry, I provided a moonlight and roses view of the desert, but it also has a very hostile side to it as well. Well, it's time for me to go.

If you're in the praying mood, please pray that the elections go off with as little loss of human life as possible. This is a historic moment for the Iraqi people. If you are news hounds dig a little deeper and take note of the dedication of so many Iraqis to pull this off. To put it in a broader context, what is happening there took years to take place for us when our country as born. The American Revolution lasted longer than this war. The implementation of our nation took longer. And by golly the "American Experiment" has worked pretty well since. The "Iraqi Experiment" will take time, and patience, and energy. I believe though that democracy is the best tool to combat the causes of terrorism. It will definitely be cool to see how democracy will take shape in Iraq. No one believed the iron curtain would crumble, but it did, and quicker than we could have imagined (especially those who had been behind it). Eastern Europe emerged from the darkness, and so will Iraq. Freedom is an intoxicating thing. God bless you all. Bye for now. Chappy

"Sentimental Journey" by Les Brown

Last night, I opened a can of Copenhagen. I have had it on me since the Sunday before departing for Kuwait. I am carrying it as a remembrance of one of the coolest men and legends I will ever know. There was, however, despite all the Okie talk no myth about him. (When I have some time I'll elaborate about the Okie talk, put it this way, his brothers and sisters tell/told stories about him that jived amongst them (which is a miracle for Oklahomans considering some usually purport to know more than others, and they also tell you "Aw don't listen to them, hell, they don't know what their talkin' about."

Well with Opa (Marion pronounced something like Mayrn), the stories not only are in synch but delivered with an almost hyperdulic (hyperdulia is a good SAT word that describes the Catholic reverence of Mary, and hopefully I'm not wrong or I'm sure Bill Smith will hunt me down and haunt me, "Listen here friend (Big Al) you'd be wise not to use too many ten dollar words, you might hurt someone (the obligatory fur ball cough follows (with utmost respect I imitate the man, who was a true champ in the cemetery, I mean seminary) reverence). (Which reminds me, when I collate these reflections for the book, I will have to put the parenthetical expressions in the format of footnotes, cause the breaks and sub-references are getting difficult to juggle. (Kind of like chainsaws.) All in all, I must present a few of these legends (from the Arbuckle Mountains) some day because they make for a great read. *(Evidently I did not heed my own advice at least for this edition.)*

Anyway, last night after ten years I smelled a smell that just cut right to the bone. The familiar smell that surrounded Marion James Wyatt, but I called him Opa (German for grandfather). That scent of Copenhagen Snuff sure brought all of this into perspective. He was a veteran of three wars,

World War II, Korea, and Vietnam. His life as a soldier made him the man he was and shaped the spirituality that he embodied. Now his only grandson, that would be me, shares something pretty special with him, soldiering. That scent really touched me, and I became aware of something I know is true. That he is with me. "Boy Ahm tellin' you, Lord, you better watch over him now. That's my grandson." His advice to me, I can hear ringing in my ears, it would go something like not being a "sorry damn lew tenant" and he'd tell me to fly straight and "You git home safe now. Y'hear me?" So what I'm saying is this; I AM IN THE BEST OF HANDS.

I know that Opa will be watching over me and praying for me and guiding me as I minister to my soldiers. Two days before we left Fort Drum I dreamed of him after a long time of no dreams of him, he was with us shopping for my gear at the military store, he was shaking his head in amusement, marveling at his grandson's hectic gathering of supplies. I could almost hear him say, "Yeah, its the same Army." It was a comforting dream, coupled with the words of a Salesian priest the day Opa died, "Now you have a saint in heaven." And that my dear friends is no myth.

You might be wondering about that can of Copenhagen. I will be carrying that with me. In my times of fear, I will open it and get a whiff. In my times of homesickness, I will open that can and take a whiff. In the times when I feel overwhelmed, I will take that can out and take a whiff. He was a great soldier, and I pray that I can follow in his footsteps, with the same dignity and poise and honor, through the tumult and the strife and back home again to the land he loved so much. It is a privilege and an honor.

Love and best wishes to all, and Ma hugs and kisses for you and please kiss the kitties on their foreheads for me (Smokey and Sportie, Cee-Cee and Iggy), Jordan (the dachshund), and also Oma. And now onward to victory.

2

TIKRIT, IRAQ

1 FEB 05 09:40 Here
"Welcome to the Terrordome" by Public Enemy

Well after several days of travel and delays I have arrived. It was a pretty cool trip flying in planes and helicopters under the cover of darkness and in complete darkness. Air traffic at night is awesome to hear and impressive to see when you happen to see a plane or a helicopter flying with no light at all. Believe me it is better than being a visible target.

Two days ago was my first helicopter ride ever, which was completely awesome. We flew in on a Chinook, no lights, and with all the doors open. It sure is a rush to have wind in your face flying at night sitting next to a gunner seeing the lights of a city or a town and occasionally to look at the window in front of you (but your not facing front) and be looking straight down at the ground. The sound is absolutely amazing, hope 1 don't lose hearing but it just pumps you up so much. Rock n Roll all the way.

Well now I am here. I have yet to see the civilian Iraqi world, which has been described to me to be destitution and poverty. In contrast, this place one of Saddam's palace complexes is a testimony to the American mission. To see how he siphoned off Iraqi money into these opulent buildings is proof that the government that he presided over was contemptuous of the Iraqi people and no more than a confederacy of thugs, criminals, and sociopaths. (One of the palaces has a lake, from which divers have in the past recovered the bodies of women who had been raped and executed by one of Saddam's sons.) If birds of a feather flock together then one can only see the danger if a relationship existed between this government and terrorists. Don't forget, that Abu Nidal lived in Iraq for many years, as a guest of the government until he was assassinated mysteriously (it was presumed it was an inside job one surefire way to get a guest to move on rather drastic however.)

Well for you who have ever been to Rome, the closest I could describe where I am is the Janiculum. Just substitute cupolas for minarets and leave out the stunning view of Rome. The buildings are really quite interesting. Oh yeah, I saw the Tigris River. Wow and yuck all at the same time. The river is not clean. There is oil (black) on the surface (kind of like contrails from planes in the sky) and a lot of oil (rainbow discoloration) too. The pouring of sewage into the river is also a common Iraqi practice.

A few cool things. Nice digs (I have a cool bed/cubicle and an office too). Great food. Flush toilets, scattered about but here at least (although the ever present Porto-sans also can be found). Awesome people. Interesting scenery. Cool sounds (choppers and jets and the call to prayer five times a day). Great work and all with the security of knowing I am being prayed for and am cared for by so many of you.

I apologize for the sketchiness of things at times. There are certain things I would love to tell you but am unable to for safety and security reasons. So if you see me just vague out on you, you know why. Safety and security. And for those who have written and I haven't written back mea culpa, mea culpa, mea maxima culpa. Adieu.

6 FEB 05 09:48 Hey Strangers!
"Stranglehold" by Ted Nugent

Sorry about the lag in updating. Life is good here. Busy busy busy is the operative phrase, however. I just said Mass a few minutes ago. I had three yesterday. Yesterday, I also made my first convoy. It was blessedly uneventful, unless you think that driving in a foreign country, and a war zone nonetheless is uneventful. It was also the first time that I saw the residents of this country, and it was a bit heart gripping. Especially seeing so many children, waving to us as we passed by. My first adult wave, in Iraq, was from a shepherd and I saw some sheep.

The weather here has been nice for the most part. The skies are gorgeous here. It's been in the mid-70's. And occasionally there has been rain. We are entering the rainy season, so it will be pretty wet for a month or so. There is some more vegetation, and that has helped in getting ready for Ash Wednesday. I have been burning palm branches, and I will soon be collecting palms for Palm Sunday.

Iraqi Election Day passed pretty peaceful, thank God. And hopes are high that we will see positive results in the coming year, as democracy is both learned and practiced. It is a process that will need a lot of patience and work. The overall social structure here holds family as the key social structure, then extended family, then tribe. With a tribal social structure, it is not easy to embrace national identity. Some tribes have age disputes with other tribes. In Saddam's day it was easy for him to put forth a national identity shaped in his own image, in which some tribes received great benefits while others were subjugated.

I am getting my feet wet with ministry and administratively, as well. The training I have received is starting to take shape and now I am seeing how all the pieces fit. Being a priest here is like being a celebrity. As soon as people find out I am a priest people tell me how few priests there are and how much we are needed.

I am grateful that my exposure to the news is limited now. I do keep up with things, but I am missing a lot of stuff. It is interesting to watch the news now and see how ridiculous and out of touch some people are with what is really going on. All the predictions by the naysayers about the elections are a perfect example. Is it all moonlight and roses? No, but the strides being made here are amazing. The worst part of this, though, is when we hear about a soldier dying and then we hear Americans ridiculing the mission we are performing. But that is just my opinion. I just know if I had family or a loved one over here I would not appreciate the nay saying. But I didn't like it, even when I was home.

I am going to be asking for some help soon. I definitely want to get something started for the kids here. Looking at collecting children's clothes and maybe even supplies (medical stuff) or essentials that a household should have if they have kids. I will be talking to the powers that be on my end to see the logistics and all. It could be a seriously awesome Confirmation project or community service thing for some of our kids back home to be involved in, as well. I'll supply more details in the future. Believe it or not, things like that really can help us in our mission and show to the people here what we really are all about. The poverty here is great and the squalor is mind numbing. To be able to make a little bit of a difference would be awesome.

Just in case I am getting too heavy know that I am still the same old me. Having a lot of fun, and trying my darndest to make my soldiers smile and nagging them to no end to take care of themselves. Bye for now, R

6 FEB 05 10:33 For the rock n rollers out there
"Mind" by Last Tribe

Just found out that John Smith has a new band called Bent Blue. John and I were altar servers eons ago, and I have been following his musical career since I was in high school. He has done some amazing stuff with the Last Tribe, Jak Tweed, and Unspun and I am sure that this group is no different. He is a soul warrior and even if you never heard of these groups before, you should have because he can knock it out of the ballpark with his talent. And although, you always got to be compared with someone else in our world, he has always been ahead of the curve and not playing a trend. Who else could fit "Born in the Bayou" by Credence Clearwater Revival right along side "Cemetery Gates" by The Smiths and also "Peace Frog" by the Doors and make them all sound like his songs? Oh yeah, rock n roll never forgets. ("Mind" is an original song by Last Tribe that they played live all the time, back in the day, and it really was one of the most perfect songs I ever heard, and it should have been on an album).

9 FEB 05 12:40 Ash Wednesday
"Dancing In the Streets" by Martha and the Vandellas

Had Mass at 1000hrs, and distributed ashes. I'm going to hit the rest of the FOBs (that's what we call a Forward Operating Base) later and get to the people who couldn't make it to Mass (if Mohammad can't go to the mountain...ah well you get the gist). The ashes I am distributing were made from burnt palms extracted from palm trees indigenous to the FOB, which is pretty cool. Speaking of Mass, the chapel I was in today is fairly small, but beautiful worship space. The other place I will say Mass, this weekend, is a theater, also nice worship space.

The congregations here have surprised me because they sing (no shy ones here, and they sing like angels). Another funny observation, the people here don't leave Mass until after Mass. Maybe it's because I don't have a collection or maybe because there's no rush to get to the parking lot. Also is funny to see my congregation come to Mass armed (definitely encourages me to "land the plane" with my homilies (or as they say here sermons).

That's all for now.

13 FEB 05 18:04 First Sunday of Lent (reflection)
"Spirit In The Sky" by Norman Greenbaum

God wants to continually fashion us in His own image and likeness. He wants to lift us out of the dirt and transform our very being. He wants to conquer our sinfulness and lift us to the very heights of His Heavenly Presence. This Lent, let us look deep into our hearts, remember we were formed from the dust, that we are not a finished product and invite the Lord to perfect us. It can't happen if we are deluded and think we are perfected already or not in need of Him in our lives. And it can't happen if we are convinced that dirt is all we are. We need to have a healthy spiritual self-esteem and be open to the miraculous nature of relationship with God.

Homework: Check out Jesus' interaction with Satan and note the phrase of "Son of God" and compare with Jesus' latter interaction with Peter regarding who people say He is and His answer up to the rather caustic retort, "Get behind me Satan". So we're talking Matthew 4:1-11 and Matthew 16:13-23. Interesting stuff, indeed.

15 FEB 05 16:53 Thoughts about Cindi
"Somewhere Over the Rainbow" by Eva Cassidy

One year ago today, my friend Cindi died. For about a year Cindi battled an aggressive and vicious cancer called leiomyosarcoma. When I met Cindi there was an instant connection. She was already ill, and the prognosis was not good. But Cindi defied the dire predictions of doctors, the savagery of her illness, and the temptations to be a defeatist. Cindi's frail frame bore a spirit that was tremendous. Ravaged by a fierce opponent, Cindi allowed the virtues of her faith, hope and love to radiate through her, usually finding its expression in her signature smile. Her illness Her ever-present pain knew no comfort but despite this she tried so hard not to dwell on it. I didn't get to know Cindi very long, but in the short time we did know each other it felt like a lifetime. She made me feel as if I had known her all my life.

I am grateful to my friends, the Quaids, who introduced me to her, and honored that I could share time with her. I am a better man for having known her. I hate talking about her as if she's gone, but I also hate the fact that I can't sit and talk to her over some ice cream and that I can't see her smile or hear her laugh. I know she is not gone, in one sense. She definitely lives on in the presence of her children Ryan and Scotty, two really fine young men, and in the love she shared with her husband Don. She definitely lives on in the lives of her parents, Joseph and Margot, and her brother Ronald. And she definitely lives on in the lives of her family and friends. I know to Cindi lives on in the presence of the Lord. She is one of those remarkable persons that you know is delighting in His presence. Knowing Cindi, she is keeping tabs on the family, and putting in a lot of time (despite the eternity thing) praying for those treasures in her life; her family and friends.

One year ago today, I stood at her Calvary, in Beacon, there with her as she was surrounded by a few of those near and dear to her. It was a place of honor and privilege to be there with her sharing those last moments of her life here in this world with her. I will never forget looking into her beautiful blue eyes the moment before she died. In those eyes, I could see a well-deserved peace. She had fought a good fight. Her eyes were not those of a victim, they were the strong eyes of a victor. That last glimpse of her eyes also spoke to my faith. I knew, I know, and I will always know that death is not the end. Death has no power to separate us from God's love. I know Cindi is in that better place but it still doesn't mean that the hurt is gone. So today, I ask that you keep her husband and her children and her parents and her family in your prayers.

I feel as if Cindi was victorious in her sufferings and death. She defied all expectations and showed all of us who she really is, a person of great courage and grace. Cindi set a standard that those who know her will look back on for many years to come. She taught us lessons that will continue to live on in us, and given an example of how we should meet adversity, with love, a kind word, a laugh, a healthy dose of fear and a determination to persevere, the obligatory tears but also the necessary hope, and a deep faith not of convenience but rooted in God's truth and love.

Cindi would probably disapprove of this kind of tribute but I think she deserves it. Sharing memories is one way of keeping her memory alive; another way of keeping her memory alive is outreach. Leiomyosarcoma is still a horrible disease and there are still men and women suffering this rare form of cancer. Please visit www.nlmsf.org. Cindi was optimistic that this cancer could be defeated, perhaps in the macro view she was right, and perhaps we can help make her dream a realization. Pax

16 FEB 05 19:59 A black cloud really hanging over me
"Play With Fire" by The Rolling Stones; "Paint It Black" by The Rolling Stones; "Back In Black" by Shakira

This morning began with a rude awakening. *A car bomb exploded in the city, killing one civilian.* Awhile later, I went back to sleep and awoke again to a day that unfolded in strange and surreal ways. All morning the sky was impossibly blue and it looked and felt as if it would be a slightly cool (upper 60's) yet perfect spring (eat your heart out, cause I said spring!!!) day. About lunchtime, the sky grew grey to the north. *Apparently, saboteurs attacked the oil pipeline in Beerat, just north of Bayji.* It looked like a big storm was going to hit. The clouds grew darker and darker in the north. The scent of the air was devoid of the pleasant ozone scent that usually foreshadows a rainstorm. Instead it was putrid. The clouds formed an ominous mass. The edges of the mass were frayed in a gaseous manner. Slowly but surely that cloud slid across the sky until it was off to the east and the north and we were became by the greasy filmy haze that robbed everything of sharpness and color. Crawling down the Tigris like a wounded animal, the smoky oil fire cloud moved over the countryside, a staggering malevolent sign of the unseen evil that haunts this country.

The cloud was like a pall that hung over the land, a perfect metaphor for what the decent people of Iraq have in the past had to endure and what they are enduring now. Hostages to vicious and evil men who have sworn and dedicated their "lives" (for lack of a better term) to unleashing their evil on anyone they can. Their abject hatred for human life is beyond belief. They have hijacked culture, religion, and a proud people. They have shown themselves implacable and are unable to understand the harsh reality that evil will not prevail. The spark of liberty is touching a land thirsty for justice and mercy and peace. That is why I am here now. Personally, I have no tolerance for evil, injustice, or for these disciples of slavery who are bent on robbing civilization of freedom. My prayer is that the freedom of the human person can flourish and that civil freedom can be enjoyed here as I enjoy it back home. The lingering stains of that cloud remained well into the evening, but that cloud will not last forever and a new day will dawn. Not optimism, just fact. Until freedom is fact we must remain steadfast.

17 FEB 05 20:57   Rock and Roll Hall of Fame and Museum
"Half A World Away" by R.E.M.

Ah the torture...Homesick...I'm missing Mom and Oma, my dear friends, my cats, my parishioners, the glorious Hudson Valley, and the simple pleasures of life: coffee at the Ground Hog, used record stores, clean air, bookstores, oh heck the list could go on forever I guess. And yes it sounds superficial but the concerts. This year the list of premium rock concerts is staggering: my new found guilty pleasure Styx, the triumphant return of the bad boys of rock Mötley Crüe, the transcend U2, the New Jersey fever of Bon Jovi, and the always fresh Peter Frampton. Last June, I spent a week of delight seeing (with Mom and Anthony and Carol) the fantastic Van Halen ("It's About Time") who rocked the Meadowlands, the following night Styx who were absolutely incredible and who that night, and not just because I was able to go back stage and meet them (along with the usual suspects)(thank you John Regan) and not just because they dedicated a song "These Are the Times" to me and my Mom and my sister (?) (Mom was equally surprised to learn I had a sister, but despite the confusion it was still a nice dedication by JY (James Young is called JY)) in which he announced that he met a priest backstage who was going to a very bad place to bring some good.

If that wasn't cool enough, the cherry on top of that rock and roll pie, the next day I got to hang out with John and Kathy. We had a nice couple of hours walking around; I took some great pictures in Central Park. Then it was off to rehearsal, which was an interesting experience. After rehearsal I had a nice dinner with John and Kathy on Sixth Avenue and then it was off to the Hard Rock Cafe to see the legendary Peter Frampton. That night was incredible. Not only did Peter play a great show despite some equipment issues but I also got to hang out with Styx, their manager and road crew guys and meet the Nelson twins. Gunnar and Matt Nelson opened for Styx the night before and they also dedicated "High Enough," which they sang with Tommy Shaw, for the soldiers in Iraq.

It was cool that after hearing so many of his stories, I finally got to see/hear John play live. What a week for any rock fan. When I thought it couldn't be outdone, a couple of days later John presented me with a guitar signed by Peter Frampton and the band, Styx, Matt and Gunnar and check this out (!) the entire road crew (that's when the tears welled up in my eyes, their sentiments were touching.

Just as an aside: The night at Hard Rock Café did not end there by a long shot. It was followed by a trip down to Atlantic City where I met up with Danny O'Gallagher and Brian Murphy and spent a night at the Pai Gow tables. We finished up around six in the morning, with a little dough in our pockets. We then hit the International House of Pancakes (which I wonder how "international" this house is since there is no IHOP in Iraq). And then still without a bit of sleep I went right back up to Wappingers Falls where my pajamas were waiting, beckoning me to put them on and get some shut eye Live like you mean it.

Having said all that. To miss the Rock and Roll Hall of Fame Induction Ceremony this year is the ultimate rock and roll insult. Especially when my favorite band this side of Led Zeppelin is being inducted; U2. So when the going gets tough the tough get going (and if the mountain won't...yada yada yada) I fired off an e-mail to the Hall of Fame explaining my plight and the plight of my soldiers and quicker than you could say "Ladies and Gentlemen, from Los Angeles California, the Doors," I got this awesome message I have pasted to close my entry this day. Totally awesome!

So, thank you to the Rock and Roll Hall of Fame and Museum. And thank you to all you patient readers who expected something more. Yesterday kind of wiped me out. The pipeline fires are still polluting the warm (70's) air and it was weird to see the news explaining why I was seeing smoke clouds yesterday but this was a welcome respite to share with you a little of one of my favorite pastimes.

Pax and bye for now, R

Father Bob,

Thanks for the email. It's always great to hear from music fans anywhere and your situation just makes it that much more special.

It also suggests the power of this art form that we celebrate and call rock and roll.

Unfortunately, I cannot supply you with the unedited version (4+ hours) of the Ceremonies. What I can do is send you the edited show (2-3 hours). This should be available around March 25th. If that works, please let me know where and in what format, i.e. DVD VHS.

Give the troops all our best.....our thoughts and prayers are with you all.

Peace and Soul
Rock and Roll

Terry

Terry Stewart
President
Rock and Roll Hall of Fame and Museum

---

20 FEB 05 21:37 Second Sunday of Lent
"Let It Grow" by Eric Clapton

Right now, you are exactly where God wants you to be. The question then is: Have we placed ourselves at God's disposal to carry out His plan? Jesus offers us the clear and concise prayer that we need to say, and He preached in word and deed on the cross. "Into your hands Lord, I commend my Spirit."

22 FEB 05 10:04 Some words about courage

"Courage is being scared to death and saddling up anyway."
   - John Wayne (orig. Marion Michael Morrison)

"Courage is resistance to fear, mastery of fear - not absence of fear."

     -Mark Twain (pseud. of Samuel Langhorne Clemens)

"Courage is doing what you're afraid to do. There can be no courage unless you're scared."

     - Edward Vernon (Eddie) Rickenbacker

"Be not afraid."

     -Jesus

22 FEB 05 20:45 An e-mail to Anthony

T,

55 and driving against traffic. Wow. Wonderful. Had to go do a visitation of our folks off post. The convoy was delayed. Our delay put us in traffic so we kept going, as Malcolm X says by any means necessary ergo the wacko-driving scenario. Amazing to see the faces of people looking like "these Americans are nuts" and them swerving out of our way to avoid getting hit.

Luckily, today I was not driving. But then we had to stop for a bit while Army folks removed an IED from the road. Always interesting to have everyone in kill position ready to unleash holy heck on any possible ambushers. Gratefully, the jerk that put it there decided to plant and run and spares their miserable lives from meeting their Maker and dealing with His wrath. Good thing for lateness and inefficiency, though. Proof it saves lives.

Always nice to look back and see God's hands moving about. Other than that, everything is fine. Just a bit rattled still. That and the idiot that insists that five thirty in the morning is the right time to fling mortars at our base. They sure are loud.

It is pretty much in synch with their morning prayer. Imagine that. Yeah, you got to love it, a little prayer, mortar some Americans and have a dull (swineless) breakfast. Well that's all for now. Hope you are well. Say a prayer for me,

R

24 FEB 05 11:09 War, weapons, and a solution for world peace
"Peace Is Just A Word" by The Eurythmics
"Success" by Iggy Pop

A lot has been going on. Our "friends" (Monsignor Smith use of the word) are stepping up their presence and a lot more is happening. I worry sick about my guys who are going outside of the wire all the time. A car bomb went off in town this morning as I was leaving breakfast. Saw the mushroom shaped cloud and it makes you sick when you hear an explosion and see the cloud of smoke and you just know something bad just happened. And then the machine gun fire. It's like the Wild, Wild West (with that I have to give a shout out to my cat Smokey, that's his favorite Will Smith song). And then you wonder what your guys (soldiers) are getting into. The burdens of being a Padre. The explosion this morning killed a bunch of civilians. *Ten people were killed and twenty-five were wounded when a suicide bomber blew up his vehicle at a police station at shift change.* Not everyday that you witness things even if it's beyond a wall knowing that a few more people have left this world. I would rather report on the moonlight and roses side of things, but it does get hairy. I feel very safe physically, but as I said I get worried. In fact, as most of you know beneath the carefree exterior is a genuine worrywart. Bet you didn't know I grind my teeth when I worry?

Please keep my soldiers in your prayers. And please keep

me in your prayers. I don't fake optimism but I do try to reassure them with my presence, knowledge and the ever-present sense of humor (in fact, dare I say it but my humor is getting more outrageous). Amazingly, I am finding the best weapon in my arsenal is a smile. It gets the job done. A smile mixed with the love of a spiritual parent (so that's why they say Father). I am blessed by some great folks, who keep me sane. My minions include: Justin (doing his parenting/brother/adviser thing - "Hey Chappy, why aren't you wearing your leg brace?" (Yeah the old patella is back to slipping from its groove (like Stella) thanks to my lax ligaments, which also makes for interesting walks as I tumble from time to time with the ankles too) or "Jeat chet?" which is Okie for did you eat yet) and Jerry (the enforcer, brother in arms, consigliore, the befuddle dispeller who makes sure I remember everything I'd forget, sacristan) Mike my roommate, and Nicole.

Poor Mike has to deal with a new surname each day from my limitless ability to draw specious and ridiculously moronic new appellations, who always happens to find new and innovated ways to make me crack up laughing. And so there it is; the tensions of a war, the camaraderie of soul brothers, and the constant wrestling match to get the job done with passion and grace and care. If you have a loved one over here, know that we are looking out for each other. We are protective of each other. We know we are making life long friends. But well have one over arching intent and desire, to get home safe after our mission is done here.

I do have a solution though to the insurgency problem. Cats. Yes, I said cats. If they had cats to look after - to clean litters and feed the cats - And attend to every whim and meow - these guys would collapse under the pressure. They would be so occupied by their responsibilities as cat owners (well, we know who owns who really) they would have to abandon their mortar attacks and vehicle born explosive devices and improvising explosive devices and sabotaging oil pipelines and the rest of that laundry list of terrorist stuff these guys do. Yeah, cats. That's my solution for world peace. Plus they can kill the mice and introduce to this side of the world the beauty of what windows are for (not shooting out of but sitting in and enjoying watching the world).

That's all for now, Chappy

24 FEB 05 02:52 An e-mail to Mom (Under Pressure)

Madre,

Sorry about not calling. The day was just that, a day. A lot going on here. Our "friends" are stepping up their presence and a lot more is happening. Worried sick about my guys who are going out side of the wire all the time. A car bomb went off in town. Saw the mushroom cloud and it makes you sick when you hear the sound and see the mushroom cloud of smoke and you just know something bad just happened. And then the machine gun fire. It's like the Wild West. And then you wonder what your guys are getting into to. Sorry for unloading. But...the burdens of being a padre. The explosion this morning killed a bunch of civilians. Not everyday that you witness things even if it's beyond a wall knowing that a few more people have left this world.

Today I am a nervous father, I will be a lot happier once I hear they are home and safe. If you intermingle the idiocy that exists with some of the Staff and I think of what dear Opa used to say about the Army. There are some great people that really kick butt and then there are some that need a swift kick in the butt. The lack of a sense of urgency among a few of my comrades is alarming. They forget the business we are in.

Jerry is a rock. Had a bit of a cry with him. I feel so vulnerable when I know my soldiers have to step into crazy situations. God gave me a hot-blooded temperament for a reason. I am seeing that now. I show my love to the ones who need to see it but I get so angry with the guys who should be stepping up to the plate and showing the love and showing the passion for keeping their soldiers alive.

Whew. Things are going well though. I am slogging through a lot of inefficiency and frustrated with how things are run. Picture ineptitude mixed in with a lack of real coherent understanding of where we are and what we are doing. Luckily, I have surrounded myself with really capable people and aligned myself with like minded individuals who are determined to get the job done and will keep people alive in the process.

I miss you terribly and am going through serious cat withdrawal. I haven't seen a real cat in so long I wonder if that would not be the solution to this conflict. Perhaps if the bad guys had to change litters and feed cats and wait on them hand and foot and attend to their every whim and meow we wouldn't have these jerks running around blowing crap up.

I am safe. Rich said he talked to you the other day. He said it was great talking to you. I love you dearly.

Please keep me in your prayers. I am bombarding our guys with a lot of love and care and can use any bit of a good word in prayer to support my actions. I am becoming more and more each day the man Opa was. I am seeing it and am honored. I understand more and more his seemingly limitless patience and also how he cultivated it. This is a good thing that I found myself in. I have the tools God wants for this mission. I enjoy it but vent when I need to. I look forward to talking to you a bit later.

Love to Oma, and the cats and the Jordan,

Rob

3

LEARNING THE AO

1 MAR 05 20:22 I'm alright
"Ripple" by The Grateful Dead

All is well. Busy busy busy as Pooh Bear says. Sleepy, too. Forgive the break, I will be back in a day or so. Just to whet your appetite: I did see my first Iraqi dog today. And this is a cat person talking. Also, had a mini-scallion today. Picked it myself and after smelling it (in order to confirm that it was what I thought what it was) I ate it. It was tasty. It's great getting back in touch with the simple things of life even here in Iraq.

2 MAR 05 16:44 A Camp Don Bosco story
"As Tears Go By" by The Rolling Stones

So there I was...miles away from nowhere...visiting soldiers, and I see that one of the soldiers has a name I recognize from back in the day. Later on, I see her pass by and I ask her, "Excuse me, are you related to a Billy?" She looked at me for a second, hesitant, and says, "Why? Um, yeah Billy's my brother." She looked as if I were playing a joke on her (Yeah imagine that, me playing a joke on someone). I then told her, "One of my camper's at Camp Don Bosco, in Newton NJ, was named Billy D..." Her face relaxed. (She knew I wasn't joking) "He'd know me as Waldo," I added. Pretty wild stuff, but its a small war after all.

Things are really heating up here. Today its about 82 degrees, but it feels a little warmer. Snow is just a fading memory. The mourning doves (who sound much more intelligent here than back home) are cooing, which sounds like a tone on Zamfir's pan flute (females), and cawing (the males) like mini (counting, Cameron, Russell, Sheryl or black) Crows with less squawk. The sky is colored like concrete and I can just imagine how much more it will heat up here. Recall, 21 June 04 it was reported to be 140 degrees here. No joke.

As I mention CDB, I am reminded to ask you to please keep a friend of mine from CDB, David Blakes, in your prayers. Sadly, his mom Dorothea died last week. There is no doubt to her coolness having raised a great son like David.

Bye for now, and for old times sake, I sign off as Waldo

5 MAR 05 22:25 Great Adventure
"Surrender" by Cheap Trick

WAZUP!?! Just needed to be a little indulgent with the introit. I got to mix it up a bit, you know? So enough of the excuses on why I haven't written for the past few days. I got the best alibi. I'M IN IRAQ! That should buy me a little sympathy. What can I say? Some days the words are there, some days they aren't and some days in order to maintain operational security I can't say nothing about anything even if I wanted to say something. The past few days have been like some episode of some demented reality show. Too much talking. When you work with people day in and day out sometimes juggling the personalities is like juggling chainsaws.

Anyway, lets talk about my subject line: Great Adventure. Today was pretty rad as today was the first time I flew on a Blackhawk helicopter. Wow, what a rush! Better than any ride at Great Adventure. It was a smoother ride than I expected and awesome as I got to see more of this amazing country. This is definitely an amazing place. Sad, but amazing. I can't wait to see what the free people of Iraq do with their home. You know with all the talking heads on television talking about getting us out of Iraq it is often neglected that we are helping to improve life here, life that we didn't mess up in as much as Saddam never let it be enjoyed. When security is taken over and the people can take ownership of their country and feel that pride and start seeing their lives get better they are going to make this a truly amazing place.

Germany and Japan had a lot of rebuilding to do after the war. But take East Germany their development was put on hold until they became united with West Germany. Now not only the scar of Communist architecture is being dealt with, but the ruins of World War Two are being healed. Back in the eighties, there were still bombed out buildings in the East, from 40 years prior. The same will happen here eventually. Once the terrorists are neutralized and brought to justice, and the wounds of the Saddam era can be allowed to heal, the Iraqi people can then attend to their cities and restore and enhance them to grandeur in proportion to their spirit. Sounds naive maybe, but recall I am a man of hope.

The freedom of non-service oriented Vermonters is uninspiring in comparison with the men and women here who are putting their lives on the line each day serving their nation. Police Stations here in Iraq are constantly being attacked and scores of police have been killed and scores of recruits and yet the terrorists are unable to stifle the seeds of freedom growing in the hearts of the Iraqi people. The volunteers keep coming forward and risking it all to build a free Iraq. That makes me proud to serve my country. That nourishes my belief that this is all going to turn out just right. The Thug Life era is over. Now it just means driving that message through the insurgency's thick heads.

Probably not one of my best entries but at least I wrote

something. And while I am just writing anything, what is up with life in the States? Hunter Thompson is dead? What's up with that? Adieu, R

6 MAR 05 17:14 Lars and the Fourth Sunday of Lent

"Enter Sandman" by Metallica

In the past few weeks a couple of cool packages have come in. Mom really outdid herself and answered the call of Roberto with flying colors. Cleaning supplies, the arrival of which has coincided perfectly with the liberation of Martha Stewart (one of my heroes) (and let me say this about that, everyone who knows of Martha knows that Martha does things perfectly, so that is how I know she is not guilty of insider trading, because had she did, she would have done it perfectly and not got caught). Anyways, my room and our bathroom at the house are greatly appreciative of the influx of clean scents and material. Also, the essentials cheddar popcorn and instant oatmeal. Bear in my mind there was a ton of other stuff, such as the obligatory cat paraphernalia, and in the midst of it all a great book on Metallica. I have devouring the book that coincides with the release of their movie (included also in the package, YEAH!!!) and the book, language aside, is pretty cool. It is has caused me to re-evaluate my own mental state right now and make sure that I am properly communicating with others and not letting frustrations build up inside.

Had a great weekend, off FOB ministering to soldiers and also attending to some of my own spiritual and mental needs. As a communications person, I had to look honestly at how effectively I have been expressing myself. As a chaplain, it is very easy to be overtaken by the nice guy syndrome and thus being labeled a pushover. So this was a perfect time to after action review (AAR) my own situation and see how I can be even more effective in my ministry. To quote Pink Floyd on the Division Bell album, "We've got to keep talking."

This also melds well with my thoughts on the Gospel today. There is more than meets the eye, and our human perspective falls so very short of God's perspective. We make judgments that at times are based on our own limited perspective, prejudices, ignorance, or even fear. Case and point, who would think a priest could benefit spiritually from reading a book on Metallica? And yet, it gave me food for thought. Sometimes we are blind by circumstance, but other times we allow ourselves to be blind out of convenience. As we approach Easter, it might be a good time to re-evaluate how much we in our limited vision, limit God's ability to operate in our world. Then we need to do something about it. Let God be God, and let God bring us closer to seeing things from His perspective. It is an eye opening, heart opening, world opening experience that can expand us in ways we never imagined possible. All the best and rock on, R

P.S. FYI - Lars (Ulrich) is the outspoken Danish drummer for Metallica and like he is like a totally awesome (feeble attempt at imitating the So-Cal-Dane sound) percussive metal force.

6 MAR 05 20:06 A note of thanks
"Thank U" by Alanis Morissette

As I mentioned earlier, some packages have come in and I thought I'd say thank you. Most especially, a big thank you to Mom for the packages filled with goodies like coffee, a coffee maker, DVDs and some books and the sacred texts of a New Yorker: The Post, the Daily News and the New York Times, also for sending me my guitar and a few things that I left at home. She also sent a box of goodies from the Smiths of New City (John's family) and many thanks to them for the Jak Tweed and Bent Blue CDs, they are excellent. They also sent some cleaning supplies.

Many thanks to Richard and Elizabeth (the Smiths of Wappingers) for their keeping me spiritually nourished as I await my subscription of Magnificat. Also, and I will say more about this later in the week, thank you for keeping me up to date with the obituaries. Although it is sad to hear such things, I appreciate being able to pray for them and their families. Richard and Elizabeth Smith's daughter, Susan sent me two things. One the invitation to my dear friend's fiftieth wedding anniversary, of which it saddens me deeply that I can not attend physically, but of which I will most definitely be there in spirit. The other being a most excellent box of toiletries, snacks, and games some of which put the finishing touches on a care package I assembled for some of my soldiers that I visit. Thanks to my friends and cousins (note we share the last two letters of our names) the Ng's for their lovely Valentine's Day card. Also, a big thank you to Jeanne and John Tamigi for their box of magazines and newspapers. It's great to see what is going on back home besides the Drudge Report and Billboard.com.

I owe a belated thanks to the children of Saint Mary's. I distributed a lot of the holiday cards to soldiers as they were departing. Literally, as soldiers were getting on the plane to come here I was handing out your cards. There was a whole batch of cards, however, that I kept to myself because they were addressed to me, and there were the flags, which I intended to respond to once I, got settled here (I'll get to it). Some of the sentiments expressed were truly beautiful and some even brought a tear to my eye (please note there is no sarcasm in this statement). Also, there have been quite a few of you who have e-mailed me. Duly noted, might I add? I read them and I also read the comments and sometimes I can't answer right away and I tell myself I will get back to them tomorrow and then the CRS (can't remember stuff, kudos to Bob Dunn for that acronym) kicks in.

Even at this moment, I am afraid that I am forgetting

someone. Please be assured that I do so only because my absent mind is tired right now. Well, I think this sets a more suitable tone for the week. Be good. R

7 MAR 05 20:28   More kudos and some rambling thoughts about NY
"My Hometown" by Bruce Springsteen and the E Street Band

Just when I thought I was all thanked out...two more packages arrived. Many thanks to the Quaids for the cookies, coffee, coffee maker (now I have one for the office and one for my room (well you know I used to practically put coffee into my system intravenously)), a rug, toilet paper (which is like gold here), tanning lotion (ha!), the Southern Dutchess News and the Poughkeepsie Journal, and assorted goodies.

I laugh looking at the sunscreen because we need it here, but also because I will probably be the palest I have ever been in my life this year, here. Why? Well we wear our helmets (Kevlar) outside, and our sleeves are always down (prevents all sorts of problems like bug bites and sunburn (hey remember I am government property right now)), and so there is not much room to get tanned, save for the hands, nose, neck, and part of the face.

I was writing Shannon B. today and it dawned on me one of the things I really miss is being home in America. We are truly lucky living where we do, and having what we have. Over the past few years, I have fallen in love all over again with my adoptive state of New York (bear in mind I was born in Virginia, so I always felt like a bit of a visitor even though I grew up here). Christmas Eve, I kind of rekindled my love of Rockland County driving with Mom around Orangetown and just trading stories with her about the days of my youth. I think I astounded her with my memory and my driving roads I haven't been on in twenty years as if it was just yesterday, and my savant like recollection of some great family moments and haunts.

The past few years, I connected with some of my favorite pieces of real estate in the universe (this side of Rome). My last year in seminary school, I went up to West Point and/or Graymoor every single weekend. Just seeing that part of the Hudson River brought so much refreshment and peace to my spirit. I also, had a secret love of the Wappingers Falls that I had been nurturing since I was a wee lad. In fact, just before leaving Saint Mary's they (the infamous cabal of unknown entities we call "they") tore down Banta's Steak and Stein which was a blow to me because I had eaten there as a child with my Oma and Opa. I remember also, from our trips to Montgomery (which we affectionately called Monkey) Wards, when Burger King was not on Route 9 but rather it was Carroll's Burgers. The bridge over the troubled waters of the Wappinger Creek was the old bridge with the trestle (is that the right word?) back in the day. I had my first and only real car accident after visiting Father Desmond (little did I know I would have the same office as my "godfather" many moons later) at the South Hills Mall where I was hit by a parked truck (ah the warped perceptions of a sixteen year old).

Anyway it was a blessing to spend three years in one of my favorite places on earth, and in the process of living there to discover some truly sacred and special places nestled in the glorious precincts of Wappingers and her environs. One of my favorite pastimes was to take an evening drive (invariably winding up at Barnes and Noble) finding a new short cut here, or an innovative way to avoid certain stoplights, or a creative way to make a dull drive interesting. One thing I learned to do was go from the IBM in Poughkeepsie and pop out all the way down by the VA Hospital without touching Route 9 or 9D once in between, which is quite a feat indeed. And then when I joined the Guard after a lackluster few years in the Army Reserves (a priest from which told me I should resign my commission because I was not fully trained and the Army "couldn't use me" (if he only he knew)) (this encounter occurred the same day Father Jerry Miller, the Episcopalian priest in Wappingers Falls met me and told me we can use you in the Guard (he was right)) oh heck, I lost my train of thought sub referencing myself into silence. Ah yes, there it is...

Once I joined the National Guard, I discovered Kingston and the glories of Ulster and I started loving New York even more. By the time, I saw Windham, courtesy of the enigmatic and energetic Father Bob Dunn my guru and mentor, I had seen the light. New York is awesome. The first night I stayed up at his place, there was a power failure and I was too scared to stay in the house all by myself so I went for a drive and went into the mountains and drove many miles relishing the rural shelter of the Catskills. And I haven't even mentioned the Seven Lakes Drive. God I love that place.

And that has been a transition from small town boy, to suburban child, to the urban adolescent, and then spending the next 14 years in the nexus of all realities New York City and its urban sprawled aura, Yonkers, never mind the year of exile in Pennsylvania which was the equivalent of Martha' Stewart's West Virginia excursion, and then back to enjoying being in the Suburbs. Even now, it would be kind of weird to go back to the city, to live. But it is a nice place to visit from time to time.

It might be evident that I love my home, and I do, and I am very grateful that I can call such a place my home. I can't wait to get back there soon. Hopefully, if the weeks keep going as quick as they feel they are going, I will be able to soon enough watch the sun set against the Ramapo Mountains (hardly an accurate word to use - mountains) and see the moon rise through the trees spilling its light over Rockland's intimate valley.

Hey, God bless you all for keeping up with me. I have been just letting it all hit the screen, trying to hold back the edit monster and just letting the heart speak. Please be patient with me. I look forward to the day that I can go over all this and see how much I have finally committed to (virtual) paper thanks to Iraq and my time here. Then in the luxury of peacetime, the edit monster can have a ball. *Or not.*

As I conclude this evening, I have a special prayer request; please keep my friend Pat Manuli in your prayers, especially this week, and especially Thursday (for the surgery). That's the beauty of life with the Lord; no matter how far apart we may be we are only a prayer away. *Incidentally, Pat was the first person to encourage me to write about this experience, and that I probably had a book in me. Hmmm. What does she know? Ha.*

Bye for now, R

8 MAR 05 15:49 Projects (2)
"What You See Is What You Get" by Hall and Oates

Hola sports fans: Once again, I am hatching eggs, no I got that wrong, once again I am hatching plots. The plots are twofold.

Operation Keep the Troops Happy - I am in need of goodies for care packages when I visit my soldiers and also for little goody bags here. The standard fare is always needed like shampoo and soap and suntan lotion and odds and ends stuff. Flea collars are out this season. Seems they attract other insects that have a propensity for biting soldiers especially where the collar is. So we (army not our unit) had folks in the past that had pretty bitten up ankles wearing flea collars. Socks are always welcome, bandannas (not bananas), handkerchiefs, lip balm, Kool Aid powder packets, paperback books, crossword puzzles, (dollar store type stuff), also if you have old movies either on DVD or

VHS they will not be wasted. But also, we need some feminine type things. I asked one soldier to give me a list and here are some of the things she wrote down that she said would be a big pick me (well not me) up for ladies: shampoo (she suggested Paul Mitchell - Do they make little bottles of the stuff?), hair dye (normal colors though its the Army not ALIAS), conditioner for dry hair (the water here is weird), nail polish (clear for hands, I don't know about for feet but its not visible so I don't think there is a uniform expectation for that), Krumpets (whatever they are), nail files, foot stuff, brown and black hair ties or scrunchies. These are just a few suggestions, they might not seem that essential but they are a nice pick up (that sounds better).

Operation Kids in Iraq - Collecting things for kids like clothes (culturally sensitive, however, like no shorts and no shirts with graphics that might be offensive (like Mom said even Barbie could be considered offensive)) but some things are very practical like towels, blankets, wash clothes, socks, sneakers or shoes. Hoping to get this underway in a few months, but I have to work through the proper channels.

That's what I'm thinking right now. If you can help send me an e-mail and I can beam you my address. Many thanks!

9 MAR 05 19:58 What's Going On?
"Stagefright" by Def Leppard

The response from so many of you is a little staggering. I had no idea so many of you are out there reading this (which is a funny statement, as if some of you are not reading this?). It makes me a little nervous, almost like stage fright (yeah, I know what that is) that this is being widely read. I am truly humbled. Brian Murphy, one of my dear friends from the Camp Don Bosco era, set some lines to digits today and really made my day. He shared with me that part of his daily routine is to check out "A Day in the

Life". Hopefully, I won't disappoint y'all. And please forgive me for getting a little acerbic at times or for expressing my political views, I know that my sentiments aren't shared by all but I still believe it is better to say it than holding it inside. Communication is the key. That's my new mantra here, "Let it fly" or as Shrek in Shrek II says, "Better out than in". What a wise ogre that Shrek is. Every time I have adhered to this principle and maintained open and honest communication and expressed myself and put words to the thoughts or emotions I have been met with inner peace. It may not solve anything other than doing that, but I think it is worth it.

This has been a great medium, thus far, at communicating. As you probably have guessed by now, I enjoy dipping my toes into the stream of consciousness. I, also, have fallen in love with the parenthetical phrase (and "if you can't hear me its because I am speaking in parenthesis," a favorite Steven Wrightism).

Things are taking real nice shape here. My assignment for visiting FOBs to say Masses is almost official. You see, I not only am the Chaplain for my own battalion, but I provide denominational coverage to Catholics, or in military speak, RC. Within a few days I should know all the places I will be going to say Mass and visit soldiers. I have been doing some traveling but it is increasing. It is definitely a neat experience and also satisfies some of my curiosity as to what this country is like, albeit only a little bit. Each week, Mass attendance has been increasing. In fact, I am adding a Mass in the next few weeks. The locations also have been quite interesting. I have yet to say Mass on the hood of a Humvee, and it's not if I do, it's when. I think that is the pinnacle of being a priest Chaplain. I have said Mass in a theatre (like the ones with a stage), a room (duh), in a palace, that (the room not the palace, stay with me here) has become one of our "chapels", a little prayer room, a dining tent (which was kind of cozy and made me think of the early Church when people would gather in homes for the Eucharist), in a tent (this one made feel like Bono's "preacher stealin' hearts at a traveling show." In fact, at one of those Masses I was preaching and something came over me and I felt like Robert Duvall in "The Apostle" which is an amazing movie (a little violent, in one part) but still an amazing movie), and I started preaching about us all being "glory bound" and I thought whoa this tent thing is pretty wild. But hey, I'm comfortable in a tent or a cathedral. It's all good to me, and it's what you're doing that's important more than where you're at.

The latest news is the grisly find of numerous dead bodies in Baghdad, killed by the insurgents. What a horrible legacy these diverse groups have forged for themselves. Murdering men, women and children. And for what? What do they want? Can any ideology justify this malevolent conduct? Can anything justify murdering the innocent? And, again, I need to understand how, while we are here trying to bring to fruition a peaceful society, how Americans can be opposed to this war? How is it that evil in the world is tolerable? What has become of us? How did we become such complacent cows? How can any sane loving human being accept that men and women and children can just be killed? When did this become acceptable? Where did the non-linear and the logically anemic concept emerge that we are not a perfect nation and therefore we should not dictate to others how to live? Who preaches this nonsense and how could they not be a hypocrite when they said it and not keep their mouth shut to, since they were imperfect? ("Now I don't want to go off on a rant here but" (thanks to Dennis Miller) I tell you these Vermonters really have stoked my Irish with their resolutions, what are they against the FACT that we are fighting evil people. Dare I quote a movie I refuse to see, but in Spiderman don't we learn that "With great power comes great responsibility"? If we pulled out now we are only saying that this murderous conduct is allowable. I wonder then if Vermont would be welcoming of these evil persons to their state and set up shop there. It would make sense, if we shouldn't be here, because we do not have a just cause, why don't the resolute people of Vermont have a big barbeque and invite our insurgent foes to it and they can all just have a nice time, while we soldiers, here, help bring justice and peace to the people of Iraq.

When did Americans lose their moral fiber? Where did it all go wrong? I ask myself every few weeks why is it that I am here, other than the obvious cause: that I signed my name to a piece of paper and took a couple of oaths (uphold Constitutions of United States and New York State). Well the latest answer to the question is: it's a matter of justice. I am here, serving in the capacity that I can, to bring justice to a land thirsting for justice. I am performing my role in bringing right to a very wrong situation. I am satisfied with this reason, and I can live with it. I am honored to be here and I believe that if there are folks who have to endure a lifetime of injustice I can endure a year in doing my part to contributing to the cause of justice. It's a price worth paying. If we won't fight evil what have we become? Love and peace!

11 MAR 05 22:15 Dreary
"God Put A Smile On Upon Your Face" by Coldplay

We are in the deep freeze here with temperatures plunging into the 40's the past few days. Mix that with rain and what do you have? Dreariness. But alas the spirit is stronger. All is well. A low key day, but in this business we welcome low key. I apologize to those of you who really are cold. Just remember in less than two weeks this miserable thing called winter is over. For those of you who think that I got off lucky this winter, just remember I was at Fort Drum exercising outside when it was 20 below zero before Christmas! That's the big league chill. As I write this, though, I might as well tell you a little story.

One day, up there at Fort Drum, I was freezing and in the

midst of meditating on the misery of the frigid weather I sarcastically considered that being "upstate" I was closer to the Canadian border. My ruminations then migrated to the sarcastic notion that since Canada is closer to the North Pole would the Northern Lights be visible. That started me on a bit of regret that I am thirty-two and have yet to have seen the Northern Lights. Well to make a short story long... That evening I was having a "cold one" and hanging out with a few of the officers when someone knocked on the door. Coming in they were all excited because the Northern Lights were visible outside. (Just for the sake of setting the scene and adding a Stonehenge sound effect kind of whoooooooooowhooooooooooooooo spooky soundtrack vibe, Yassar Arafat was lying on one of his deathbeds at the time.) So I went outside and there they were off to the north of all the strange places, green and wavy just like the pictures I saw in books, the Northern Lights. Wow what a treat! Bye for now, R

12 MAR 05 17:25 A perfect day
"Perfect Day" by Lou Reed

Today was a perfect day for going to the golf course. The kind of weather that compliments so well a visit to the driving range, hit a bucket of balls and have a nice dirty water dog with mustard and ketchup (the horror!) and some onions. The sky was impossibly blue. A bit windy. The sun shining makes even this land look pretty darn friendly. Hope the weather is improving back home.

13 MAR 05 22:16 The best laid plans...
"Take It Easy" by The Eagles

Ah! The best laid plans of mice and men...(There is a brilliant British comedian, Eddie Izzard, who really attacks Mr. Shakespeare's quote with the observation that he doesn't know what plans mice are laying)...today was another beautiful day, I had a brief opportunity to sit and eat lunch watching the sun glisten gold ripples over the breezed upon surface of one of the two man-made lakes here. I sure wish I was up at Lake Askoti, up there in the Seven Lakes Drive area, just south of Lake Tiorati. That there is another of my favorite places on Earth. When I get the chance I'll throw a copy of the poem that I wrote about that lake that was inspired by an Easter Sunday experience. Stay tuned...I'll try to put it up on Easter Sunday.

But those plans...man they get frustrated...Today I aimed to be where I had to be with time to spare and try to keep the pace of the day and Masses a little less hectic and rushed and guess what...Stuff happens...And that is where the challenge lies, when our plans for improvement get frustrated do we cease to plan? No, it means we need to adapt to the challenge, but it shouldn't mean that we stop trying. Sometimes it is the effort that we put into a project or a plan that means more than even the net result. Sometimes God speaks directly to us in the frustration. Sometimes that is exactly the thing God wants us to work on. For instance, if you are like me noise can be a blessing or a curse. I like the noise of music and interesting noises, but certain sounds especially repetitive sounds or inconsiderate public noise like whistling on line at grocery store or incessant tapping drive me nuts.

Now lets sit in a metaphorical pew in church and lets deal with that annoying person next to us who may be disturbing us while we are trying to pray. While we may see a frustration of what we are trying to do and then get angry with the person for it (hopefully not expressing that anger). A different view would be to start inserting that person in our prayer. Maybe they are nervous, and just fidgety, dealing with a problem the only way they can at the moment. Maybe they came to church because of this issue. Maybe our reaction or reactive look may influence them in a negative manner. Maybe... Well you get the gist. I am not a perfect practitioner of this myself. In fact, I am awful at it sometimes. But I am trying.

15 MAR 05 15:50 Source material I wrote for Catholic New York Article
"Who Are You" by The Who

I am stationed at FOB (Forward Operating Base) Danger in Tikrit. Tikrit is a small ancient city, believed to have been founded by Alexander the Great. Tikrit really has earned a place in the world's eyes as being the birthplace of Saddam Hussein. Ironically, it was just on the outskirts of Tikrit that Saddam was captured, just over a year ago.

I am the Battalion Chaplain for the 250th Signal Battalion, based out of New Jersey. My home unit is the newly formed 104th Military Police in Kingston, New York.

The base here is one of Saddam Hussein's palace complexes. The property here was not open to the general Iraqi populace but some Tikritis grew up on the grounds before Saddam and his government seized it and made it his property.

There are several very large buildings and numerous smaller palaces. Most are decorated with elaborate garnishments but on closer inspection one can ascertain poor craftsmanship and it evident that the builders cut a lot of corners to create a stylish atmosphere but one with little substance. (A great example is seeing how there may be marble floors in a lot of these palaces and yet there is just simple concrete grouting done.)

There is a place that was a bit of a "hangout" for one of Saddam's sons. The lake it overlooks is one of two man made lakes here. In one of these lakes divers discovered the remains of women who had been raped, murdered and then dumped.

Tikrit is located in what is known as the Sunni Triangle. There are some insurgent hotbeds in this country, but it is difficult to characterize this area or even this country as insurgent country.

Their presence is felt. They are active, but the nature of the insurgency must be understood properly. Insurgent is a label that covers a multitude of factions and groups with varying goals, motives, and techniques. Some of the insurgency is based on the religious differences of the Sunnis and the Shiites. Others are ethnically different as is the case with Arab and Kurdish tensions. There are many clans that live in Iraq and there are some rather long standing conflicts that exist between various clans. There is also a diverse political landscape, which at times blends seamlessly with the aforementioned rivalries. The insurgency is not a unified group adhering to one set of standards or principles. Mixed into the religious and political ideologies of the insurgency, there is also the criminal element that has taken advantage of this situation to establish their own presence here in Iraq.

In all then, the level of caution is always strong. One does not ever leave a FOB or a military installation without having prepared for the worse. There is nothing routine about traveling here. Anything is possible, and we do not look at any movement casually. Preparation, training, and the flexibility to deal with an ever evolving and adaptable adversary is a challenging endeavor. There is a certain healthy degree of fear, which is present at times, this fear is not a hindrance to our mission but a reality that must be acknowledged and transcended. We have a job to do, for the most part we do not have the luxury to not perform that job, and so we need to put our fears aside and do the best we can in our mission.

I arrived here in Iraq on the eve of the National Elections. At the present time, I am unable to disclose a return date.

In May, I will have been in the New York Army National Guard for two years. I am currently a First Lieutenant and am awaiting promotion to Captain. This past summer, I went to the United States Army Chaplain School and Center, at Fort Jackson, South Carolina. I participated several years prior while in the United States Army Reserves in the first stage of the Chaplain Officers Basic Course and this year completed that training. In it we had a modified Officers Basic Course. I say modified for the reason that weapon training is not part of Chaplaincy training. Chaplains are non-combatants and are not to bear arms under any circumstance. This prohibition is both a military policy and a principle of the Geneva Conventions.

I wear the very same protective gear as my soldiers wear. As a designated non-combatant I am assigned a Chaplain Assistant. Together we comprise what is called the Unit Ministry Team. My assistant is a man who wears many hats; a veritable sacristan, administrative assistant, driver (although, I do my share of driving, too), an extra pair of eyes for discerning soldier issues and he is responsibility for my safety and defense in times of jeopardy.

As a Chaplain, my mission is straightforward: To uphold my soldiers' Constitutional right to free exercise of religion. Concurrent with this mission is providing Catholic religious support for Catholic soldiers. I must also ensure that the moral and spiritual climate of the unit is in good order. This is a vital service for soldiers. It can save lives and careers if they are staying spiritually centered. When they go astray and do not deal with their moral and spiritual welfare they will find other outlets, which may be illicit or pose a danger to themselves or others.

As one would imagine, I interact with people of varying faiths and must ensure that they each are able to worship according to the tenets of their faith. I also get to work with Chaplains of different faith groups. This gives me the opportunity to dialogue on a personal level about our respective beliefs and has aided me in understanding different perspectives a little better. I find enjoyable to ask questions and have had a lot of misconceptions dispelled by this opportunity.

A majority of the soldier's issues are related to the work environment and the stresses that accompany deployment. The normal stress of being away from family and friends for an indefinite amount of time places a two-fold burden on the soldier. Add to this mix, job stress, combat operations and combat related issues and anxieties and one can get an idea why a chaplain is indispensable to a unit.

My role as a Catholic priest is no different from being at home. The major exception is in this environment one has to be very flexible. Mass times, through no fault of my own, may be fluid or changed on a dime. I also must be conscious of time and be sensitive to the fact that soldiers may not have a lot of time to be away from their stations. I also have to set aside some of the creature comforts that priests usually expect. One place I said Mass at had only a very small table that I could use as an altar, I had to bend down pretty low so I could see my Sacramentary, and it looked kind of silly in relation to someone of my height and stature all hunched over. One place, I had to compete with the loud helicopters outside of the tent. The other day I was saying the prayer over the gifts when a mortar went off near enough to shake the chapel. A slight pause was all I had to register what had just gone off, and deal with my own emotional response, and continue on with the Mass. It was a good reminder that what I was experiencing was only a hint of what these men and women experience on a daily basis.

My ministry can be described in these terms, availability, presence and communication. It is very important to the soldiers to know that they have someone who is there expressly for their needs and concerns. My availability is a necessity. It follows then that I must also be present among my soldiers. Bishop Gerald Walsh, many years ago once told me of the priest's role as a ministry of presence. I have had, thus far, some truly grace-filled moments talking with soldiers and because I was in the right place at the right time. And in that much of my time is spent listening and aiding in communication. At times I can be a fresh set of ears with a fresh perspective that may help in the situation. Sometimes I am the bridge between two parties that might have very different views, and every so often I must be an advocate for a soldier that has a grievance with another soldier. What is key though, is that I am considered one of the soldiers. I may have some privileges but in all we share a common experience being away from our family, friends, and our lives back home.

As a priest, an essential part of my life as an Army Chaplain is saying Mass and administering the sacraments to my soldiers. This is done each Sunday and also throughout the week as I visit the FOBs that I am responsible for as a Catholic Chaplain. There are three other priests, and we cover an area, described as, about the size of West Virginia.

As a chaplain, I have a direct link to my commander. I advise my commander on religious and moral issues and am considered the resident expert. I am responsible for designing a religious program for my commander and then seeing that it is implemented. The religious program is not my own per se but hers since this is her unit. As I provide her with an estimate of the spiritual climate of the unit she offers guidance as to what she would like done to meet their needs.

This particular mission Task Force Liberty is a National Guard led mission, one of the first times since the Korean Conflict. The 42nd Infantry Division leads Task Force Liberty. The soldiers of Task Force Liberty are focused and have embraced their mission with vigor and enthusiasm. The overall tenor is good. We are encouraged by the great strides and developments here. The elections were a great sign of hope and demonstrated that the work here is not for naught. There is certainly much work to be done, but it is not an impossible task. The majority of Iraqis are glad to be free from an oppressive regime and are weary of those who insist on frustrating their aspirations for a better life. Each day that dream comes closer to be a fully realized reality as men and women embrace democratic principles and shape the future. Despite threats against their lives, Iraqis by the thousands have volunteered to serve their nation as police or military personnel. And many more have entered into the burgeoning political process and are staking their claim in service to their nation. This offers us with hope and a sense of satisfaction that we are able to assist the Iraqi people in this defining moment in history.

Additional personal tidbits:

I have been a musicologist for most of my life. I grew up in a home where Motown was on par with sacred music. Oldies were a major staple of my musical diet growing up. My first real personal preference was expressed in my devouring John Lennon's Double Fantasy album when it came out. I was nine. "Watching the Wheels" is probably on my top ten of favorite songs. When I went to Cathedral Prep I lived with a student from Wappingers Falls, of all places, who taught me, through immersion, the sublime beauty of hard rock and heavy metal. In my four years there I learned all about Van Halen, Led Zeppelin, AC/DC, Pink Floyd, as well as the now so-called hair metal bands. The latter is probably one of my guiltiest pleasures. My musical journey has taken me into almost every kind of music and style. I can enjoy gangsta rap as well as something from Senegal. I am not a musical snob except in regards to the so-called Nu-Metal of Korn and Limp Bizkit. My favorite group of all time though would have to be U2. They just move me like few others can. I have an I-Pod with an obscene amount of music on it. I have yet to find a radio station here, not because I haven't tried but because the radio hasn't arrived yet. It's on the way. I am however devouring cds and DVDs. Today I picked up the new Lee Ann Womack album, which is pretty nice, and has an old school country ambience.

We have four cats at home now. Iggy, the newest addition, Cee Cee who joined our family about a year ago, and Sportie and Smokey both of whom have lived on our property for almost ten years. All the cats mentioned appeared on our doorstep. They were preceded by Toonces who we had for almost twelve years. She was the gateway cat. She taught us that we had not yet lived until we had become cat owners or rather until she owned us.

The blog is a new addition. (I have been writing poems for about fifteen years but I am very shy about it, despite having cultivated a pretty solid voice and style.) Writing though for me has always been more about editing that coming up with ideas. I spend much more time editing and rewriting and shaping what has been written than generating the initial idea. With the blog the exact opposite is occurring. I am keeping the editing down to a bare minimum and using this as an exercise to express my self candidly and yet with in the strictures of operational security. Much of what I experience can't be written because it could reveal information concerning operations and mission sensitive items. So there lies the secret to the schizophrenic hopscotch that occurs on the website. This limitation has opened up new possibilities for me as a writer. By being confined in what I can talk about I have become flexible enough to delve into new avenues of expression. Now telling a story has become not an interest but something vital. Here I can truly appreciate the vital connection writing has. Interestingly enough, I now have an audience and they are not as harsh the critics as I imagined an audience would be. I have yet to meet a harsher critic than myself. Be that as it may.

As a final note, I forgot to mention the people of Saint

Mary's. A number of people have taken advantage of the technological opportunities to impart to me messages of support and affirmations of my ministry there and beyond. I am humbled so often by the kind words and deeds of my parishioners. It is hard to believe that when I come home I will not be returning to Saint Mary's. I am not sure if I have really processed that yet.

15 MAR 05 21:36 Where does the time go?
"Tuesday's Gone" by Lynyrd Skynyrd

Tuesday's almost gone. Time is rushing by. I was made aware of that today with the news of the death of Father Floyd Grace. Ordained just a year before me, I had known Floyd for maybe ten years. Lived with him at the St. John Neumann Residence and at Dunwoodie. A good man. A good priest. Relatively young, too. I ask that you remember his family and his parishioners in your prayers. For some strange reason, Floyd always smiled, would shake his head, and inevitably burst into a restrained laugh whenever I talked to him. I could say something as innocent as "Hi" and I could be assured that a volley of jocularity would come flow out. There was no guile with him. In my book, that says it all. Regarding prayers and prayer requests, please keep Pat in your prayers, as well. Another kind person, with whom there is no guile.

The weather here has been glorious. Blue skies. A growing greenness. The night skies here have been equally glorious. The night sky is resplendent with constellations pronounced even more than home by the lack of the amount of ambient light pollution we New Yorkers are accustomed. The days have been busy as one can imagine as I begin planning Holy Week. That seems to be an interesting endeavor coordinating with out the luxury of musicians and lectors and altar servers. This little cowboy is tired so allow me to bid you all adieu. Bis Morgen.

17 MAR 05 18:49 St. Patrick's Day – Happiness & Joy
"No Excuses" by Alice In Chains

Happy St. Patrick's Day! Have a leprechaun on the door from the Rumleys, a little card with the leprechaun in a glass of green beer. I bet that would be a fun swim. Had lunch with Phillip today and hung out with him for a bit. (I baptized his son on New Year's Eve). He is one of my sanity people. Hanging out with him even for a few minutes usually generates some laughter and good vibes. The past few days have been taxing. The best way to describe things here is to say that different weeks we ride different waves. Yesterday was one such day. I'd rather not go into further detail, at least right now. Things are going well. The weather here is nice and getting warmer. Keep up the prayers, they are working! Bye for now, R

18 MAR 05 19:10 Friday already
"Three Little Birds" by Bob Marley and the Wailers

All is well. It was a mad cross between a slow week and a busy week and then the dragon of office work (yuck) arose to cast a shadow on my days. In all, the week has been going rather slowly, but there has been enough in it to fit three weeks. On Wednesday, a few of our soldiers were involved in an accident. Thank God, all emerged fine, although a little banged up. That same day, in I was supposed to go on another convoy, in the very same vehicle. The convoy that went in our stead on the way hit an IED. (improvised explosive device planted by God only knows. You guessed it, terrorists not Americans!). Again, luckily, no was killed. A honey wagon (that's Army talk for the truck that sucks out the waste from the Porto sans) was damaged, however. The newly promoted Staff Sergeant Swain and I went to visit our soldiers who were in the accident. Their guardian angels deserve a bonus, considering the HUMVEE rolled over twice, and that they were thrown out of the vehicle in the midst of the rollovers.

Seeing the wreckage, one would have expected them all to be dead. After that trip was complete, we officially have logged-in thirteen convoys.

Yesterday, I earned my money tackling the logistical horrors of preparing to minister to soldiers scattered over quite a distance for Holy Week. Sadly, I will not be able to go to all my areas of responsibility each day, and when all is said and done, I feel a bit like a bad parent not being able to provide for my "children". I wish I could be with them all, and since God does not approve of cloning, I have to do the best I can with what I got. But the planning has been done, and now I just have to implement the plan.

One of my plans was to hit one of my FOBs today. Thanks to the grace and power of a Blackhawk, I had a great commute to work today and was able to bring Palm Sunday (early) to some of our soldiers and civilian support personnel. After meeting with one of our Chaplains and working on a schedule, we caught our Blackhawk back to our - home away from home. When we arrived here, the big news was that our friends, in the Monsignor Smith usage of the term, here had been a little aggressive in their hazardous occupation as terrorists. Targeting soldiers at lunchtime. There were some injuries, but thankfully guardian angels are diligent workers. Please note: the bad guys like the cowards they are had to launch their attack from a staging area near civilians, so we couldn't respond proportionately.

The best way to describe the bad guys would be to call them the Meredith Baxter Birney of terrorists. They may have the made for television movies locked, but they will never be the next Faye Dunaway.

I hope this note finds you all well. Happy Saint Patrick's Day! And a very Happy Saint Joseph's Day tomorrow! Have a Saint Joseph zeppoli for me, the Italian pastry for St. Joseph's Day. The Groundhog should have them, and if they don't tell Mike I am shocked. All the best, R

20 MAR 05 15:47 In the face of evil
"If I Die Tomorrow" by Mötley Crüe

Many of you, for almost a year have been with me in some manner on my journey as a military chaplain. This is a very intriguing ministry because there would seem to be an inherent contradiction in terms. No one really has called me on this, and asked me how it is that I as a clergyman could find it consistent with my call to wear a military uniform and to (guilt by association) condone the military action that is now in its second year, here in Iraq. I have been consistent from day one in seeing this war as necessary and a matter of justice. Whether one is pro- or anti-George W. Bush is beside the point, for me. The Hussein regime was an intolerable evil in the world. There is nothing that can be said good about what Iraq had to endure during his tenure as dictator and "first criminal." Saddam Hussein and his network of sociopaths that enjoyed the subjugation of the Iraqi people for over two decades needed to be removed. The fact that Hussein was a sponsor of terrorism is undeniable. There is no credible or reality based argument that can deny this fact. Rehashing the subject again, rewards were offered to the families of suicide bombers in Palestine, by the Iraqi government. Thousands of dollars were provided for death and destruction while Saddam Hussein allowed his own people to wallow in poverty and oppression. In Saddam's world, rape, torture, mutilation, intimidation, mass murder, environmental destruction, persecution, extortion and a pantheon of other evils were commonplace and tolerated. The scars left on the Iraqi people by the tyranny of Saddam Hussein will take generations to heal.

And yet still, there is a belief that stains reality like an oil fire cloud that seeks to deny the facts and to twist reality on its head. This mentality seeks to look at Iraq and what has happened here, and to place the blame on the shoulders of the United States of America. It seeks to place the onus on men and women who advocated the invasion of Iraq and to deceive the world into believing that we have perpetrated an evil far greater than anything Saddam Hussein could ever have possibly done. In the face of evil, we cannot sit idly by. In being a member of a just society inaction is action. When we allow women to be raped, human beings to murdered, and allow innocents to be subjected to hell on earth we are not being true ambassadors of peace we are collaborators. At times in our nation's history we have allowed evils to exist, but this time we got it right. It is morally repulsive to me that anyone would advocate allowing evil to flourish. Pacifism would exclude using force to prevent an evil act from occurring. I cannot subscribe to this, because this is not justice. Justice is defending the defenseless. It means stopping evil even if this requires the use of force.

The law of war is very precise as to when the use of force can be authorized and is permissible. There are criteria that must be adhered to very similar to the criteria that police officers must adhere to and almost identical to the just war tradition. As a seminarian, I studied this subject with Monsignor William Smith, a man who often gets quoted here for his quips but whose true genius is his extensive knowledge of the realm of morality and the study of moral theology. In all of my studies, I have encountered the constant confusion of terms that need to be precisely defined and used very carefully.

As a Christian, I must look to the person of Jesus Christ and his teachings. Given his proclivity for delving into controversy, I find it curious that the Lord never issued a prohibition against conflict. In fact, our Lord speaks of the blessedness of peacemakers yet when he encounters military persons he does not chastise them for their choice of profession. There are a multitude of curious observations regarding military life that should be noted; 1) Roman soldiers are some of the first witnesses to the identity of Christ, 2) Christ heals the Centurion's (equally shocking) slave, 3) Christianity's rapid spread is attributed to how the faith spread with great speed by way of the Roman military. I could continue, but this is a good start and makes my point. Jesus gives the command to some to change their life (i.e. telling prostitutes and tax collectors to repent and sin no more) and yet he does not do the same to the soldier. On the contrary, Jesus highlights in the case of the Centurion the man's great faith.

So either Jesus Christ was coward or he saw nothing intrinsically evil with the profession of soldier. It would then follow that Jesus saw even some moral possibility for one serving even as a Roman soldier (the occupiers of Israel)! Where then is this primacy of pacifism. Where is the foundation of pacifism in the life and teachings of Christ? Are we to maintain that it all lies in the Lord's instruction to "Turn the other cheek"? Are we also to consider the Lord in violation of his own teaching when he takes the chords and fashions a whip and drives the merchants (with force I might add) out of the Temple, after peacefully over turning their tables. Hmmmm. I am not a pacifist. I do not believe that we are called to sit idly by as evil runs rampant. I believe that when we allow evil to flourish we are actively (albeit with passivity) cooperating with that evil. If one does not protect innocent human life one is (in the moral sense) performing an evil act. This war has seen the loss of innocent life. At times, this has been done intentionally by individuals, who have not acted in accord with the laws of war, regardless of sides. To put the onus entirely on the United States of America is disingenuous and erroneous.

Fact: The United States has put on trial and convicted soldiers when they stepped outside the boundaries of internationally accepted rules of engagement. But we cannot forget that an adversary infests the peacekeeping operations here, an insurgency. Insurgents do not operate within any internationally accepted rules of war. In their cowardice they hide among civilians, they wear no uniform, they intentionally target non-military personnel and non-military targets and many of them have either received their training by the former regime or by foreign powers that sponsor terrorism.

Forgive my passion on this subject, but as a man whose mission places me in situations that are at times dangerous, as a man who serves with men and women who find themselves in dangerous and life threatening situations, as a man who ministers to soldiers that must at times make life and death decisions, as a man who knows what it feels like to be hunted and defenseless, I do not take easily to suggestions that the presence of United States soldiers in Iraq is wrong. I believe this is probably one of the most right things this country has done in many years. This is a just cause, it is a mission that is just, and it will produce real results. It may take time, it will take patience, but it is worth it. There are men and women here who have yet to understand the concepts we Americans were born into. Freedom, rights, true justice, these are concepts that the Iraqi people are capable of learning but theory needs to be practiced. Right thinking needs to be complimented by right action. Some speak so smugly that the Iraqi people will never be able to have a true democracy. This is silly. Of course, they will be able to have true democracy but they need instruction.

Maybe we as Americans need to re-evaluate what democracy is, maybe we need to re-learn some things. Maybe we have become a little to secure in our concepts and have lost track of what freedom is. We speak of freedoms in convoluted ways. We speak of the murder of innocent human life as freedom of choice. And why don't "pacifists" don't protest this destruction of human life? I suppose I could go on for days, but as you see I see no contradiction in my line of work. I do now that I am a changed man, I believed in justice and freedom, but now I appreciate it more having seen the face of evil and seen the wounds it has caused. To all the men and women in uniform, live justly, act faithfully, and may God be with you.

My comments can only be characterized as the words of one still distressed. I watch the news, now feeling more divorced than ever from a public that still uncomprehending of how bad it was here in Iraq. There was such an abject antipathy to the human person, and human life was seen as so disposable in the ruling party's view that the Iraqi government was a threat to our nation. The record of atrocities perpetrated by Saddam Hussein and his rogue government provided sufficient hints as to the direction that they were aimed in. With Afghanistan no longer offering the safety terrorists crave, and without a government to be a big daddy to them, terrorists were on the prowl for another regime that they could cozy up to. Saddam's government was a prime successor as the protectorate of Al-Qaeda as it had been for various other terrorists and terrorist groups. The Michael Moores, the John Kerrys, the Hollywood elite, and the other self proclaimed spokespersons for civilization were wrong. Their facade as being counter culture figures whose goal was peace turned out to be a popular celebrity cause devoid of moral courage or rectitude and awash in animus against our President.

So while, people march protesting the war, I stare at a television screen in Iraq, saddened by the display that mocks my soldiers. Hey instead of protesting, and waving your chicken feet and rainbow bright flags why not put some resources into building instead of tearing down. Maybe the Kumbaya chanting, prisoners of the sixties, and all the other folks should start sending some clothes and money to charities (oh no not faith based initiatives!) and doing something useful and winning hearts and minds. If they want us home, why don't they stop whining and start doing stuff to bring us home by fostering peace here? And please know that your misplaced expressions of sympathy can bring s a lot of sadness to people who pass by, and have to live without their relatives for almost a year at a time serving this nation.

It would behoove people to be aware that in the pocket of every soldier is a card that reads "Rules of Engagement." *See Appendix D for more regarding ROE.*

21 MAR 05 17:43 Thank you (plural)
"Lovecats" by The Cure

"We in government have a duty to protect the weak, disabled and vulnerable."
  - Governor Jeb Bush, Florida

Words like this restore my faith in the political process and that some politicians still are aware of their responsibilities and obligations. (As if he would be reading this, but it's the thought that counts. Right?) Thank you, Mr. Bush.

Additional thanks are in order. Thank you to Jerry and Gwen Ng for the nice box with some Easter candy and some fun cat books. Which reminds me, it has been sixty two days, at least, since I have seen my last real authentic cat. I'm going through withdrawal, I tell you. Hope everyone is doing well. You are missed very much. Please keep up the prayers too, they are working.

Adieu, R

23 MAR 05 10:44 Holy Week, Psalm 22 and life
"Praying For Time" by George Michael

A blessed Holy Week to all! Today is known as Spy Wednesday. The name is derived from the Gospel reading of the day where we find Judas covertly aligning himself with those seeking to deliver Jesus to death. The intrigue continues to develop this week as we journey through the Lord's last days prior to the Resurrection. As we meditate on the Passion of Our Lord I cannot help but think of another Calvary occurring in our own beloved nation, what has become the deathbed of Terri Schiavo. This horrible tragedy that has unfolded is another clear example of the continuous assault upon human life.

Again, truth has been veiled by the emotional whims of an individual. A moral ethic must be grounded in absolute principles founded on truth. Life is sacred. We have a duty as human beings to protect life in all its stages. This particular case is alarming because it is eroding the moral landscape. Food is being equated with extra-ordinary means. Whether the food is being delivered by a spoon, a fork, hands, or a tube, food is not an extra-ordinary treatment. Fact: We need food to eat or we die. What causes confusion sometimes is the use of artificial means for respiration or ventilation. Some of these processes go above and beyond the scope of the ordinary means of preserving life. At times, persons are taken off respirators and they are still able to breath and still able to live. One cannot live with out nutrition. If they cannot ingest food they will die.

For all the drumbeating about keeping legislatures out of the practice of medicine, which is inherently a false premise, there are inconsistent thinkers who will do anything to attack the life ethic including betraying their own principles to further their pro-death agenda. So, if it means killing a sick person, let's have a judge dictate medical procedure. If it means killing an unborn child, let's have a judge turn his/her not legislate on medical procedures and let doctors do their job. Hmmm, there is something fishy in the State of Denmark, as old Bill once said.

Starvation is a horrible way to die. Even more horrible is

the fact that because Terry may have diminished reasoning, her husband (the loathsome toad) sees fit to be merciful and let her die in this manner. Is this how America treats those who are already suffering? This seems to contradict the works of many dedicated Americans who have been advocates for the innocent, the weak and the defenseless. In this month in which we celebrate the contribution of women in our society, I can't help but think of Eunice Schriver and her work establishing the Special Olympics and raising awareness to the plight of those who may suffer diminished reasoning. And what about those who suffer other debilitating handicaps? Should Christopher Reeve have had his life terminated because he was dependent on machines for breathing assistance?

Life is sacred.

A segment of the population wishes to deny this with their false and emotionally charged arguments about dignity and quality of life. Let me say this about that, my dignity comes from being made in the image and likeness of God. I believe this holds true for every single human being in this world. I believe quality of life is too subjective for one to base a moral principle on. One person's definition of quality of life is a death sentence for someone else. But nowadays this is the end all be all. Quality of life. The truth is that we all want to hide from suffering. I do. And yet, there is no hiding from it. It is there. In has to be accepted and it is possible to triumph over it. I have seen it done. In my view the dignity of the person is never lost.

Quite honestly if I didn't believe in the sacredness of life I would suggest that all the death lovers just do themselves a favor and end it. Interestingly enough though, most of the death lovers, prefer harming others and have no qualms about living themselves. Those who hold their own life in contempt seem to have given into the conventional idiocy that the helter skelter morally vacuous have been promoting. Terri Schiavo's husband undoubtedly is obsessed with her demise. And being a New Yorker filled with a slightly cynical inquisitive nature has to ask the big question: Why? What's in it for him? True love? Yeah, believe that and I have a bridge in Tikrit to sell you. Mark my words there is money to be had, or an inconvenience to be relieved by her death. This is not a rational man. In fact, like all benders of truth he has shown that the rational is not opposed to the spiritual, but it is often at times with the emotional. As he becomes ever more consumed in his emotional response he is showing his lack of rationality. And people accuse the religious minded folks of being unreasonable (I chuckle).

So there you have it. The drama of Holy Week unfolding in macro vision. Another innocent condemned to die. Psalm 22 for me is where it's all at. Written hundreds of years before our Lord's Passion we witness so vivid a depiction of his sufferings, death and his triumph. "My God, my God why have you abandoned me?" Those words on the cross are scriptural shorthand referring to this psalm. The speaker in the psalm it becomes apparent is the Lord. Where is his dignity as he suffers so shameful a fate? Is it diminished in the least because he is suffering? No in fact, his dignity is not diminished but made manifest to all. In the most horrible moment of his life he is glorified. That is why the cross is not seen as something shameful but something we Christians boast. We see the triumph of our Lord.

"I thirst." As we meditate on our Lord's Passion and Cross may we pray for all those who suffer, that in their time of trial they may experience union with their Savior and also share in His Resurrection. Let us pray also in a special way for our sister, Terry, and for her family that they may experience relief of God's abiding presence as they cry out with him these words. Enjoy and God bless and may you all have a Blessed Holy Week.

24 MAR 05 16:27 Holy Thursday
"Mass in B Minor (Qui Tollis)" by Dominic Miller

Holy Thursday in Iraq is a little different, but also there is something glorious found in the sameness of ritual. There was a little less liturgical panache but I did do my best to live by Fr. Anthony Sorgie's credo back at St. Joseph Seminary of offering the liturgy in "noble simplicity". I had two Masses which were rather small gatherings but still beautiful. My homiletic message was pretty simple. We need allow the Lord to was our feet. In other words, we should not be ashamed to allow God to minister to our needs. Who doesn't need to be cleansed by the Lord? This gesture of love and humility, though, needs to be offered to those around us. We need to minister to all the people we encounter, following the Lord's example. He did not pick and choose the persons he would love. He loved all. Some times it was tough love, but more often it was a tender love filled with understanding and compassion. Are we willing to roll up our sleeves and love even those who have hurt us?

If it sounds hard, then the message is being heard. It is virtually impossible on our own. That is why the Lord linked this lesson with the gift of the Eucharist. On our own we are powerless. The Eucharist is our fuel. It is our strength. The Eucharist offers us the graces we need so that we may no longer try on our own, but so that we may share in the legacy of union with Christ. We then can be His hands in the world. We can be His voice in the world. Union with Christ. That's what it is all about. Union in purpose. Union in spirit. Union in truth. Union in love.

And to counter our arguments of unworthiness, Jesus says to us, "Yeah and so? Let me wash your feet." He wants us to avail ourselves to his ministering. We need to allow him into our lives, and He will provide for us. In this, we are granted a worthiness beyond our expectations. God has deigned to share Himself with those who are unworthy.

God knows what He is doing. So let us let Him do what He must.

25 MAR 05 16:45 Good Friday
"The Cross" by Prince

This morning we had a nice Good Friday service here. One of the things about religious services and Masses in the military, that is weird, is you never know how many people may be there at a given liturgy. It could be sixty or it could be eight. Yesterday, my first Mass had eight people. The second one, twenty two (ish). This morning, I had about twenty six attend the service. (These are rough numbers; recall memory is always a little flimsy.) This evening, I have no idea what attendance will be like. I am hoping for an increase. Again the buzzword for the liturgies is "noble simplicity". The message for the day is that we need to look at the cross as the point where humanity and divinity meet in the person of Christ and His Passion. Usually we relate to Jesus in His resurrected person. Perhaps it brings us comfort to relate to Jesus in mostly divine terms, but on this day, we are called to relate to Jesus, as He is divine and human. On the cross, we find his humanity waiting for us. We are called to embrace Him in his suffering and death, and to realize that in our sufferings He is embracing us. His death is a sign and reality of God's solidarity with humanity. He understands our lives intimately. The Cross is a magnificent point in which our lives intersect with God, and we are invited to enter into new life with Him. This day, let us be with our God and realize that He is with us.

Prayer request: Please remember Fr. Rich Gyhra's mom, Mary, in your prayers. Fr Rich is a great friend and through him I have found great friends in the Gyhra's. Mary recovered from cancer a few years back but now it has come back. Her outlook is nourished by her faith but still let's pray that she get through this ordeal and experience healing and for strength for her family particularly at this time.

27 MAR 05 20:23 Happy Easter (Resurrection Day)!
"God Moving Over The Face Of The Waters" by Moby

Jesus Christ is risen today! Alleluia! Easter Sunday in Iraq, talk about a memorable event. Four Masses. (Mind you, this year was a little daunting without the guidance of Monsignor Bellew. No safety nets and also no predictability. Just fifteen minutes before the Easter Vigil, some soldiers were performing "No Sleep Till Brooklyn" by the Beastie Boys, in the very area I was supposed to be offering Mass. And would you believe I could not find any of the lights in the corridor leading to the makeshift Chapel so the whole light vibe was a little spoiled. But rolling with the punches, which is becoming an art form for me got me through without losing hair about it. The amount of improvisation necessary here kept me on my toes but in all nice Masses were offered and in a way that was both fitting worship and with a touch of intimacy. We even had music provided by Major Paradis and a sung Exultet.) Two convoys, actually these were called Combat Logistical Patrols (CLPs). Would you believe, four fairly different homilies, too? Two of the homilies focused in on how we experience the resurrected Jesus in our lives. From that, I could not help but recall one of my favorite Easter memories (one I alluded to several entries back) of the Easter morning I spent fishing with Opa (my grandfather).

If memory serves me correctly, it was the Easter of my freshman year of college. I had been the Master of Ceremonies at Saint Augustine's for the Easter Vigil and had Easter Sunday off, so to speak. Opa, Mom and I got up about five thirty and went fishing. Actually, Opa and I went fishing, Mom was our driver (recall I didn't start driving till I was about 26 or 27 after a brief debacle (parked truck hit me as I was pulling into a parking spot) at South Hills Mall (how is Media Play surviving by the way with out me as a customer there?) when I was 16, visiting Father Desmond when he was an Associate Pastor (before the term Parochial Vicar popped up into Diocesan parlance) at Saint Mary's (incidentally I would have the same office twelve years later).

Back to the fishing story. First we stopped at a bait and tackle shop on Route 17 in the Sloatsburg vicinity to pick up a Styrofoam cup of night crawlers for bait and then off to Lake Askoti (more precisely the lower tier lake on the other side of the road up in the Seven Lakes area). This is one of my favorite places in the universe (I hope you all are keeping track of all these places) and it is linked so much to he and I fishing there at various times as I was growing up.

So the sun rose behind us, as we stood by that serene lake, a thin layer of morning mist added a slight chill to the air and there we were fishing. This was the last outdoorsman experiences I had with Opa and also one of the only times he did not admonish me not to throw rocks into the lake (that was something I enjoyed doing on previous fishing excursions despite his protestations that this activity scared the fish away). For me it didn't matter if we caught anything, what mattered was that we were doing something together. It being Easter was significant for me, reminding me of my favorite Gospel account when post-resurrection Jesus appeared to His disciples while they were fishing.

All told, I could not resist putting that experience to paper and I wrote a poem about it and so without further ado here it is Resurrection Day by yours truly.

Resurrection Day

Early that morning, Opa and I were fishing,
down by the lake, while on the far shore,
in a grove of evergreens, I thought I heard a choir of angels singing.
The water was still, glossy beneath the shady veneer of pine and wood.
And a rippled ring appeared on the surface
where the cast had reached its end.

It was the Resurrection Day.

The early ones were already in church
while I learned these holy lessons
as the line tugged slight in his hand and he reeled it in
and it quietly clicked in time and there was a splash
and a passing gurgle as he pulled a fish from that lake
and grabbing it with his big hands he went about taking out the hook.

It was the Resurrection Day.

"Boy Ahm a tellin' you, that's one Hell of a big one," he said,
holding the bass level up to his pale kind eyes
and then a moment later,
with a peaceful smile etched on his ancient face
he tossed the fish back with a singular heaved arc
and on the far shore I thought I saw someone walking
and I recognized the face and I felt the stirring in my heart.

It was the Resurrection Day.

And them angels were singing louder
and the figure bent down stoking a charcoal fire
and the centuries separated our fishes
and the distance separated our lakes
but there was no doubt in my mind
that all this talk of His wasn't just idle chatter,
the faith was burning in my soul
and the joy in my heart
a memory forged in the peace of eternity,
my grandfather and I celebrating together
the good news to be proclaimed:

Hallelujah!

It was the Resurrection Day.

4

SPRINGTIME AT FOB DANGER

1 APR 05 18:50 Prayers, thanks and what not
"Half A World Away" by R.E.M.

News travels fast around this world, so you are all probably in the know of the Holy Father's serious condition right now. One of the on-line papers had a headline about Catholics being afraid for him, and I thought this was a nice sentiment but probably misappropriated. It seems hard to believe that the man we have looked to as shepherd for over twenty-four years appears to be nearing the end of his life. I remember the first time I was conscience of his existence at my First Communion when I received from Grandmother Elaine a copy of a book commemorating Pope John Paul II's first visit as pontiff to the United States. Over the years, I have been privileged to come to appreciate the great gift we as Catholics were given in the person of John Paul. I have been blessed to see him several times, in person, and to have met him when, as a seminarian, the students at St. Joseph's Seminary made pilgrimage to Rome in 1997. He is a true original. So original, that his persona has completely eluded many people and it is most evident in the pigeonhole portraits and caricatured sketches that have been attempted in making John Paul known to the world. So many look to him, even in the Church, as rather stiff and fairly unimaginative. They look at his moral leadership as being based more on orneriness as opposed to having deep spiritual and philosophical roots. They fail to appreciate a man who has always been ahead of the curve. His head may be in the clouds but his feet are firmly on the ground.

We have seen in Pope John Paul II a man of deep holiness,

faith, hope, love, humility and profundity, a priest, a bishop, keen intellect, a brilliant statesman, an author, a poet, philosopher, playwright, a moral theologian, an actor, a humorist, an athlete, and a linguist. He has been a tireless defender of the Catholic faith while he has witnessed the Church go through some turbulent crises. His consistent message for us has always been, "Do not be afraid!" (I must note that I said humorist: It is a fairly ill kept secret that our Holy Father has a brilliant sense of humor. I am fond of the story that the Pope took Bono's sunglasses when they met several years back. It should also be noted that the Pope tried those sunglasses on as well, but the Vatican would not release photos of that moment for fear that it would be disrespectful (bad move, they should have published it). Also, I can't help but recall that miserable day in Central Park when John Paul II brought sunshine to the throngs by singing a childhood song in Polish. And then there are the stories of Monsignor Lorenzo Albacete, who wrote a phenomenal book several years back called God at the Ritz (which is dedicated to Karol), which used to delight us as students back in seminary.)

"Do not be afraid!" How comforting it is to have heard that message resonate through his papacy as he has called the world to not be afraid. This from a man who lived through some pretty frightening things. And as if to give us more courage, for the greater part of a decade, he has been a sign and symbol of strength and resolve as he confronted perhaps our worst fear, mortality. In the years of his dealing with Parkinson's Disease and in dealing with the aging process he has stood steadfast, a sign to all who suffer that it is not for naught. His courage is one of the most inspiring things for me. I am awed by it and determined to live enlivened by it.

I am not afraid for Pope John Paul II. If I were to be afraid for anyone it would be for us, losing such a fine shepherd. But, alas, the Holy Spirit will provide a shepherd when that time comes. I do feel sad though, to know that a man who has given so much of his life in selfless service faces such painful moments. I pray that he can meet these moments with the peace he needs, and that he receive a just reward for all that he has done for the Church as Pope. I am not anxious to see Pope John Paul II go. As he faces these trials now, let us pray for him.

On a totally different note, I wanted to thank Susan Lueck, again, for graciously starting this up about a year ago and having given me this web log as a gift. She was kind of enough to get the ball rolling and pay the fees for this to happen. (Can you imagine that they (that nefarious cabal of minions and unknowns known as they) don't pay me for this stunning web log (I'm trying my hand at not sounding humble for the sake of shamelessly promoting this web log)?)

And finally the what not. Just thought I'd say that this has been a truly interesting April Fool's Day (also known as National Atheist Day). I feel like the joke is on me today being here. The past few days I have been pretty introverted and really mulling over things. I am a pretty infamous muller as you may or may not know. Mulling, however, really impinges on my ability to blog. So hopefully, I will get out of the funk and start to blog. Maybe after the weekend. Please be assured of my prayers for all of you out there in blog land. Please keep me in your prayers as well. Bye for now, R

4 APR 05 19:11 What does one say?
"Sometimes You Can't Make It On Your Own" by U2

I'm kind of at a loss for words. So, please be understanding, I'm going to keep a little quiet. I will post some things, as I come across them that I find interesting. So far, I have been intrigued at the very amazing coverage Pope John Paul II is receiving, deservedly so I might add. I can't help but be annoyed though at the subtle little jabs some in the media feel they must make. A great example is the New York Times obituary. It is a pretty thorough and long piece, but their complete lack of comprehension concerning the Pope and moral teaching is stupefying. It'd be like praising Santa Claus but not understanding his duty of bringing children toys and gifts. Well, that's all for now. God bless all of you and please pray.

At this time, in what is called the interregnum, please pray for the College of Cardinals, as they perform their duties in the coming weeks. Also, now would be a good time to begin praying for our future Pontiff that he will be prepared for the mission that will soon be entrusted to him. If you are watching the news, pay a little attention to the different Cardinals they mention. It will be interesting to Monday morning quarterback who the news was focused on and who was eventually elected, as well as seeing whether the new pope was fairly visible or kind of in the background at the various ceremonies. Please pray, also, for the safety of all those going to Rome, and those in Rome, during the next few weeks. Both those paying their respects and participating in the Holy Father's funeral, and for those who will be welcoming the new pontiff.

7 APR 05 20:59 You are very special!
"40" by U2

The past few days have been a bit difficult. There are obvious reasons and not so obvious reasons, too. If you must know, I have this really weird habit comparable to the nesting thing that pregnant women do before they give birth. Strange comparison, but I have never used the term nesting and just thought I'd throw that one out now. The nesting thing is like this: I have living space, here, there, anywhere and what I do is I play a room sized version of Rubik's cube until the room is conformable to my living standard. The modernists (not of the dreaded Modernist Crisis (sorry Tom) out there may refer to this as connected to Feng Shui. Whatever. I just always love to transform a room so it bears my mark and style and also is functional. Back home, I had the luxury of Pier One. In Iraq, well one improvises and so the other night I got hold of a bunk bed. Got rid of the lower bunk. Transformed the lower section into a storage area. Cleaned the room up of clipped newspaper articles, magazine articles (Dimebag Darrell tributes and Guitar magazines), greeting cards, poem fragments, pamphlets, books, prayer cards...ah yes, prayer cards...

1. I found the vocation prayer card from Father Ed Cipot, which has on one side a beautiful picture of Our Blessed Mother and the Infant Jesus entitled In Vobis Matrem. That is an awesome painting Pope Pius X gave to Cathedral College. Everyday I walked into Cathedral Preparatory Seminary at 555 West End Avenue my eyes would be drawn to that glorious image that hung above the fireplace in the lobby of the Prep.

2. I have my Prayer of Saint Francis Card.

3. My Irish blessing/Fran Connelly card. (The other Saint Francis)

4. And the card Officer Steven MacDonald gave us at St. Mary's School. On one side is the Iron Cross from Ground Zero, and on the other side is a poem entitled "You Are Special!"

The sentiments on that card warmed my heart and I thought some of you may need to hear these words as well. Also, while searching for this quote I found a brilliant bit by Mother Theresa that really kicked me back into gear. Hope this does the same for you if you are in need for a little spiritual infusion.

God bless you.

You Are Special - Author Unknown

In all the world there is nobody like you.
Since the beginning of time,
there has never been another person like you.
Nobody has your smile, your eyes, your hands, your hair.
Nobody owns your voice, your handwriting,
your unique way of communicating with others.
You're special.

Nobody can paint like you.
Nobody has quite your taste for food, music, books, dance, or art.
Nobody in the world sees things as you do.
In all time, there has never been anyone who laughs in exactly your
way.
What makes you laugh or cry
or think may evoke a totally different response in another person.
So you're special.

You're different from every other person who has ever lived.
You are the only one in the whole world who has your particular set of
abilities.
There will always be someone who is better at one thing or another.
Every person is your superior in at least one way.
But nobody has your combination of talents and feelings and tastes.
Through all eternity,
no one will ever walk, talk, think, act, or love exactly like you.
Remember: you're special.

You're rare, and in rarity there is value.
You're special, and it is no accident that you are.
So realize that you were made for a special purpose.
Life has given you a job that no one else can do as well as you can.
Out of billions of applicants, only one is qualified.
Only one person can do what it takes, and that is you.
You are very special.

and from Mother Theresa:

People are often unreasonable, illogical, and self-
centered; Forgive them anyway. If you are kind,
people may accuse you of selfish, ulterior motives; Be
kind anyway. If you are successful you will win some
false friends and true enemies; Succeed anyway. If
you are honest and frank, people may cheat you; Be
honest and frank anyway. What you spend years

building, someone could destroy overnight; Build anyway. If you find serenity and happiness, they may be jealous; Be happy anyway. The good you do today, people will often forget tomorrow; Do good anyway. Give the world the best you have, and it may never be enough; Give the world the best you've got anyway. You see, in the final analysis, it is between you and God; It was never between you and them anyway.

11 APR 05 20:08 Doldrums
"Under Pressure" by Queen and David Bowie

It's hard to believe how mundane and repetitious life here can be. Even with the fact that things happen from time to time that make it interesting. Even with the fact that certain duties are very interesting. For instance, I do a lot of convoys. But after awhile it's business as usual. By the way, since I started working over here and I am now up to thirty two convoys.

What then is needed is a disciplined practice of making the days a bit different. Adding variety. Waking up at different hours. Switching up the routine frequently. Making sure that one does not sink into the mistaken belief that things are really boring. Boredom here is an illusion. But the business as usual attitude is like boredom's twin. "Boring" here is not boring back home. Hearing gunfire off in the distance is "boring" now whereas if I heard it back home I would not think it was "boring" at all.

I am so desperate now to keep things interesting I have resorted to physical training. Today Jerry was showing me some personal defense moves. I felt kind of awkward learning how to block hits but also fascinated at how amazing martial arts are more than just an attack or repelling an attack but it also involves physics and logic and an awareness of ones movements and the movements of ones opponent.

14 APR 05 15:22 Wake Up!
"Wake Up" by Rage Against The Machine

At five thirty, I awoke from a bad dream.

Several minutes later, I fell back asleep only to awaken about an hour later to a very loud explosion. This one was close. It was near enough from where we were, although not on the FOB proper, for us to see below the jet black billowing smoke the bright orange glow of the raging fire that had consumed the interior of the building. Interestingly enough, the blast was distinguishable to my developing combat ears: quickly one develops an ability to categorize the various sounds of gunfire and explosions. This explosion was very discernible to my ears as that of a car bomb. There is a certain signature that becomes identifiable that is unlike anything that would correspond to my civilian life.

As I speak of the acoustic signatures of explosions, I might as well add that the same thing occurs with gunfire. We tend to refer to gunfire as small arms fire, and even gunfire has a distinct sonic quality. Strictly speaking as one who is a relative novice to the combat scene, I am amazed that I am able to distinguish the various munitions of gunfire. I am not yet versed in the difference between Ak-47 and M-16 gunfire, but I am sure that will come in time. There is no confusing either of these two types of gunfire with the sound of a .50 cal.

A suicide bomber blew up a car outside the front gate, the "Horse Gate" of our palace complex. The torso of the bomber actually landed next to the gate. The car blew up in front of a house, originally owned by one of Saddam's relatives, and which was being used by Special Forces. One American soldier was injured, and two Iraqi soldiers were also.

14 APR 05 15:47 Thank you's are again in order!
"Livin' On A Prayer" by Bon Jovi, This Left Feels Right version

Another set of thank you's are in order! I'd like to thank the student's of Mrs. Friel's 5th Grade CCD Class. For me it was as if I was sent 22 reminders of the importance of the mission here as a soldier in Operation Iraqi Freedom III. Thank you to the Smiths (Wappingers Chapter) for their most excellent box of toiletries, magazines, newspapers, puzzles, videos, candies, muffins (breakfast fare), and sunglasses.

Thank you to Paulette Maggiacomo for the paperback books, gum, and the boxes of popcorn and oatmeal.

Thank you to the Rumley's for kindly lending their father and husband to me and the Division and who watches out for me (and vice versa) and for the excellent Irish Whiskey flavored cigars, which unfortunately or fortunately depending on whom you ask, I did not smoke. I did, however, cement some friendships and brought some serious laughter when I was giving them to people saying, "It's a boy!" Also, for the lovely Easter Basket!!! Yum!

Many thanks to the Duke's (Debbie, Bill and Kristen) for their box of goodies: socks, candy, gum, two awesome nail kits (for the ladies), wash and dry, face cleaners, suntan lotion and chap-sticks.

Thank you also to the Lange's for a most excellent box of clothing, toiletries and books. Thank you also to the Tammy Salaun and her delightful children for lending me Mike as a war buddy and movie viewer (even though he falls asleep after five minutes) and for the awesome bunny that sings, "Jesus Loves Me". All I can say is at least it wasn't the Cracker Barrel monkey that Mike uses to compete with my Cracker Barrel cat (which looks like Cee Cee the Alamo cat.

And then there is Mom! Yo mama! Wow! Five boxes of goodies! One labeled snacks and yet if I ate any of the contents I assuredly would die a painful death because it was jammed pack with cleaning supplies (for our bathroom). Two boxes of clothes for indigenous personnel (winning hearts and minds). One box of newspapers (da paypahs, paypahs). And one box of toiletries, and games (badminton and beach-balls and razors).

What I have been doing is a fair share of sharing and spreading the wealth. The socks have been a big hit. The scrunchies have also. Books are always welcome. I put together boxes for our soldiers who are in remote locations. I throw in some soup cans and some things I scrounge from around here and whallah I become Santa Chappy. Thank you for all you do, and to all my unseen angels who keep showering us with your prayers. So muchas gracias and remember, "Love, Peace or Else!"

P.S. Happy Anniversary to Shannon and Justin! Today's the day. I wished Justin Happy Anniversary last night about 12:30 after we finished watching Elektra (Shannon I know you're a Jennifer Garner fan but OMG what a stupid movie).

15 APR 05 13:34 Twenty five ways to be a rebel
"Working For The Weekend" by Loverboy

I wrote some words of advice for a young lady in Texas from whom I received a letter; I thought I'd share them with you all. Bear in mind this is not a comprehensive list, just a random list from a random mind.

1. You are unique, so be yourself and be your own person.
2. Follow your dreams.
3. Have a neat handwriting. And have manners.
4. Don't be afraid to give and give thanks for what you have.

5. Do your best and be willing to improve.
6. Look for God. He is here. And don't forget to pray.
7. Appreciate how unique you are.
8. Don't waste your talent.
9. Be open to the newness of life each day.
10. Read. A book = a chance to flex the mind.
11. You're never too old for stuffed animals.
12. Treasure family and friends.
13. Stand up for what's right.
14. Ask questions.
15. Be humble.
16. Always keep a sense of humor in case you need it.
17. Presence is important. Be there.
18. Remember we define success.
19. Life is a precious gift. Live it like you mean it.
20. Care for/about others. If you don't, who will?
21. Be safe. Always.
22. Whatever part of the heart is missing love is also dead.
23. Control is overrated.
24. Don't be a follower.
25. Walk, look around, and take notice of the beauty around us.

When I was writing the letter I mentioned an historical figure that I find interesting. His name is General Tadeusz Kosciuszko. He is the brilliant man that has brought a great deal of joy to my life, indirectly, of course, for he selected the sight of West Point.

If you would like a nice little excursion, I encourage you to go to West Point and if you really want to be a rebel and see something few people see find the Officer's Club and you should see a sign for Kosciuszko's Garden. It is located below the Officer's Club on the steep overlook of the Hudson River. Directly across you will see Garrison Landing. It is a beautiful little space and a place of quiet and beauty. One of my favorite places on earth. Enjoy. And while you're there say a prayer for my soldiers, it's a nice place to remember them.

17 APR 05 16:21 The Good Shepherd and another dear friend.

The weekend round of Masses came to a close a couple of hours ago. Six Masses, and six variations of lying on the floor, demonstrating Jesus' statement, "I am the gate" and how this relates to His being the Good Shepherd. Tying in the Cross as the gate and how the crucified Lord is the gate, and how he lays down his life for his sheep. The question: If we were on the cross right now, how would we act? Like Jesus. Reflecting on my own state of mind, I would probably want to retaliate, or curse at my persecutors or even spit on one or two of them. Hardly admirable. But at least it's an honest appraisal. From that I brought in St. Peter's message of enduring suffering with patience for the sake of good, as Christ endured the sufferings of the Cross. Again, those crosses in our lives! They are opportunities to be more like Christ. They can bring us closer to our destiny to be true images and likenesses of our God. Random thoughts by the grace of the Holy Spirit some how connected together with the encouragement that we should seek to be like sheep and not the wolves that come after us. Imagine a sheep doing a wolf impersonation and that was the image I presented. Instead of acting like a wolf, lets be like the sheep and come to the Lord. Even bleating, "BAAAAAAAAA," when we come to the Lord, the good shepherd who is able to deal with the wolves in our lives.

Well, I got back here. Checked my e-mail, and received some heartbreaking news. Mary Gyhra, Fr. Rich's mom died at 1 a.m. on Saturday, out in Nebraska. (You all should know by now that I hate speaking of people in the past tense, so bear with me.) Mary is a spiritual giant. I only have known her for something like seven years, and yet I have known her all my life. After first meeting her, I was promptly informed that I was now part of the family. Spiritually adopted.

The woman was a saint already what with us (Rich, Frank,

Jerel, Dan, Mark F., Phil Persico, the homeboys from Lincoln, a host of other characters I didn't know, and the various siblings who would pop in for cameos and guest appearances) at the farm. Our exploits are the stuff of legends. From the hastily enacted rabbit hunting expedition that yielded a pheasant, to the time I got "lost" on an ATV for an hour or so in the farm fields of Nebraska. From my Metallica videos of pigs and road trips to the COPS/ATF re-enactments. From the big breakfasts and dinners to the mid day naps. From the romps with the kids out in the yard to just sitting around and telling stories from the seminary. From the epic family barbeques, one of which roused an entire barracks of Nebraska State's finest to the highways and by-ways to the splendid Masses celebrated at St. Anthony's (with three or four priests and Emmett and Mary too). And through it all Mary stood as patiently delighting in our *joi de vivre*, grateful that we would choose to spend time with her family.

And amidst all the fun, and frivolity I was assured with the beautiful heart to heart conversation that was inevitable when Mary would just draw you into and you left her home feeling as if only you were the only one who got to talk to her. And never did she not ask me, at least once, "How's Mom?" And she'd expect a real answer and she'd listen and share her maternal concerns and in all you just felt so privileged and loved.

Mary Gyhra is a woman of great faith. A hearty soul. Right now she is most probably looking out a kitchen window in the Mansion of our Lord, praying a Rosary for her dear husband and her children completely aware of the dark clouds they are facing right now. Praying with that intense fervor she had, doing all in her power to get it done. I know she probably has a tear in her eye. Completely absorbed in praying them to the peace they will need. Not a tear of sadness. But a tear of effort, and love and compassion. If that's what lesson I gleaned from her was that when you pray, pray like you mean it. Pray with intensity and pray like people's lives depend on it.

The world is little darker, knowing that I won't hear her voice again in this world. But it has been left a better place. Her legacy lives on in her wonderful children and grandchildren. The lessons she taught will echo on for many a year and be passed on. Please keep Father Rich and Emmett and their family in your prayers, that they may be comforted in this time of sorrow with the assurances of faith, which nourished Mary in this life. Now she knows the Good Shepherd in a way, God willing, we all will know, someday.

19 APR 05 15:48 No lounging for this freedom loving lizard.
"The Changeling" by The Doors

So there I was last night in our kitchen, and there he was in the corner of the room, on the floor, lying on a glue trap used for catching mice, a little lizard whom we named Justin since yesterday was his birthday and also because we rescued the lizard just in time. Mike and I felt terrible, fixing popcorn in the microwave knowing that this little creature was dying or doomed to die on the glue trap. So with his Warrant Officer technical prowess and my creative idea we pooled our resources in approaching this task. Luckily it was a lizard and not a mouse because we would have probably been bitten or scratched up in the process but lizards being lizards Justin just relaxed for the most part until he realized we were getting him gradually looser from this torturous device then it would get excited and squirm around a bit. We decided that if we soaked the trap and the lizard in water we could loosen the glue that bound Justin and also we could slowly with deliberate and cautious manipulation we could pry the little lizard from this sticky situation. Needless to say, we were able to transcend the absurdity of this predicament and offer Justin a new lease on life. After we had removed much of the glue from him and him from the glue we placed him in the yard and released him back into the wild. A simple episode and yet a nice break from the seriousness that surrounds us from time to time.

Today, I was able to see some more lizards, different variety; less snaky and zanier than the fellow I encountered last night. Not for nothing, these guys can move very, very fast. I didn't photograph Justin, but I did get a few of the ones today. (You ask what I mean by zany? One of these guys looked as if when he stopped he was doing push-ups.)

19 APR 05 16:23 Another round of thanks
"Gratitude" by The Beastie Boys

Thank you to Alison and the kids for the socks and the sneaker type things for the kids. And also high voltage thanks to Laura and Brian Murphy for the most excellent six cds 80's hair metal/ballads compilation.

20 APR 05   An excerpt from an e-mail to Mom

Still in Kirkuk. Went for a visit to As Sulay Minayah this morning. A good two hour trip into a strange part of Iraq. It was all green, big hills and lots of rocks. The most striking thing is going through this Kurdish region and constantly witnessing people waving to us. Sometimes we would not have noticed the people had they not been waving, meaning they were a good distance away. The cool thing is the kids waving. You can see that they genuinely like us and see us as a force of goodness here. You don't even see that in our own country. Am tired despite the time of day. I was very surprised at the outcome of the conclave.

21 APR 05 16:39   Oh hi!

Was out of the loop for a few days. Now am back. Need a bit of recovery time. Am tired. Will be back tomorrow. Please pray for our new pope, Pope Benedict XVI. A German pope! Pardon me if I gloat. Talk to you all tomorrow.

22 APR 05 20:51 My first article for the 250th Signal Battalion's Newsletter.
"You Better You Bet" by The Who

An Industrious Lot by Chaplain Robert B Repenning

Wasted time is a big fear of mine. I have been approaching this deployment as a two-fold project. On one side I have a mission to do and on the other hand I personal goals that I wish to achieve in addition to my responsibilities. I think it would be a shame to have spent so long away from my loved ones and not have more to show for it than pay stubs and a mission accomplished.

With this in mind, I have approached this deployment almost like some people welcome in a new year. My resolutions are to grow physically, mentally and spiritually. In the physical arena I hope to get in better physical shape, lose a few pounds around the waist and do some muscle toning. I, also, want to read more and to spend some time studying some things that interest me. Finally, I would like to grow deeper in my spiritual life, to pray more from my heart, to grow in patience and to appreciate more God's work in my life and through my life.

These resolutions or goals are personal but they are concrete examples of what I would like to do while I am here in Iraq. Wouldn't it be great if we could make this time as productive as we can? So whether we are languishing in the day by day grind in the heart of

Operation Iraqi Freedom or we are slogging it out on the home front juggling the day by day with a few less hands and a lot more responsibilities we need to resolve to use this time wisely. We can transform this time in the actual or metaphorical desert to a time of great fruition, which can bear immense fruit when this deployment ends.

It may sound like a daunting task, but it doesn't need to be. In fact, I believe God offers us plenty of instruction for us to glean guidance from that can assist us in our endeavor. For me, I gleaned guidance from a very unlikely source, the Iraqi ant. Several weeks ago, a virtual army of ants caught my eye, as I was walking to dinner. I stopped for a moment and noticed some interesting things. The ants were traveling in long lines that looked about 20 feet long (that's human feet!) there were several of these lines, moving to and from the entrance to their domicile with distinct purpose. The lines of ants were remarkable but what really was remarkable was that they all were engaged in labor. They all were carrying wheat-like flecks of amber grass, into their headquarters (they are an army, and they don't really look like hills here). Others were carrying, what could best be described, as chaff from out of their headquarters.

Since that initial encounter, I have spent a lot of time on the way to or from chow stopping momentarily to see what the ants are up to. On a given path, I may see up to seven of these ant work crews absorbed in labor. Where once I though of ants as frightening, now I see them appreciatively, in a new light. Perhaps, my anti-ant biases were trapped in my inability to look beyond their bug-ness. I jut saw these tiny animals as targets to be exterminated by any means necessary. My ignorance of their ecological purpose, if any, and the reasons for why they do what they do, other than for survival, placed them on the outs, until now.

I still am not keen to share living space with them nor do I desire to share my personal foodstuffs with them, however I have grown to see ants, not as mere pests but as mini-teachers. They have taught me a few things, which I plan to put into practice in my life and which will compliment my resolutions that I have previously stated. I have not arranged them in an order of importance but I did limit them in number to something simple.

So here they are, the ten ways I have found one can live a better life by imitating ants:

1. Make good use of time.
2. Be a team player.
3. Work hard. (Ants can lift 9X their body weight).
4. Be goal oriented.
5. Be determined.
6. Be ambitious. Think big. Dare to dream. (Think of that long line of worker ants.)
7. Look ahead and prepare for the future
8. Communicate. Be a team player.
9. Know when to take a break. (The ants stop working during the heat of the day.)
10. Enjoy sweets.

Having earned a newfound respect perhaps I may not use that derogatory word "bug" anymore. I definitely will take their lessons to heart. Remember, this time of deployment can be a valuable learning experience for all of us. God willing, we can glean from these minute messengers some possible ideas of areas we, as an industrious lot, can grow in and areas that make us better people when this chapter of our lives draws to a close. God Bless you all!

"Go to the ant, you lazy bones; consider its ways, and be wise."
   - Proverbs 6:6

"The ants are a people without strength yet they provide their food in the summer."
   - Proverbs 30:25

23 APR 05 21:16 Happy Fiftieth Anniversary*!*

About two years ago, Richard and Elizabeth Smith asked if I could be there for their Fiftieth Wedding Anniversary. I answered first with a hem and haw and something about having something I had to do that day and then after some more teasing I gave an enthusiastic, "You bet, I wouldn't miss it for the world."

Well it seems the world came knocking. Since arriving in this part of the world I have missed several things I wish I didn't have to miss. There are quite a few weddings I had lined up. Sadly, several funerals that I have had to miss, particularly Dorothea Blakes' and Mary Gyhra's funerals. And now this.

I just wanted to take this opportunity to thank two very remarkable people, Richard and Elizabeth Smith. They have been great friends, great parishioners, great co-workers (in the sacristy and in the Church (I would be amiss to not point out how often Richard's cough has saved the day and I looked up to get a bit of silent direction from him. And I would also, be amiss not to mention the many times that Elizabeth saved the day, either by getting something in the nick of time or passing a message on to me about some much needed information. And both deserve medals for dealing with my last minute improvisations and changes)) and great examples of the Christian life.

Fifty years. Wow! Pretty impressive. But not surprising because you are two very impressive persons. Thank you for the gift you have shared with all of us, your love. As I have said, at every wedding I have had, the love between a husband and a wife is supposed to remind us of God's love for His people. Thank you for doing just that for me. May God continue to bless you and many more happy and healthy ones to come. See you at your fifty first. I wouldn't miss it for the world.

24 APR 05 20:01 A year (ish)
"The Future's So Bright" by Timbuk 3

It just dawned on me today that it has been just over a year since my world was turned upside down and my long journey here began. I recall a horrible week last April in which I received the news of my being activated for deployment and the same week having to say goodbye to the parish in a very hurried and rushed fashion. Our Lord, with His divine sense of humor, delayed my departure a bit, and put me through a waiting period that was at times very nerve wracking. Then it was time to go to Chaplain School and quicker than you could say South Carolina I was graduated and waiting for my report date. Soon thereafter it was off to Fort Drum and eventually to here FOB Danger here in Tikrit.

Wow. A lot has happened this year. I look at the coming year with a lot of anticipation but no expectations. I am kind of intrigued what the Lord has in store for me. In a few months, I will start looking at the parish landscape back in the Archdiocese of New York and see what parishes will have openings. I welcome the chance to work with a new pastor and learn as much as I can before I end up in the pastor seat, myself. As the old saying goes, it will be interesting to see how it all turns out.

I definitely don't want to disappoint anyone, but to all of those hoping that I would return to St. Mary's, I am sorry to say, that will, in all probability, not be happening. This does not mean that St. Mary's does not have a special place in my heart. St. Mary's has a very special place in my heart and always will especially because it was my first parish. As I serve here, very much in the capacity of a pastor, I see how much my priesthood has been shaped by St. Mary's. I see that the people of St. Mary's have made an imprint on the man I am now. My first parishioners taught me the value of being an authentic and real priest and to do so unafraid of being human in the process. That lesson has made this experience here almost a seamless transition ministerially. My "parishioners" here are slowly growing accustomed to the sight of Fr. Rob walking on the streets of the FOB with a book in his hand like back home. Many thanks to all who have been so kind to me this past year. I cannot stress enough; your care and love carried me through some tough times and continues to do so here.

Please keep those prayers coming and be assured that my prayers are always with you, as well. Blessings and peace!

24 APR 05 20:52 Sandstorm and the heat
"Hot, Hot, Hot" by Buster Poindexter

We broke a hundred degrees for the second day in a row here. And man is it a hot heat. And then to add more spice to the desert life. A real doozy of a sandstorm. This is not the first sandstorm we have had. But it is the closet to what I had imagined sandstorms to be like. Luckily, I had my goggles with me, because the wind just began to blow real heavy and although it is mostly a fine chalky dust, debris does fly about at some radical speeds and could do damage to unprotected eyes. Visibility crashed in quickly closing in and obscuring anything beyond a quarter of a mile, including the sun.

The heat here is exhilarating. With this sandstorm it has cooled off quite a bit but during the day it is beginning to feel as if a hairdryer were turned on a few inches from one's face. It is brutal and unrelenting and compared with the negative 20 degrees back at Fort Drum, I am in heaven. I really like it, feels like Oklahoma. I am in awe of such heat though, and it hasn't even really begun to get hot. We still have thirty or more degrees to go! How cool is that?!

28 APR 05 13:54 A rough sketch of a poem

Tigris

Wrong, so very wrong the way this river flows
Waveless, the greasy river slides downstream
A sickly skin over the green decay
Mingled with the sewage and oil, miracles and death,
A disaster careening toward the sea.

The grey waking sky cools the air and warms the face
A yawning sunrise pales golden beams and halos the clouds
And it's ponderous what has brought me to this point
Standing here, on this cliff, a stranger to my own world,
The logic still abides, but the gravity weighs me down.

Maybe it is all for naught, not the reason
But the explanations, the empty words, the imprimatur
The human stain, inevitably corrupting,
The poison that can't help destroy what it touches
That corrupts everything that is beautiful and right.

28 APR 05 15:30 Wrestling with faith and God.
"Bullet The Blue Sky" by U2

Genesis 32:24-32

"It's a mystery!"

In my line of work, this is a frequent answer to a number of
questions. Sometimes the answer is in relation to some
article of faith. In the Catholic Church, the faith is awash in
mystery. The mysteries of the Resurrection, the Trinity, the
Eucharist, are just a few of what are known as Dogmatic
mysteries. Tenets of the faith that we believe yet cannot
fully be answered. It is not a matter of ignorance that these
answers are inaccessible but rather it is the great depth of
what is believed that makes it impossible to be contained
entirely in human terms.

"It's a mystery!"

There have been times when I have uttered these words and wondered to myself if this was a copout or a legitimate answer. It is hard for me to say those words and not remember when those same words were said to me. I never could understand what the point was. What good is a mystery if you can never solve it?

The way of approaching mysteries of faith is to appreciate the process. Certainly where one ends up is of great value. But we should not lose sight of the fact that the process is also of great value. I certainly believe that when I depart from this world into the next, all will be revealed. I believe God will be able to explain these mysteries, but at this point I do not feel that I am able to comprehend the realities our faith informs.

Mysteries demand a response from us. When we are presented with mysteries we have a choice to engage them or not engage them. Some mysteries overwhelm us. Some seem less formidable and yet all of rationalization and attempts to convey the meaning fall flat in comparison with the interior logic we experience.

For instance, believing in a Triune God makes sense for me. I see no contradictions in believing in One God, who is Three Persons. This mystery is one that I contemplate fairly often, yet my thirsting knowledge is never fully quenched. There always is something more, a horizon I strive for that seems to retreat as I draw near. Such is the dynamic of faith.

Is it worthless, though, to ask questions that cannot be answered? I would say it is not. I believe it is always valuable to ask questions. Granted my curiosity may never be totally satisfied but I may come to some degree of insight I was missing before. In this way, I have deep respect for process.

This is a rather strange story plopped into the Genesis

narrative in which Jacob, a rather dubious hero, encounters this divine being and he emerges a changed man. The cycle of the Jacob stories is one that paints a picture of a less than perfect person who has, nonetheless, a relationship with God. This relationship seems to find its synthesis in this story, in which Jacob "wrestles God." It is from this encounter that Jacob's name is changed to Israel meaning, "wrestling with God."

It is Jacob or Israel that becomes the personification of the people of Israel and in a sense the personification of all who believe in God. This story then eliminates the clean cut black and white antiseptic concept of faith that many of us have. Perhaps, you like I believe at times that faith is meant to be something peaceful and neat and ordered and everything needs to be in the right place.

People often tell me, when they get themselves right then they'll come back to Church and pray and start being religious. My response is always pretty much the same; Good luck with that.

This is not how it happens. Relationship with God is a tumultuous event. It is the Main Event. Sometimes it feels like Smackdown, in which we find ourselves overwhelmed by our divine adversary. One of the reasons for this is that in our estimation we fall short of God's hopes for us. We may look in our hearts and be embarrassed by our sinfulness, our imperfections, our inadequacies…the list goes on…We perceive many obstacles to relationship with God but we don't really think that maybe we are the biggest obstacle.

We are the ones with all the preconceived notions of how it should be, of what God wants from us, and what the right way is. But it seems we do make these decisions blindly. We would all probably agree that Jacob is not a person with an impressive character. In fact, he shatters our misconceptions and in his person God invites us to something new.

God is inviting us into a relationship that is not idealized or sentimental but something that is real. In this relationship there is give and take, it is rough and tumble, it is kinetic and demanding. If you want a spectator sport, then you are out of luck. If you want to doze off, or put it off you better think again. Faith is not static. It is not a mental exercise. Nor is it a fantasy. It is wrestling around on the dirt, or the mud, wrestling with our humanity with God's divinity and all the mysteries in between.

28 APR 05 19:34 Under a rock
"Breadline" by Megadeth

Hola. The past few days I have been getting up earlier than usual. Even stranger, I have been waking up without the assistance of my alarm clock. Fear not. The apocalypse is not upon us. It is however a good indicator of how things have been going. Let's just say I have wanted to crawl under a rock the past few days. Yes, the truth is even caregivers get to feeling YEECH. Had a day yesterday. One of those, where you feel like someone is running over you with a steamroller. I am still recovering. Sometimes kindness is in short supply here.

Alas, life moves on. One can get so absorbed in their own down feelings that they may develop the tunnel vision are called to avoid. Jesus called us to love one another, not lick our wounds and feel pity. He also calls us to pick up our mats and walk. Today, I offer my feelings up for those who are genuinely dealing with heavy things: Pat M, John Bailey, Elizabeth K, Danny O, Bo, Rich and his family, the family of those helicopter crash/murder this past weekend, The Scalzo's on the first anniversary of Richard's death.

We think that things are so bad. And sometimes they are and sometimes we just get caught up in the drama. It could always be worse. As we travel on the way we wrestle with life, and faith, and ourselves, and the world around us, and that's good. That wrestling match is an opportunity for us to be with God and wrestle with Him and come to understand Him and ourselves more and more. (Genesis 32:23-34) Recall that this wrestling match transforms Jacob and even changes how he is known. It is here, that Jacob is renamed Israel ("he wrestled God"). No retreat, no surrender!

29 APR 05 17:59 Elegance and a few editorial comments
"Ripple" by Grateful Dead

"How you making out, alright?"

Just thought a little editorial comment was in order, I'd like to say a word (or more) about the substance. I hope this experiment is going well. I have a lot of rules operative in writing this journal. They are an unwritten, self-imposed set of rules that I try to abide by. Not having any reason to read other blogs I began with an unbiased vision. Having now from time to time skated about the web I have seen other blogs and been considerably disappointed. Apparently elegance is a word that is out of a great many people's lexicon. Vulgarity and foolishness are familiar tools. So it is with some sense of relief that I look at what has accumulated here. I have my silly moments, and at times I have felt embarrassed but I can live with it. At least I know I am not compromising my values or myself in my presentation.

What you have been getting is a fairly unedited treatment. I say fairly because from time to time I do rephrase things and tool and fashion sentences and try for a bit more style. I try to be open, but I also try to maintain sensitivity as to my audience. I appreciate that you come to these pages not to hear rants and raves but to maybe hear a story or learn something new. I am one of those people who is always interested in both of those things.

This has also become a great tool of communication, but I am a slow learner. I learned only recently how to respond to comments. Sometimes I fall behind responding. If I haven't answered in awhile I may have lost it and may also need a reminder. Feel free to remind me, but also check where you left the comment, I may have responded. Also, if you have prayer requests send them to me. The ones I mention usually are at the forefront either because there is an anniversary, or I received e-mail, or someone reminded me. My memory doesn't always stick.

Finally, I hope this is upbeat. The way things are here, there are cycles. Sometimes it is busier than usual sometimes it is very quiet. Sometimes the worst time is when it is quiet. One just then feels that dramatic tension, wondering what's going to happen next. If you look for an update on what is happening, this may not be the best source of information. One reason is I am limited in what I can say. Another reason is that there are family members of my colleagues who read this and again I want to be as sensitive to them as I can be.

All in all, hopefully this blog is doing its job. Be assured I love interaction, and I especially love when we can have affecting discourse. A few weeks ago, someone sent a verse of "Chopin's Piano" which really rocked and really had some people talking. I must confess, I enjoy the artistic flourishes like that. That little verse brightened my day considerably by its sheer beauty. That was a little a great example of what my expectation for this is, a break from the vulgar and the foolish, an opportunity for us to learn something new and a smattering of elegance.

All the best. Robert

5

WARMING UP

3 MAY 05 12:17 More editorial comments
"All You Need Is Love" by The Beatles
"Sorry Seems To Be The Hardest Word" by Elton John

I apologize for the lack of entries the past few days. 'Tis the ebb and flow of life in a war zone.

Let me say this about that, though. I finally watched Michael Moore's Fahrenheit 9/11, albeit it bootleg version. (In honor of May Day, the closest I can get to ultra-leftist political protest).

I watched the program (Please note: I didn't it call it a movie, documentary, or a film). I am glad I saw it. Certainly entertaining. I must admit I fell asleep for about twenty minutes and had to go back and see what I missed. It was hardly worth the hype and it did raise some interesting points. Unfortunately, it was a scatter-shot approach of attacking President George W. Bush, as opposed to presenting all of the facts. The treatment of the war was haphazard and degrading and very misleading. Sadly, some of the negative portrayals of conduct must exist but it was made to look endemic and endorsed by the military. The context was completely one-sided: Moore's side. This is not to say that all of the points raised were not valid. But an evenhanded and balanced approach lends better to getting to the bottom of things. Some of this movie was just down right ugliness. (I was a little amazed that one would cast judgment of how the President reacted to the news he was receiving about the attacks on this Nation. I also, don't think it is a dignified way to refer to anyone by talking about his or her Daddy or Mommy.)

Much to Mom's chagrin (because when I am home, I subject her to hearing all of the other side's interviews and speeches) I am open to hearing the argumentation of those with whom I disagree. Hopefully, those who feel a political kinship with Michael Moore will take his movie as an example of how not to present their point of view. Perhaps, before the next election we can elevate the political dialog and eliminate some of the rhetorical flourishes that many of us find demoralizing. Maybe we need to encourage our politicians, from all sides, to be issue driven and call them to task when it digresses to personal invective. Whether one thinks this president is a good president or not is a moot point, but one thing I like is that he associates with people from various ends of the political spectrum. His inclusion of the past former presidents, for instance, in the Tsunami Relief was not only, I think healing for the nation but also seemed quite genuine. That is the kind of spirit that America needs more of. Wouldn't it be great to see Howard Dean and George Bush talking together? We would then see people who have different ideas interacting and not get caught up in a seeming personally driven contest.

"That's just my opinion," to quote the great Dennis Miller, "I could be wrong."

By the way, if you'd like to see a most excellent and touching story, I highly recommend "Finding Neverland". Great film, great acting, and a really nice message. Bye for now, R

4 MAY 05 16:48 Thank you, thank you, thank you
"Friends" by Michael W. Smith

More opportunities to say thank you have presented themselves and so I say thank you. Unfortunately, I usually give a thumbnail sketch of the things that have been sent to me, but please know I feel the love and care that goes into sending these things and am very appreciative.

Today, I received newspapers from Tammy Salaun. A big highlight was the "Pope"-ourri, and the cat magazine. Regarding "Pope"-ourri, I must thank J.D. Dworkow for his contribution of newspapers and some magazines involving the Holy Father and his death. In addition, he also sent a monster toilet paper (a friend indeed) package the size of which could keep a small family in hygiene for a year (ha ha ha), as well as a cool Black Crowes shirt. And finally, I received a most excellent assortment of Guitar Magazines. Coolness.

The 250th Signal Battalion's Family Readiness Group sent a very cool care package to each soldier. Mine was pretty mint, right down to the James Taylor Greatest Hits CD. A big thanks to all you FRG elves!

Sheila McGayhey also sent a mint box stuffed with candies (Werthers Ma!), nuts, gum, mints, and Girl Scout cookies (so, when I come home overweight, you all know who to blame (ha, ha). Sheila, the calorie content of those cookies has been the subject of many of my jokes, and also a great reminder of St. Mary's when I would buy a case of those cookies just in case we were under a Level Orange Terror Alert.)

I would like to thank the three angels Marilyn Johnson, Vinnie Fitzsimmons, and Lori Heneka who sent two immense boxes of goodies ranging from toiletries to fun snacks. Debbie, Bill and Kristen Duke sent two boxes of books and goodies, as well. One box arrived without a return address so I am not sure whom to thank but it had a lot of goodies in it as well. American Recreation Military Services in Red Bank sent an excellent box of goodies, also.

I am deeply appreciative of everything that is sent. I waited a little to long to say thanks, but please be assured that you not only make my day, but you make my soldiers' day. I am a notorious sharer yes, but I am also a realist (right now I can't wear a scrunchy, partly because my head has been shaved bald, but also because I am a guy, so I share). My calorie intake too, would be astronomical unless I shared my booty, so please know that it is going to good use.

I have a few soldiers who don't get much because they don't have family back home so I try to hook them up as well with some fun things. In all, thank you so much.
But I would be remiss if I didn't mention my Mom. Thanks Mom for the "Pope"-ourri newspapers and also the goodies and toiletries and snacks and for the mail and the toilet seat. Only in the Army would such toilet related items be so welcome! By the way thanks for the plethora of Pope related articles I am going to make a scrapbook, so thank you for breaking the ice.

I hope I haven't forgotten anyone. But in case I did, thank you anyway. Till tomorrow.

5 MAY 05 13:17 The Skinny
"Working For A Living" by Huey Lewis and the News

A few words on what is going on here. First, in my estimation it is freezing. Today it is in the sixties and I am a frozen chunk of ice. Its overcast, but the aesthetic reality here is that overcast does not mean rain, but only an occasion drop or two (note this is literal and not figurative, you will actually feel a drop or two and then nothing. Not a sprits, or a quick shower, or even a spit, just a drop or two). Temperature outside however is also indicative of the inside. Since there are no thermostats the air conditioners still pump out air and so it is equally frigid inside.

Second, work is interesting. Spent a goodly sum of time in meetings and planning sessions. Right now we are looking at long-range goals into the autumn. Logistics is an amazing and intricate affair, and with the military the amount of movable parts makes for interesting planning and preparing. The rest of the time is presence. Being available to the soldiers. Here is as good place as any to ask for continued prayers for my soldiers.

Third, attitude readjustment. 1/3 (ish) of the tour complete, this is a good opportunity to step back and assess my own attitude. It seems as Catholic guilt has permeated some of my Protestant colleagues ministry, so too has the Protestant work ethic permeated Catholic circles. Its funny, a lot has been said of how we have influenced each other and here I see how true that is. I have been operating in a very work focused, get the job done attitude which at times has embraced the take no prisoners, by any means necessary "git 'er done" attitude. My maniacal urge toward being productive has left me a bit of a wreck. In ministry, one has to remember to be kind to people and to oneself. Care of the caregiver. This caregiver has been ruthless, mainly to myself. My assistant, God bless him, has had to deal with me and my relentless drive, and I must say he has been incredible. After some reflection though, I realized I need to let up a bit for my sake and his. Always set reasonable expectations, huh? So reasonable is one of my new buzzwords. Kindness is always somewhere in the mix, but kindness to self is now part of this caregiver's lexicon.

Fourth, social readjustment. After more than a few months of being immersed completely in constant social interaction, I am now taking a bit of a retreat each day for some quiet no-people time. Although, most people think that because one does extroverted activity or is outgoing that one is an extrovert, which is not necessarily true. I have found that I need quite a bit of time away from people to recharge and get energized. Sometimes it works, sometimes it doesn't. Where I live, I share a large room that has been divided up into eight by eight living areas with two other fellows, Mike whom I mention fairly frequently and Ed. I sometimes feel bad because when I get back to the room in the evening I am either very talkative or deathly silent. Part of what I am learning to do is to let people know that I work with or live with: Hey forgive the silence, but I need some quiet or alone time. The other day, I really needed to explain to Ed this because I hadn't been talking much, and I saw the effort talking and I wasn't responding. So I told him what was going on, that I was in one of my moods. In all, I am learning to communicate more effectively and leaving less for people to have to figure out. None of us are mind readers.

Fifth, I'm looking forward to the day when all of this is over and my soldiers and I are safely back home. I don't spend a lot of time thinking about it, but from time to time the very thought brings warmth to my spirit. Alright friends, bye for now, R

6 MAY 05 15:43 Patience: A Newsletter Article
"Patience" by Guns N Roses

One common expression is "Everyday is Monday here." As a Chaplain, I like to say, "Everyday is like Sunday." But in reality, everyday is most like a Wednesday. The days blend into one homogeneous blob of time marked by whether it was good or bad. There is a cyclical way those days greet us. These days, need to be greeted with a certain degree of patience and especially when we go from having a great day to being hit with "one of those days."

I have been having a bunch "of those days," lately. You know the kind of day, where things just go askew, or things just take on a life of their own. One perfect example is this very column. I have, in fact, written five columns and all I have is this one to show for the effort.

One column grew to such epic proportions and when I tried revising, it proved too much a task. The key word was wrestling, and it was based on a Prayer Breakfast talk I gave a few weeks ago. Another column focused on the palaces here in Tikrit and perspective, but when I left the computer for a while, when I returned I had no idea what my point was. Yet another column I wrote was on balance, and that also grew to great lengths and needs to be tamed, this was my second attempt on the subject. The first attempt at a column on balance fell victim to not being saved on the computer and thus lost. That column on balance focused on how we communicate with each other with all this space between those here and Iraq and our families and friends back home in the States.

For whatever reason, the aforementioned columns were lost or jettisoned. I am sure, there are a couple of spoilers there, and that you will see these ideas come to life in upcoming issues, but that is not the point. The crux of what I am trying to say is that plans are great, goals are great, but we need to be able to roll with the punches when things get out of whack. That's the lesson here. Sometimes we got to take things as they come. Over here, that is the one point that keeps repeating. It would be most wise, for us to learn this lesson. So dear friends, lets pray for each other and for our patience. And let us not forget that we can learn this lesson in solidarity, with each other.

6 MAY 05 18:28 Happy Birthday, Ethan!
"Birthday" by The Beatles

Just wanted to wish Ethan Bowden a very Happy Birthday. I know he isn't going to read this, but I write in anyway. No, he is not a curmudgeon who refuses to use a computer. No, the truth is Ethan can't read. But it's not that bad. He's happy not reading. In fact, he is probably having the time of his life with one exception, his father. Right now, he doesn't see too much of his dad. But again, it's not as bad as I am making it sound. Ethan turns one today. Ethan's dad is none other than Justin, my bud from Missouri (he says Oklahoma). My prayers go to Justin and Shannon (Justin's wife and Ethan's mom) and Ethan particularly today. But they also represent all my soldiers who drive on each day and deal with the difficulty of separation from their loved ones. I have thanked a whole lot of people for the various and sundry material gifts that you have sent to us, but please know I am very appreciative of your spiritual gifts, as well. Please keep my soldiers in your prayers, and their families. If you'd like maybe you can spiritually adopt a soldier and his family. They need all the prayers they can get, because we all can relate to not having a loved one be with us. It is definitely a challenge to hold a family together thousands of miles away. So, whatever prayers you can offer my soldiers is definitely appreciated.

Just as a side story. I had e-mailed Mike's family and I was trying to encourage the kids to do well in school and not be slackers so. Hold on, I want to tell the story but I need a sentence break. Anyway, I was encouraging them not to follow Ethan's example. I went on by saying that Ethan doesn't do well in school, and even clarified that Ethan doesn't even bother going to school, and that they should not follow in his footsteps. Needless to say, when I did tell them that Ethan was a baby, they reprimanded me promptly defending him (I was joking) and saying that he would show me when he started going to school and to leave the poor baby alone (they were teasing me too.) Their e-mails definitely brought a smile to my face. Well, bye for now.

7 MAY 05 17:53 A Day Off!
"Saturday In The Park" by Chicago

After ninety-nine days in Iraq, I am finally taking a genuine day off, and loving it. I slept a little more than usual. Watched a bit of a movie. Did some reading. Checking the e-mail. And I am genuinely relaxing. I'm going to hit the shower in a few, shave, and put on one of my freshly cleaned and ironed (believe it or not, I found a way to get my uniforms ironed (like on M*A*S*H)) and have some chow with my buds before I hit the 1830 Mass. Hope all of you are well.

8 MAY 05 17:54 Happy Mother's Day!

Happy Mother's Day, Mom! Here I am, probably the farthest I have ever been on a Mother's Day making my annual wish and also expressing my deep gratitude for the gift of you in my life. This day affords me one of the rare moments when I can recall being small. One of the best memories I have is not confined to a set moment but a collection of moments encapsulated under the classification, "Gold Chair moments." Growing up, the Gold Chair (and yes it was so significant an entity that it deserves the capitalization) was the place reserved exclusively for me and Mom (and occasionally the dog (!)(Yes the secret has been revealed, we were not always cat folk (!))) It was on that seventies monstrosity of upholstery in a gold hue that has now gone the route of bell bottoms and shag carpet that Mom and I would share family time. Each day, we would have dedicated time there in the living room by the fireplace and there Mom would read me stories or just spend time talking to me or teaching me something new. Truly cherished time.

Its funny, we have the tendency to look back and say, "Ah the good old days," and fail to see that some of those magic moments never really ended they just grew and matured and diffused into the rest of our life. That chair eventually died the death of material things, and one day ended up on the curb and taken away by the garbage-men. But the memories, they have remained. This collective filed in my memory as "Gold Chair memories" will never die. They will remain with me through out my life. And they are reminders of how much Mom loves me and how much I love her. How cool a God we have to give us gifts such as these.

Happy Mother's Day Mom, you're in my heart, always! I am so proud to call you Mom (Ma, Madre (Bill?), Gristel Stew). I owe you a nice dinner when I get home. Also, I must ask your forgiveness in front of all these readers. I bought your card and Oma's too at the end of March, but I have not mailed them yet. Yes, yes, I am badness (however I have witnesses now that there are no numbers on my scalp, which I recall you looking for when I was a wee lad (ha, ha)). The cards will be mailed tomorrow. Scout's honor. May this be a day, not of sadness, but a day of great joy and happiness, and hopefully the others (cats) will treat you well this day. Please extend my love and best Mother's Day wishes to Oma, as well. I owe my former Long John Silver compañero a nice dinner, as well. Tell her that, and translate the word compañero (wing it) to her, as well, and I know she will be delighted.

To all the other mothers out there this day, happiness and joy! Enjoy your day! God love you all.

9 MAY 05 20:20 Beautiful day!
"Beautiful Day" by U2

Today was a beautiful day. Hot, hot, hot. But by evening it is glorious. Had a flight today, which was awesome. I got to sit by the window. But there was no window, the door was open completely. Exhilarating. (To all the worriers, this warrior was safety belted in.) This evening, I sat outside and had a nice dinner (Raviolis) and I was enjoying a beautiful warm breeze and the lowering sun. All the doves and pigeons are enjoying that breeze, too, flapping up high and then soaring/coasting and riding the current as far down as they can. It is cool to watch other creatures appreciate the beauty of this world. I have been taking dinner more frequently in quiet, which gives me a chance to recharge and keep the mind fresh. God bless you all. R

10 MAY 05 15:43 Something humorous
"Ship Of Fools" by World Party

J.D. sent me this, credited to some vintage roadies, but soldiers could very well have written it;

> We the willing, led by the unknowing,
> Are doing the impossible, for the ungrateful.
> We have done so much with so little for so long,
> That we are now qualified to do anything,
> With absolutely nothing at all.

11 MAY 05 17:15 Protest

All is well. And yet the tension that surrounds us is palatable. What you see at home is disconcerting. You hear of the wave of violence and terror bombings and the death toll, but there is little context to understand these events. Most of you may feel the nervousness thinking of the endangerment of Americans' lives. Over here, we are very safety conscious, however, we are greatly disturbed by the constant threat against human life. Again this morning, most of us in Tikrit were awakened to the sound of a loud explosion. The enemy here is a morally depraved minority determined to impede progress for the people of Iraq and prolong United States involvement here. They continue their campaign, devoting most of their energies to killing Iraqi citizens.

The scandal of silence regarding the loss of innocent human life at the hands of Muslim Fundamentalists is deafening. Several weeks ago, when the minority masses of anti-war protesters took to the streets wrapped up in their own egotistical self righteous accusatory manner they like the terrorists showed their cowardice once again. Instead of condemning evil they selectively flaunt their political thoughtlessness than to actually make a cogent point. If one points the finger of accusation at the United States so loudly at our involvement, why is their not a fair and balanced accusatory finger pointed to the insurgency? We need to pressure leaders to begin condemning these acts of evil and call it what it is, in one voice.

Forgive me for getting all political again. But it is so disheartening to hear of people condemning our presence here and refusing to acknowledge a foreign presence here that is determined to kill innocent Iraqis. Should we abandon Iraq to these killers?

13 MAY 05 15:34   A Great Quote
"Lovecats" by The Cure

"There are two means of refuge from the miseries of life: music and cats."
       -Albert Schweitzer

14 MAY 05 15:08 Hot hot hot
"Hot, Hot, Hot" by The Cure

The temperatures have returned after a week or so respite to what I am told is the customary summer temperature of infernal. If one is traveling and wearing a flack vest the temperature only rises above and beyond that. Sitting outside during the day here is a neat way to sweat off a lot of pounds but also it is a great way to celebrate no snow. Most people think I am nuts but I prefer this heat to the opposite end of the spectrum. Now the only thing I must do is get the water drinking thing down. Hope all is well. Bye for now. R

16 MAY 05 16:14 The latest from Tikrit
"Ride Captain Ride" by Blues Image

Hola sports fans. I have been a little sporadic the past few days writing. Perhaps it is the hundred degree heat mixed in with a heavier workload and a helping of the usual soldiers issues. In the interim, SSG Swain and I had a few convoys and a few Blackhawk commutes. Our Battalion had a skit show on Friday, which was a lot of fun. A good time was had by all, except for one sour pussed miserable Captain type. One of the highlights for me was the music. Swain, Dale, and Schrivner played some good ole rock n' roll and brought a lot of cheer to us. (Nothing like live music.)

Country music fans were jubilant here; Toby Keith paid our FOB a visit and played for the soldiers. He and another fellow performed a set and we even had a fly by courtesy of a military jet. Pretty cool stuff, though I must confess I did not go to the concert. I like classic country as opposed to the new fangled stuff. *What was I thinking?*

The heat is kind of wild. But praise the Lord that there is little humidity. Last evening a dust storm blew in and it was a doozy. It resembles a fog, but windy. It is bizarre how the sun disappears completely. It is however not same as the sandstorms that you hear about. Yesterday, there was a grit to the air nonetheless that could be felt on the teeth.

This is most definitely an exotic locale, but I am getting in withdrawal for my beloved Hudson River Valley. They play a commercial on the AFN (Armed Forces Network) channel that advertises for some place in Germany called Edelweiss, and one of the pictures looks just like Bear Mountain. I can't wait to do some hiking up there when I come home.

A few months ago, I put out a call for donations of clothing items for Iraqi children. Many thanks for the donations that have been sent thus far. At the end of the month, I will be turning in the first batch of swag (hipster lingo for the stuff). I would also like to call attention to Operation ICAN, which is going on and is being run by our Civilian Affairs soldiers here in Iraq.

The Internet address is http://www.operationican.com/ please pass this address to as many people as you can. I am hoping for the widest distribution possible. This is incredible outreach and we really have a potential to do so much good by our good will and deeds.

And finally, I have been selected to join the sacred ranks of Crunch, Kangaroo, Morgan, Jack, Caveman, Kirk, America, Kidd, Hook, Pierce and Hunnicut, the guy with Tenille, and Bowden...yes it is true, my promotion has gone through...in several weeks I will the soldier formerly known as 1LT Repenning as well as Captain Repenning. Many thanks to the powers who be, and for all my supporters.

17 MAY 05 21:17 Warm, quiet, but busy
"Time" by The Alan Parsons Project

Doing well. It's been quite warm. Thankfully quiet. And yet busy. The days are going merciful and fast, for me. Once we have mail call, I can feel another day pass and it makes me feel good. This is an amazing experience but I will be most happy when it concludes and I can enjoy life again back home.

I participated in the skit show last week and it was great getting involved in something fun. I just was commissioned to put something together for Memorial Day which I anticipate to be stellar.

I am considering, also, putting together a few videos commemorating our time here. A little balance makes such a difference. It is so important to get the job done, but I am learning that you can't get the job done well with out that balance. Well that's all for now.

Bye for now. R

19 MAY 05 20:49 Four years
"Homesick" by Soul Asylum

Four years ago, I was lying on the marble floor at Saint Patrick's Cathedral, lying before God and His people prostrate (I hope I spelled this right). How bizarre that that decision would lead me to this place four years later. My prayers and best wishes to Frank, Fidelis, Stephen, Luke, James M., James P., Jerel, Edward, and Norbert. Well the journey has been interesting thus far. In all the defining word for the past four years has been presence. I pray that the Lord may continue to guide me and lead me to be a present for others, and that I may share my gifts with them and thus be a vehicle of God's grace. My mission has led me here, I ask that you please pray for my soldiers, their needs and the families of my soldiers, and please pray that I may be a force of goodness and spiritual guidance in this time here in Iraq.

Blessings to all of you. I miss you.

P.S. See Revenge of the Sith for me, but if your under 13 see it with your folks.

22 MAY 05 19:33 Holy Trinity

Several years ago, back when I was in seminary school (hee hee), I was at a reception, I ran into a lady. She said, "I know you." Her tone was slightly obnoxious and I couldn't place her face I impatiently asked her, "From where?" She responded, "You were at O.L.A. in Pelham Bay this summer and you spoke about the Trinity. You compared the Trinity to a Bicycle wheel. I'll never forget it, what a stupid thing." Seems my quick assessment of her tone was dead on. Thankfully, my mind and mouth were in the same time zone at the moment and without a beat I responded, "Well you remembered it, didn't you," and I walked away.

Well she had been right, I did preach on the Trinity and I did compare it to a bicycle wheel. Each Trinity Sunday I have done the same thing, and used the same imperfect analogy to address this mystery. Here it is again.

The Father = the hub
The Son = the rim
The Holy Spirit = the spokes
God = bicycle wheel

You need each piece to have a bicycle wheel and in a similar manner you need each person to have God. The Trinity is a revelation from God of Himself, revealed to us so that we may come to know God as He is. The key to the Trinity is it is made up of relationships: F-S, S-HS, HS-F and vice versa. The Holy Spirit I once read described as the love between the Father and the Son personified. The spokes analogy demonstrates how powerful that love is flowing between the Father and the Son and vice versa. How do we fit in? The tire. In this relationship of persons we call the Trinity we learn about ourselves and how we fit in. The person of Christ gives us shape, and we see that God desires us to be in union with the Trinity. We can learn from the Trinity as the persons relate to each other that we are called to relationship also with God, and with neighbor. We can look at the Trinity as the perfect example of relationship, constantly directed outward not inward and aimed to the other. This is evidenced in the New Testament whenever we encounter one of the persons of the Trinity.

This mystery like all the mysteries that we celebrate are not intended to be stop signs but is meant to encourage us ever onward to deeper relationship with God. There is a momentum and dynamic to the Trinity that desires to draw us in and share itself with us.

Pretty cool stuff. Excelsior!

24 MAY 05 17:10   In the news
"Television (Drug Of The Nation)" by The Disposable Heroes of Hiphoprisy

From what I understand, there is a lot of news on the news about things going on over here. As you all must know by now, I am a news junkie, however, I am watching less and less of it as time goes on. Quite honestly, hearing the bad news about what is going on here is frustrating, especially since we all know there is more to the stories than what is being presented. I find the media's coverage abysmal. One of the most telling things to support my opinion: look at the photo-journalistic coverage of the war over here. The media was like a swarm of flies on rotting meat when it came to their desire to take pictures of flag draped coffins but if it's a live subject who wears a uniform forget about it. The fact that the media regards the men and women of this nation in the Armed Forces with utter contempt is the latest photos of the late and not-great Hussein in his underwear. It also settles the debate whether Saddam was a boxer or brief guy.

What is going through the minds of the media? Are they incapable of telling success stories? Abu Graib this and that, atrocities, any other impropriety, and or invented stories that denigrate the efforts of a majority of us soldiers here is what might sell papers and television time but really is a downer. Finally, my falling out with the media revolves around who is speaking about the war over here. Most of the folks who rush to the airwaves and deign to speak for the "boys" over here (men and women the last time I looked) are completely irrelevant.

As now being in the midst of things here, I see how so many people who took to the airwaves and purported to have such great wisdom regarding the legitimacy of our being here really have no comprehension of the facts. Things here are progressing. Albeit not at the fast food culture pace of our nature but in comparison with the way historical progress is made, it is remarkable. So my suggestions about the news, newspapers, and special reports: Take it all with a grain of salt. Most of the time it is presented stilted, with an agenda, and with error. I may have said this before, question things and double check facts. And fret not, tragedy pays the salary for these folks so before you get upset at each little news report, relax take a deep breath and consider that it may not be as it is being portrayed. 'Til tomorrow.

26 MAY 05 Road trip

A lot of road tripping the past few days. Classic story though is how our CLP thanks to an outdated map for the new computer system went all the way from Hawijah to Bayji only to find that the bridge had been blown away two years prior. On the way back, to make up for lost time we took a short cut down a road that probably no Americans had ever gone on along the Jabal Hamrin range. One of the FOBs we went to, I believe in Yachi, had allegedly been the home of "Chemical Ali" and it was said that he once hung someone above his dinner table as entertainment for his guests.

28 MAY 05 21:18 Conundrum and a rant of sorts

Oh hi. It seems like forever since I have written on this. I have to admit it is a growing balancing act that becomes more and more strenuous with each new entry. I find it hard to project an upbeat yet honest perspective to a situation that is usually requires limiting information for security reasons and maintaining an upbeat perspective for the sake of you the reader. Who really wants to hear someone bellyaching about his life? I sure as heck don't? That's what grunge was all about and just recall where it is now, as M.I.A. as W. Axl Rose.

So what do I write about then if I can't be honest and I am afraid of not being upbeat? The answer: nothing. I am not saying that I am not writing anymore, just that I will write when I do. Right now, I am doing the day-by-day thing. I am not wishing away the time exactly but I do look forward to the day when I will be back in a life of normalcy back home. At present, the days are tough. Some days are better than others. It is awful to be on the other side of the world away from the people I love and care about and the cats and the life I really enjoyed and miss terribly and the friends who I enjoyed relating to. I have little of that now. Sadly it seems this experience is an alienating one. It seems like my interchange with those back home is one sided and I end up the center of conversation and that's exactly where I don't want to be. And I don't want to discuss the war or why I am here or talk about Middle East politics and yet I get sucked into it.

I am so sick and tired of the so-called voices of America speaking their minds (empty) and voicing opinions so divorced from the truth. I am appalled by the hosts of celebrities who have stabbed the nation in the back and our soldiers while collecting our hard earned money. I am disheartened to watch Star Wars and see the cheap shots alluding to our president (and I am once more thrilled that someone else (George Lucas this time) was deprived of my hard earned money.) (Intellectual property? I believe if it lacks in intellectual qualities it can hardly be referred to as an intellectual property, so I'll just keep on raging against the machine and fight the power).

And so I spend a lot of my writing time trying to write the wrongs that the mass media mind rape passes on as historical fact. CNN, 60 Minutes, ABC News, New York Times the whole lot of them are writing the history in their image and they are writing themselves as the heroes and all I see is half truths. They are not telling the truth about what is happening here in Iraq. They are spinning a tale that is aimed at one man and one party and they will use every soldier's death not to pay honor to the fallen but fuel the fire they have against a political enemy. And that's what gets my political Irish roused, and that why I wish the record or CD were set right so people can see that the enemy tries to kill us and the media licks its chops and rubs its hands hungry to publish the photos of the flag draped coffin so it can say one more time to the President, "You were wrong." We are not wrong. The deep underlying reasons are the same whether it's a nuclear bomb or a car bomb; there are killers out there that must be stopped.

I don't want to describe what is going on over here and yet I feel compelled to do so. And yet I can't be upbeat about it, because it is war and there is nothing upbeat about war. It is dawning on me that we as humans are mired too much in the mud of violence and hatred. I think we should be here, that is not the issue, but collectively there should be more done to prevent this from happening. Individually, we all contribute in one way or another. Whether it be prejudice, lack of respect for our fellow human beings, the careless way we treat the environment, it all builds up and contributes to a down graded version of humanity. I was thinking this the other night when I found that a mouse had stepped on the glue trap mousetrap in my room. What a horrible invention, and after disposing of his (or her) body I was struck by how horrible it is that we as humans think we own the world and can do with it whatever we wish. I do not want to live in a house with rodents and I know that snakes can be enticed by their presence but I don't have the heart to kill another one of these little fellows. Afterward, I was dumbstruck if I could get all messed up about a mouse, what goes through the minds of a terrorist? What could compel a human to kill another human like these people blowing themselves and others up?

I read an article about Weapons of Mass Destruction the other day. Its funny how so many people mocked and derided our government about the lack of any here in Iraq. I have no doubt that since they existed and they are still unaccounted for that one still has to do more than laugh about not finding them and ask the question – what happened to the WMDs? Granted, although the works of Josef Bodansky (hardly a slouch, and an expert in terrorism and the Middle East) cite Syria as the recipient of Saddam's chemical arsenal, there has been little in the way of the sexy weapons promised by Powell and Rice and the rest of the administration. The question remains what is a WMD? A WMD is a weapon of mass destruction (duh). So, if a weapon kills many people does that count? Is a terrorist a WMD? A suicide bomber? No? Why not? So 9/11 wasn't mass destruction? This is why we are here. The folks that are ready to pull the plug on their lives and the lives of innocent people and on soldiers weren't created by enemies of George Bush. They were created by enemies of our nation. They existed before 9/11. Saddam Hussein founded his government on a cheap regard for human life. He found the cheapest way to destroy human life is using human beings to do the deed. Many of the terrorists here are former regime persons. They were trained for this, and taught how to do it. And if it wasn't here, it could easily be somewhere else. So we may not be finding the promised WMDs but we are finding other WMDs, which are just as dangerous.

So, I guess I digressed, I just halted my little detour but the gist is that as I write I hope I do not bring you down. It is hard however to conjure up some moonlight (which is beautiful here) and roses (we have them here too) version of war. I don't want to do that, but I also don't want to bring you negativity either (there is enough of that in the world). Conundrum. I will find the balance I am sure. Please remember my soldiers in your prayers, and throw in a good word for me, I need it.

I guess I have said my peace. Where does one go from here? What format should this take? What should stay? What would you like to hear about? How about you throw me a few ideas? Give me a little input. I am not sure who is reading this anymore. Also, I want to apologize if I laid it on a little heavy just now. And finally, some of you might think I am a big apologist for the President and maybe I am because it seems like everyone just loves to bash the guy and make serious ad hominum attacks on him as a human being. In my line of work, and in my philosophy this is just awful. The attacks at times are so outrageous and insulting that I think the truth gets lost in the sixth grade name calling as opposed to intelligent discourse.

And finally, speaking of brilliant; today David Allen Blakes graduates from college. Holy Cross. Good man. I am so proud of you. My prayers are with you, and I know who is smiling down from heaven especially today. Peace.

30 MAY 05 16:10 Memorial Day

But we in it shall be remember'd;
We few, we happy few, we band of brothers;
For he to-day that sheds his blood with me
Shall be my brother; be he ne'er so vile,
This day shall gentle his condition:

   -Henry V, Shakespeare

A difficult day to not be home. Today it would be to Frederick Loescher Cemetery to visit Opa's grave, or to West Point. One year, Mom and I went to the Intrepid. The past few years, relishing the sacredness of the day in Wappingers beginning with Mass, concelebrating with Monsignor Bellew. Well I guess I am in the thick of it this year. This morning the Chaplains of the FOB put on a Prayer Breakfast and it was a resounding success. I was commissioned to put together a memorial slide show of our soldiers in Task Force Liberty who have died up to this point. With the invaluable assistance of Jerry my "guardian angel" and Chief Salaun we came up with an amazing tribute. It was a truly great teamwork experience. Not a dry eye in the house by the end, and rightfully so. One can fall complacently into routines or forget the reality that surrounds us. As I was putting the slide show together I kind of met some of these soldiers, meditating on their photos and reading some of their obituaries. How sad the loss we suffer but how great the example of dedication. Please say a prayer for the families of these great men and women who cherished the very liberties we enjoy.

31 MAY 05 16:24 from an Iraqi poet *(I print only so that this poet and other Iraqi poets will be known to those who otherwise would never know them.)*

Everyday by Abd al-Rahim Salih al-Rahim

The stubborn donkey
returns with the rooster at daybreak
to follow exactly the same route.

At nightfall, the stubborn donkey
returns with his heavy load,
exhausted, saturated with sorrows.

The stubborn donkey,
after the usual vicissitudes of life,
stretches his limb in the dark
and caresses his thoughts
and jumps among the stars
like a distant dream,
ethereal and alone.

6

HOT, HOT, HOT

2 JUN 05 16:42 Over Baqubah
"Waterloo Sunset" by The Kinks

Things here are well. Took a little trip and was able to see a little more of this place. Some beautiful country here. Today flew over what can only be described as a tropical paradise. Beautiful groves of palm trees. Pretty neat stuff. Bye for now.

3 JUN 05 15:47 One day at a time: Another Newsletter Article
"Where Have All the Good Times Gone" by The Kinks

Back in the day, when I was a youngling, growing up near the mean streets of Rockland County , New York five words from a bumper sticker were emblazoned on my mind and are tattooed to my heart here in Iraq. The words: One Day At A Time. At the time, I was oblivious to its connection with Alcoholics Anonymous and probably thought it had some relationship to the Valerie Bertinelli sitcom instead.

One day at a time.

Patience has been blooming in my heart and mind as each day passes. In fact, this consummate New Yorker (metropolitan area) riddled with the affliction of impatience is slowly (ah, you can't rush excellence they say) but surely meeting the cure and being healed. Granted I still find myself to be impatient, but each day I am surrendering some of that impatience for something greater:

understanding that there is a rhythm to life that at times is not in synch with my rhythm.

One day at a time.

There is little we can do when we are the mercy of time but lean back into its sure hands, to become aware that the rules of time are unchanging. The past is the past. The future is the future. And now is at hand. Granted the present may not live up to its name and seem more of curse than a gift but it is what it is, an opportunity to grow. Through the ages, the great poets have spoken of time in a variety of metaphors. One of the most common images of time relates to water and the flowing of water. Are we feeling like we are fighting a tide or going with the flow?

One day at a time?

Or is it just wishing time away? From the perspective of a man who would rather be elsewhere, I can say that I am speaking from the front lines of this constant battle we as humans have with this confining dimension we call time. We will not win, however, and we must accept the rules to be what they are, immutable.

One day at a time.

Once this perspective is adopted, time begins to move faster. I am witnessing it in my life right now. This is one of the challenges we all must face this deployment, let us not forget that whichever side of the globe we are on we face these things in solidarity. As the saying goes, this to shall end. Have a little patience. Take one day at a time. And be at peace.

4 JUN 05 09:35 Lush
"Trapped" by Bruce Springsteen and the E-Street Band

Some more time spent flying on missions. Had a real enjoyable flight yesterday over some interesting area. A lot of farmland, desert, swamp, and then lush groves of date palm trees. They call these trees the Nakhla. They really are captivating. We flew over some villages that were surrounded by these trees and the lush greener is definitely a break from the usual drabness that we are used to. I have to admit feeling a twinge of homesickness looking below at the seeming paradise and thinking about the veritable paradise thousands of miles away in the Hudson Valley. I have missed quite a few things but right now I really could use a mid-seventies overcast/rainy day to lift my spirits. Blessings and joy. R

5 JUN 05 03:45 Hair dryer
"Heatwave" by Martha and the Vandellas

The image is of a hair dryer. Imagine one, turned on, right in front of your face, on high. Now look up, the sky has the pallor of concrete. The sun glares defiantly on all below. If you are holding anything metal, whether it is in sunlight or not it will be hot (I mean hot) within several minutes. This is day time, from about eight in the morning till about six thirty or seven at night. There is a breeze. But there is no hint of cool in it. Just relentless thick hot air. Praise God, no humidity, though! No matter how miserable the heat is, it sure is better than the heat of Columbia, South Carolina.) Just relentless thick hot air. Like a hair dryer. The legend was that at some point one stops sweating. I can dismiss that legend at least up to 113 degrees.

Remember I mentioned rain, well that is the extent of rain here, and something one talks about but doesn't happen until the winter. The anticipated rainfall for this month here is a big goose egg. NO RAIN. Nada. Zero. So there you have it. Now I am off to Mass. It's a about a mile walk, which means I will have a good sized sweat/salt stain on my shirt by the time I get there.

Today's message: We are sinners. We don't go to Church because we are holier than thou; we go to Church because we are sinners in need of the Lord's grace. We shouldn't have the attitude that we can't be in God's presence because we are not perfect but should go because we desire Him to perfect us. We also need to get over the fact that we are sinful. We need to acknowledge it, not revel in it or glory in it, but ask for God's mercy and then allow ourselves to be loved by God and relish His mercy in our lives. The Cross is meant to redeem us of our sinfulness. The Cross is God's gift to us.

As I write this entry I am thinking about Caravaggio's painting "The Call of Saint Matthew" which is in the church (Chiesa) of San Luigi dei Francesi, in Rome.

6 JUN 05 00:15 Dust storm!
"Ziggy Stardust" by David Bowie

So this evening was quiet. Mike and I went to karaoke. That was fun. Then we walked back to the house. It was a beautiful summer evening. We were met on the way by CPT King, who showed us a camel spider that he had caught in his room and was holding in a Tupperware container. We chatted for a bit and observed this grizzly creature that looks like something out of Aliens. We went inside and were going to watch the second episode of Band of Brothers.

CPT King left a little while later and a moment later returned to inform us that there was a massive dust storm. Sure enough he was right. An impenetrable wall of dust made visibility impossible, and the wind was extremely strong. Porto potties have been knocked over and a garbage dumpster was pushed across the street. The dust is neat because it finds its way into buildings and blows in soft as talc but unfortunately it clogs the air with a haze and is a little discomforting to breath.

I am in my office and the haze is pretty thick and a thin layer of dust is on everything. Another interesting moment here, of which there is never a shortage of interesting things to see or experience. Along the way Chief and I made some popcorn before I came over here and another camel spider was lurking in our kitchen. These spiders can grow quite large, about as big as my hand. These spiders we saw were rather small, about half the size of my hand. Chief stepped on it, and I killed a few more times with Lysol disinfectant. So that's a little taste of things at midnight. Today is tomorrow now. Today, in a special way, let's thank God for the gift of our soldiers back in the Day who turned World War II around. Good night. R

6 JUN 05   16:20   Where two or three are gathered (literally)
"Pray For Me" by Joe Perry

Today I went to FOB Wilson. I say Mass at this place in an actual bunker. As would happen, one of my brilliant chaplain colleagues still doesn't understand that he is responsible for alerting the soldiers to my arrival and he still hasn't caught on that every two weeks yours truly and my faithful assistant arrive and say Mass at this FOB. Not exactly rocket science. So today, I had one soldier attend my Mass. What may seem like a hassle turned out to be a nice and spirit filled half hour of prayer.

I have been telling the Division Chaplain the past few weeks how some of the chaplains just are not being cooperative and supportive, and he just looks at me dumbfounded as if I told him Santa Claus was not real. Also, I work with some officers who are called fobbits.

This is a derogatory term used to describe people who, strictly speaking, do not leave the FOB; I have a problem with calling someone that just because they have an assignment that doesn't involve traveling (some of my friends would be called fobbits). But there are some people who give a bad name to the whole lot. The term fobbit then is more accurate to describe the people who have cultivated a certain work ethic and an attitude that is lacking in efficiency and in efficacy and incidentally do not travel. They forget that traveling is not the most desirous activity, and that for instance in my case I have a unit to minister too besides.

In the process, they complacently make all of us officers look bad. It is most discouraging when it is an officer and even more so if it is a chaplain. Many chaplains struggle hard to maintain a level of professionalism. We try hard to present ourselves in a manner that can earn chaplains credibility and respect as Staff Officers. So it makes me upset when lazy chaps undermine our efforts. The image of chaplain needs to be liberated from the befuddled image of Fr. Mulcahy on M*A*S*H.

Oh well, that's one of those issues that I deal with frequently here but I choose not to mention in this forum, but I guess it should be noted as it is part of my experience. It does paint an interesting picture when I have soldiers here so hungry for the Mass and that are quite sincere asking when and where is Mass and grateful for at least a Mass once a month and yet back home the very same thing is taken so much for granted. We could learn a lot from soldiers. Anyway counting Jerry and myself there were three of us and after Mass the soldier said, "It's been a month and man do I feel like a weight has just been lifted from my shoulders." That's what I'm talking about.

The dust storm last night is being called a sandstorm. Wow! The amount of dust and sand everywhere is amazing. The sun is shining and it is just bright and everything is cement colored and blah and hot. And the feeling in the throat is like one who sang themselves raw at karaoke (oh yeah (oh it was a horror show last night)) and then breathed in quite a bit of dust and sand. About last night, imagine holding out your hand as far out as possible and not being able to see it at all. Amazing stuff. Bye bye.

7 JUN 05 20:35   Rebellion, dust storms, ants and reading
"Everyday I Write The Book" by Elvis Costello

Hola. Today started so blue skies and all that and has ended up overcast by dust. The sun faded into a grayish mauve screen of dust that resembles a foggy haze. Throwing rocks this evening, I took great delight seeing when they landed the poof of dust just like in the days of old when I used to throw dried mud which I called dirt bombs and see them make similar puffs dirt "smoke".

The wildlife has been very captivating as usual. Today I watched in awe as two parent sparrows were feeding their two birdlings. What I presume to be the mama sparrow would gather food and carry it in its mouth while papa sparrow would provide over watch and scan the area for potential aggressors (all this happening on the roof of our building here and the eaves (ish)). The mama sparrow then would put the food into the gaping pleading mouths of her young, and man alive those younglings really squawk a storm up.

The doves here have converted me so much. These birds here don't seem as mentally deficient as the doves back home. These doves look so insightful and almost loving as they look down on us. Some birds almost seem conceited at times but not the doves. I am amused how they will fly really high up on a hot day and then glide down sometimes it seems they are gliding like two three hundred feet with out flapping their wings. No exaggeration. I also get a kick out of how these docile creatures will let out their squawking battle cry that seems to be totally out of character.

This afternoon, I witnessed a gorgeous little lizard and took a few pictures of him. I could have caught him no problem, considering I touched its tail. Lizardy (I am the lizard king) in the Komodo dragon miniature variety.

Last night, in the kitchen a lone ant wandered across the floor. The detestable instinct to destroy was present as my tyrannical feet clobbered ever closer until my eyes caught the distinct antennae and the little legs and with such innocence he moved his way over to me like "Hmmmm, who is this" or "To whom do these Death Star sized sneakers belong to?"

And then there is the growing thoughts of rebellion and revolution as I read yet another book. I have to count up how many books I have read this far. I am so neurotic that I have been keeping a running tally of what I have read and I even have them listed in order since I arrived in country. Today I finished one and am in the midst of another, "Fahrenheit 451" by Ray Bradbury. That was one of the few high school reading list books I read back in the day because I had to, and I actually ended up enjoying it. Back then I hated reading books that were forced down my throat and in my typical stubborn or tenacious manner would read the books after the fact so I could read them for the actual pleasure of reading and not to make the grade. It is ridiculous that we force kids to read and desire them to parrot back the status quo thoughts about the books as opposed to cultivating a love of reading.

I confess, I love to read and I am so glad my Mom gave me this gift of loving to read. She never forced me to read but I will never forget the reverential way she would hold an old book, especially a book that was special to her. I love books and "Fahrenheit 451" just is reminding me how deep that love is. It was starting slow and then bang it sucked me into it and the brilliance of Bradbury is once again attested to. Science fiction or prophecy? This simple small novel is like a history book peering fifty years or so into the future and showing us how corrupted we have become by what the sociologists would call the McDonaldization of our culture (fast food nation). I highly recommend this book. Brilliant (as the Guinness gnome would say, and Justin (Oh, brother where art thou?))

Reading = rebellion. If only we could sell that truth to kids today. If only we could really teach them the value of knowledge. If only we could let them know that the written word has a power that can change the world. And if only we can let young people know that knowledge is power. Read, read, read and if you are really daring, pick up a pen and write.

9 JUN 05 12:00 Safe
"Don't Believe The Hype" by Public Enemy

I understand that Tikrit was in the news. Just wanted to say that I am safe and hard at work. Y'all know the nature of work so you can understand my obliqueness (no deception intended).

Regarding news, I hope the irony is appreciated at the vocal outrage about the desecration of the Koran (appropriate) but the absolute lack of outrage from the same outcriers about the desecration of the human person by terrorists. Again, when are we going to hear these things condemned with burning indignation on the news show? I would be upset if the Bible were desecrated, that's just wrong but it is puerile. But in comparison, I am more concerned about the murder of innocents. I am more outraged to hear that worshipers in a mosque were the victims of a bombing for example than that some idiot thought felt it necessary to fulfill their purpose by doing something idiotic.

Hypocrisy alert. I should point out when it comes to liberal hypocrisy my memory is not very forgiving. When Andres Serrano found it artistic expression to immerse a crucifix in a container of urine the liberal media didn't bat an eyelash. Now the hypocrites have found religion and now regard for religious articles, the Koran but not Jesus or the Blessed Virgin Mary, and call it desecration. Is it me or is something amiss? Is there a lack of fairness? Is it not desecration if it involves Christianity? If you aren't asking these questions what are you doing? Once again the media is manipulating our minds and twisting logic to suit their designs.

11 JUN 05 21:18 Grandparents and parents - A simple thought

Over here, in the military, I have come to a much deeper understanding of my grandfather, Opa, Marion J. Wyatt. Almost eleven years since he died, his wisdom, words, stories they seem to grow richer the older I get. At times, I feel guilty that I have not been as prolific about my other grandparents. Is there nothing good to say about them? No. Absolutely not. There is much that can be said about each of them. However, on the path I have found myself many times, I have been accompanied by Opa's presence. Here that feeling is profound. In some way, I feel I know him in a manner that no one else could. Fellow soldiers. In that identity there lies a whole world that is incomprehensible to other rational creatures. Through my relationship with him, I am beginning to appreciate the roles and identities of his fellow colleagues: Elizabeth Wyatt, Elaine Repenning, and William Repenning. The sense of pride that I have, regarding grandparents, has always been strong and remains so now and I know will continue to grow.

My relationship with Opa also has fostered a deeper love and respect for my own parents. I see in my Mom the teacher who has taught me so much about the process.

Thanks to her I have learned how to get here or there, as it were (though that destination is horizon and is a continual process). And in my father, I see the teacher who has taught me how to be there or here. Whether it makes sense or not, its the best I can do in regards to expressing it. It makes sense to me.

So, today is Opa's birthday. It is also the one year anniversary of Fran's death, Dan's mom. I look at the death of Fran as a tragic loss. She is the mother of one of my best friends. When I would see her, I always looked at her with a bit of awe. She raised my brother from another mother. That just rocks. What's even cooler is the familiar air of humility that she seemed to love to swim in. Nonchalantly walking in this world, aware though of the great gifts God placed in her life. It was always cool to see her light up at the mention of her children and grandchildren. She knew the treasure and yet she still was humble about it. In that way, her pride was louder than anything that could fly over Jackson Heights.

Humble pride. Which sounds like a great band name. That's the legacy our loved ones leave us with and carry with them in their life journey. I recognize it more and more, each day. And I feel it more and more. I know my parents have it. And Oma never lets me forget it. And that was the legacy of my grandparents who have entered into Eternal Life. I just wish they could see my now, but then again... ...they do.

Thank you for coming along with me and sharing a few moments with me. Hmmm. How odd so far away, so public a place and yet sharing something so personal and kitchen table (y). God bless you.

12 JUN 05 17:01 Please pray for the soldiers and their families

Capt. Phillip T. Esposito and 1st Lt. Louis Allen were murdered by a subordinate. There was an article written in the Journal News, which I posted on my blog, however, since an investigation was being conducted I did not think that it would be appropriate to write anything personal regarding this incident.

The night of the incident, around 2200 hrs I was outside the TOC (Tactical Operations Center) with a few soldiers. Two Blackhawks had just landed at the lower landing pad and a very loud explosion occurred in the vicinity. The two Blackhawks immediately took off and as they were ascending from the landing pad several smaller explosions came from the same general area.

The explosions stopped, and a few of us started to run to see what had happened. It was then that SGT Moon came our way and told us what he had seen. By all indications it seemed as if several rockets and/or mortars had been fired at the helicopters on the landing pad near the palace that housed Division personnel.

Shortly we heard that two soldiers were seriously injured and were being EVACed to FOB Speicher and could possibly die. The next morning, the Chaplains were called in for a meeting and we were tasked with counseling soldiers down at the palace. We also were informed that Captain Esposito and Lieutenant Allen had died in the attack.

After a long day of being present for soldiers and talking to as many as we could, and helping deal with this loss word began to trickle out that the "attack" was now a murder investigation.

14 JUN 05 20:50   Guess who's back?

Oh my. It feels like quite awhile since I have felt like this. A bit free. The rat race has been just that. A lot of pressure from all sides. Seems like even the pillow was reluctant to surrender some z's my way. Ah. Life in the pressure cooker is how I like to describe it. Take away all the things you take for granted and soak in the blahs. What has it done for me? Wonders. It is no secret that the great spiritual masters and those who sought enlightenment found it just beyond privation. Scripture places a value on the desert experience, which to the student in me seemed metaphorical as opposed to a reality. In seminary (I prefer this expression, as opposed to "in the seminary", despite the Anglican cadence to it) we heard of desert constantly in the metaphorical sense. The desert became a symbol for something. But now I see that the desert doesn't represent some reality. It is reality. When one goes into the desert one goes into a world of in which survival is watered down (pardon the Bono-esque irony) to the bare essentials.

The desert can kill you. It can suck the life right out of you and leave you charred to ash and mingled with the dust. It can strike you down like a lightning bolt, it can coil around you like a viper, it can crawl onto your skin like a scorpion, and it can bury you under the weight of ages and isolate your existence to a granule. It can forget you and pretend you never were. It is a powerful force and yet it has been tamed. And so it is a frontier, we have come to ignore, a place of myth and ancient tales, a piece of our history not too highly valued. But it here where the real wars have been fought. It is here where eternity was claimed, where man and God met, where Satan was defeated, where humanity flexed its muscles and did not succumb. The desert is so many things fearsome and threatening, but it has also become for many generations home. The desert may not have yielded, but it is a place where man refused to yield as well. And a breeze burns on across the searing tracts and my sweat has mingled with this hard land.

This desert has become my classroom. With the absence of so much that I love and value I find that I my imagination is growing more and more vivid. I can close my eyes and visualize so perfectly, for instance, the beauty of a rainy day, the midnight streets of New York City, the snow swept paths through the forests of my youth, Berlin and Rome, Riverdale and Long Beach Island, the cool waters of Lake Askoti and the open road between Beatrice and Lincoln.

Granted at times the exile is like an aching in my bones. I feel the absence. I feel the privation. I thirst to feel rain on my face, to sit by the riverside of the mighty Hudson, to hear the roar of the ocean or the simple sounds of children playing at a playground, from the taste of a cool beer with plain pizza to hearing the engine of my car as the miles unwind on a nice open stretch of Route 17 heading home from Goshen. And never mind the personal. Ah, to see my family and friends and hear their voices. This is probably the most difficult and painful. But in that pain and difficulty lies the preciousness that they are in my life. If there were no love or care there would be no pain.

This Sunday, I spoke of authority. I recounted a few tales of my youth that illustrated why some of my frustrated teachers, while I was growing up, would occasionally label me as one with a "problem with authority." I noted, that in contrast at home, where the authority of parental and grandparental love was at rule, I resembled more of an angel, at least in my own self-described mythology. What separated the authority of home with the authority of grammar school academia was the perceived presence of love and concern from home and the perceived lack of it from those entrusted with the care of teaching. And that observation really cuts to the heart of authority and its value. Where authority drifts from its mandate of service, which needs to be personal and if not loving at least rooted in care for the other, authority ceases to be relevant.

Authority for the sake of itself is worthless. Authority for the sake of the person is primary. Case and point, the authority of Christ is rooted in love and service of each and every one of us. Christ lords his authority over us so he can wash our feet, or feed us, or heal us, or raise us from the dead, or satisfy our thirst, or comfort our sorrow. So, what does that mean for us? We must strive for that power and that for that power alone. All else will pass like the sands of the desert. It's good to be back. Blessings to all of you, especially my partners in crime out there fighting the good fight and righting (and writing) the wrongs of the world: Bill, C-S-I-S, Dan, Rich, Brian, my minions from the CDB, Marley, the folks of the Wappinger's Soul Chapter.

Peace Out, R.

15 JUN 05 21:58 120 and climbing
"Rain" by The Cult

The heat has now graduated to about 120 degrees. Oklahoma is looking like Eskimo country here. It has been about six weeks since I have seen rain. If a windy stretch hits the air gets real dusty which colors the air a vague sulphur tone resembling a dry fog. When you get a good woof of dust in your face and mouth and nose it smells like dirt and tastes just a tad staler. The air now is pretty intense breathing it in. You can feel the heat down into the lungs. It's pretty heavy duty. The sky is getting paler and paler resembling less an intense slab of concrete and more like a salt flat rendering the ambient light more pale, as well. I was watching a few moments of television this afternoon and was virtually mesmerized by a commercial that showed a battleship being washed. To see so much water splashing was just wonderful. I could almost smell the water and feel its coolness. Well that's what's going through my mind right now, the fact of heat and the dream of rain.

16 JUN 05 23:41 Another Battalion Newsletter Article
"Heroes" by David Bowie

Dear friends! Well here we are just about at the halfway mark. Our Battalion has been blessed with much success here, and we are performing our mission with the skill and acumen of seasoned professionals. Each day, is a lesson in dedication and hard work. SSG Swain, my assistant, and I are blessed and very proud to serve with the soldiers of the 250th Signal Battalion. As awed as I am by the performance of this battalion and its many selfless servants I am equally awed by the spirit that this battalion possesses.

Talk is cheap though. I think that the best way to support my opinion is with some evidence. Happily, while performing the thankless task of cleaning my e-mail box I came upon a note written by SSG John Dale just as we were beginning this deployment. His words touched me then, as they do now. I felt that you might appreciate his sentiments and I am sure you can relate to this man's heartfelt sentiments. They bring honor to us as soldiers as we celebrate the Army's birthday and also they are a nice testimony as we celebrate Father's Day this weekend.

Blessings and peace,

CH Robert Repenning

Greetings All,

This will hopefully be my final email from the lovely state of New York. We will be flying from here to Kuwait on Wednesday. In Kuwait we will be getting our equipment ready, going through some more training, getting adjusted to the environment, and preparing to make the trip North into Iraq.

I heard a song the other day that a good friend of mine played for me here. It is from a local band in Marshall, which is about 30 min North of Sedalia on Hwy 65. I think they are called Renegade. They wrote a song about heroes that I think is very appropriate to share with you all. It is about a father who tells his young son to be careful who he calls his heroes, as that they can't be just anyone. His father then tells him that the real heroes are the ones who give them the freedom to enjoy this baseball game that they were watching in the stadium at the time. Later in life, the young son grows up to be a soldier and goes overseas to serve his country. A truly "American" story and one that I am proud to relate to.

My father told me a long time ago that being in the military would not be too bad of a way to go. I have grown up knowing about my Uncle Jimmy who gave his life in defense of his country during the Vietnam War. My Uncle Mike and Austin, who were blessed to make it back home, both served during this time as well. Both of my Grandfathers served during WWII. All of them showed undaunted courage and valor and served their country proudly. I took my fathers advice, combined with the yearning to be an honorable man like them someday and joined the military. I have no doubt that this was the right decision to make.

My children will know of these heroes that are in my family as well as the men and women that I have served with in Bosnia and the ones I am serving with now on this deployment to Iraq. We need to remind our kids, grandkids, and for some great grandkids, that not all heroes wear football pads, shoot a basketball, throw other men around in a ring, or swing a bat. This country has heroes that are normal people who do extraordinary things when their country asks them to. I know who my heroes are. They are those members of my family as well as the people I live and work with everyday on this deployment. And here real soon I will be right beside them in combat. Not everyone gets to be as fortunate to have their heroes close to them.

I ask of each of you to take a minute and ask the Lord to give us the courage and strength to safely accomplish our mission and come home to our loved ones. I thank you all again for your continued support. My next email will be from Kuwait.

God Bless,
John (SSG John Dale)

"Greater love hath no man than this, that he lay down his life for his friends."
- John 15:13

17 JUN 05 13:18 Tragic loss

This morning, I caught the CBS News report of the deaths of CPT Esposito and LT Allen. This is a tremendous tragedy that we, soldiers, are dealing with here, and that the Esposito and Allen families are dealing with at home. As a priest, from the Archdiocese of New York it is equally tragic, in light of the fact that they are so close to home. My heart goes out to the families, their loss is one that touches me deeply. My prayers are with them, and I would encourage you to please keep them in your prayers. CPT Esposito and LT Allen were men of service and they were highly respected as soldiers but also known as family men. It is heart rending to know that they leave behind two wives and five little children.

I can't help but be moved by the plight of some of the other victims of this horrible event. The family of the accused face now must grapple with many hard questions, the stigma and the deep anger concerning events they do not understand. Please keep them in your prayers, as well, as they deal with the unfolding events and the impact it will have on their lives.

In addition, please pray for the soldiers that are here; those who served with CPT Esposito and LT Allen in a special way, and the other soldiers serving in Task Force Liberty. This is a deeply disturbing morale issue. For soldiers there is a sacred trust that we rely on as brothers in arms. An event of this type wound that trust and so we will need to experience healing. Pray that we may experience that healing and thus do all we need to do to come home safely to our loved ones. Blessings and peace.

18 JUN 05 22:27 A long dusty day...
"Three Birds" by Bob Marley

...On the road...said four Masses at two FOBs...received a coin from General Sullivan, usually given to someone for a job well done...needless to say, it was cool after Mass, as I was putting my uniform shirt back on to be given this by him...and then it was back to here...rode with General Sullivan's Personal Security Detail back here at night (!) which was kind of cool since it was my first night mission...fact: there is more electricity being produced now than ever before here in Iraq...and yet, how sadly dim it is at night...I think New City or Wappingers is twice as bright if not more than all of Tikrit...but with the dust in the air even the moon is dim...well tired I am...bona note, as the Italians would say...and by the way, FEAR NOTHING.

19 JUN 05 22:14 Happy Father's Day
"I Want To Break Free" by Queen

Happy Father's Day to all you fathers out there. And a special Father's Day greeting to my father (Happiness and Joy) from me (his son the Father (which he gets a kick out of saying)). I can't get over the amount of fathers (and mothers) over here that are separate from their children for such a long period of time. Remember in your prayers those children who have lost a parent over here in service of our nation.

It seems most appropriate to share in this space a great Dad moment in my life. As soon as I heard that I was being deployed, I called home and needless to say Mom was devastated. I suggested that we go out and meet with Dad. I called him and he said come on by. And so Mom and I went out to Milford and met up with him. We went to one of the parks just outside of town and walked up towards this gorgeous waterfall and spent a good hour or so talking. The fear was so great that day and yet as we talked the fear was dispelled a bit. It was one of the rare moments that I have shared with my parents. We cried, we laughed and we declared a determination that I would come home safe. The neatest thing is that day we took a picture of the three of us. Although, I have to bug Dad about getting me a copy – it is the first picture in decades of me and both of my parents.

A lot of sameness going on. Happily the blahs have taken over for a bit. Sameness is dreaded and yet also welcomed. The dread is that it can lead to complacency or to thinking that things our work is done or getting easier, the welcome side to the sameness is that it sure is better than something different. Most differences are conflict induced, so any time conflict can be minimized that is a good thing.

Speaking of good things. Justin should be returning soon. That is good thing, for us at least, but I am sure Shannon would not share the same appraisal. Hopefully he has been enjoying himself and being home. His presence here has been definitely missed.

Word on the dirt road is that I will be getting home for some rest and recreation in the next few months, which is a good thing. And next week I will be beginning a four day pass (four day vacation) in my room but at least I can sleep, read and write, so that is definitely a good thing.

Speaking of reading. I just finished an interesting book entitled, Bruneschelli's Dome by Ross King. It is an excellent treatment on the dome of the Santa Maria di Fiori

Cathedral in Florence. A great read especially if you enjoy a bit of religion, history, art, Italy, science and engineering. It was one of the few breaks I have had in my Robert Parker marathon. I have to check out my count, because it may be literally a literary marathon with Parker.

When I go home, I have decided that since it takes several days to get there and several more to come back I will finally read Gabriel Garcia Marquez' One Hundred Years of Solitude. Which aside from the Bible is supposedly the most read novel in the world. Having read, back at Fort Drum, his Chronicle of a Death Foretold which is just amazing literature, I anticipate to have my socks knocked off. Well that is all for today. Keep up the prayers please. A lot of hard work ahead and the only sure fire sustenance are the prayers.

Before I sign off remember faith does not mean an absence of problems, nor is it designed to be a drug that numbs our reality, nor is it meant to divorce us from reality, it is designed to illuminate our reality (in all of its untidiness and difficulties (at times)). We should also beware of a faith life that is hooked on a feeling, and believing that our faith is all about feeling good. Feelings are not a good barometer of the strength or value of our faith life. Just something to think about and the crux of my homily this weekend (all seven Masses in two days and in a grand total of six different chapel facilities.) Adieu.

20 JUN 05 16:53 Them
"Crossroads" by Cream

Good morning, good afternoon, or good evening, which ever the case may be. Them. Do you remember them? Not the sixties group fronted by Van Morrison (Did you know Van is a nickname for Ivan? Actual name is George Ivan Morrison.) The "them" I am speaking of is the "them" that is out there. "Those" formerly known as "they." "Them."

These are the folks that we usually lump into a collective that fits our categories but usually sums up little more than our ignorance. Derogatory terms need not have hate intended, but sometimes there is hatred present. "Them" for me is a word that disturbs me at times, when its usage degenerates into the derogatory. Sometimes the term "them" is also a way in which we can encapsulate a group of people into a romantic category.

Both manners of the word disturb me because they twist reality into a vision that is inaccurate and impersonal. A number of years ago, this realization hit me while in Harlem on something Saint John's University called the Urban Plunge. It was designed to expose college students to the plight of the poor and less fortunate in the urban setting. It was an excellent concept and I enjoyed it much, except for the talk.

It seems whenever we had group reflections on our experienced the kids I was with would speak of poor people as "these people" or "those people" and it seemed like all of us college students were not only God's gift to the world but we were doing something that should be appreciated by the poor people that we were working with for a week. I noticed that this tendency could be absorbed in so many aspects of our lives. In which our worldview is divided in "us and them" terms.

I had the same experience in Kentucky working in Appalachia back when I was in Seminary school. (Again, for a week, I should add.) Again, I noted the habitual manner that we can gather a group of people under impersonal terms or in comfortable categories.
This might just be a personal annoyance or a sensitivity I have but one that I feel strongly about. It seems timely to bring this up, as I witness here the same tendencies and I find it necessary to vocalize it so that I may not only inform the opinions of others but also to ensure that I do not fall into the same mode of thinking. It is very easy to use broad

terminology that dilutes the complexities of life in Iraq. Part of the challenge is in our desire to have clear cogent and intelligible categories that can provide an ordered framework to an otherwise chaotic pastiche of ethnic, religious, political, and social entities that comprise the population of this nation. The political sphere here is incredibly complex and diverse and covers a broad span of opinions from theocracy, democracy, fascism, tribalism, possibly confederacy, possibly oligarchy (I say possibly because I am sure someone out there is advocating it), and anarchy.

Even the term enemy is deceptive because it connotes a collaborative affair when in fact the enemy is a mixture of organizations that do not all share the same goals, resources or modus operandi. These groups share at times little more than hatred for the United States or of an Iraq outside their own vision. And this is where the critics of the United States' presence here in Iraq are either uninformed or driven by an agenda. They speak of the enemy as a united front and in reality it is a host of fronts, each with its own set of goals and motives. A good analogy is crime. Not all criminals work in cahoots (what a fun word, don't you think?) with each other. Nor are all criminals of the same ilk, nor are all criminals driven by the same motivation. In addition, there are some criminals who are criminally insane (not sure if this expression is still used). One wouldn't automatically assume that just because two persons are criminals they are linked, however at times this is true, especially in the organized criminal world. So too, in Iraq the enemy is not one corporate entity.

In a similar manner, not all Iraqis are terrorists or cooperators in terrorist activity. There are some Iraqis who have taken up arms against the United States and Coalition forces and also lest we forget with the Iraqi government. They receive some support from some Iraqis, but the numbers are far from a majority. So speaking of Iraqis as them is also a misnomer. Like all societies, there is a wide spectrum of Iraqis, some of whom are deeply appreciative of the United States commitment to stabilize the nation and allow the new government to take shape and completely assume sovereign rule of their nation and their destiny.

And somewhere in there lies the deficiencies of our thinking. And it requires corrective measures. Simply put perhaps the starting point should be the little words that we use lazily and carelessly. Maybe we need to be a little more precise in our verbiage and in our distinctions and perhaps "they" may be a very good starting point. Adieu.

21 JUN 05 13:55 My Top Twenty (ish) "Night" Songs:

1. Bring On the Night - The Police
2. Thank the Lord For the Night Time - Neil Diamond
3. Nights in White Satin - Moody Blues
4. Wild Night - Van Morrison
5. Because the Night - Natalie Merchant
6. Here Comes the Night - Them featuring Van Morrison
7. Night and Day - U2 or Frank Sinatra
8. Oh What a Night (December 1963) - Frankie Valli
9. One Wild Night - Bon Jovi
10. Your Ma Said You Cried - Robert Plant
11. Night Songs - Cinderella
12. Night Fever - Bee Gees
13. In the Still of the Night - Whitesnake or The Five Satins
14. The Night They Drove Old Dixie Down - The Band
15. Strangers in the Night - Frank Sinatra
16. Help Me Make It Through the Night - Kris Kristofferson
17. You Shook Me All Night - AC/DC
18. Summer Nights - Van Halen or John & Travolta
19. Waiting for the Night - Depeche Mode
20. Tonight's the Night – Neil Young

21 JUN 05 20:32 Summertime
"Summertime" by The Sundays

Hot dusty day. It as if there is fog sans moisture and the dust is dense enough to dim the sun to a lunar luminescence and at times to obscure it completely. This all occurs as the wind blows steady and hot from the west. Day after day of it is quite a mental endurance challenge. The wind here has no taste to it. There is a gritty texture to it, but there is no scent, which can be a blessing or a curse. Just heard a fantastic song from back in the day by Crosby, Stills and Nash called "Just A Song Before I Go." Wow. I hadn't heard that song since I was a little kid, and then I heard it the other day and it just clicked in my head. Similarly, a few days back I heard a few songs by Gordon Lightfoot (Sundown, If You Could Read My Mind, and The Wreck of the Edmund Fitzgerald (great songs) which rocked me in a similar way).

Blessings and Peace. R

22 JUN 05 20:55 Happy Summer
"Heart Full Of Soul" by The Yardbirds

"Summer's here and the time is right, for dancing in the streets," as Marvin Gaye once wrote. So now, the days will get progressively shorter. The heat is on, as Glenn Frey would sing. No humidity, just a dry and persistent heat. There was little wind today and thankfully no dust in the air. In all a nice day. Had a chance to be on one of the buildings as the sun was going down this evening and got some cool pictures of the city. Now it is off to a nice cool shower and then watch a video before bedtime.

Blessings and peace, R

23 JUN 05 19:47 Anthony's Nose
"Ain't No Mountain High Enough" by Marvin Gaye and Tammi Tyrell

Status quo. Heat, dust, busy-ness, routine, planning, chores, meeting with soldiers, etc. Today I am thinking about Anthony's Nose. Within two months I hope to be looking at it, up close and enjoying being there. I have been compiling a list of some crucial tasks that I need to achieve while I am home on my two week leave (what the military calls leave normal people call vacation). The list is made up of some activities, which will energize me and invigorate me while I am home; needless to say this involves good solid family time and some time with my friends. The hope is that I will not run myself ragged and end up more exhausted than when I arrived here. The list is basic.

One of the things on this list is a hike up what Mom and I call "Mt. Repenning". "Mt. Repenning", as it were, is located just off the Palisades Parkway, up by Bear Mountain. Going north on the Palisades Parkway, "Mt. Repenning" can be seen a mile or so after the Perkins Memorial Drive exit, of the left side of the road. It appears first directly in front of the parkway but as one gets nearer the road cuts to the right of it and soon is on the left side, across a mini-valley. The "mount" is north (ish) of the larger Bear Mountain. There is a tiny tangle of roads off 9W that gives one access to it. Whence one is there, the walk/hike takes about thirty minutes or so and is lovely. The view that is afforded from the summit is pleasing and peaceful. There one can see the mighty and, I don't care what anyone says, clean Hudson River as it traces the contours of the valley from the West Point bend to the north all the way down to the northern tip of Buchanan to the south. Across the way is the hissing Palisades the fades in and out of cover of the greenery and lumbering above it the impressive Bear Mountain. Pivoting to the left is the iconic Bear Mountain Bridge, which spans a narrow stretch of the Hudson across to the Anthony's Nose.

Anthony's Nose from this vantage point looks much smaller and lower than this height and it is seen more as a part of the larger ridge, which extends from the north as far as Fishkill/Beacon depending on which Route 9 you are on to the Peekskill traffic circle. Anthony's nose enjoys a peculiar name, which hails back to the voyages of the explorer for whom the river is named. The story, which may well be apocryphal, is that the Half Moon, Henry Hudson's ship navigated up the river and as it neared this point in the valley the crew with great delight exclaimed the observation that the mount looked similar to the nose of the Half Moon's cook named? You'd be right in answering Anthony. And so the story goes a bit of a diversion but a neat little trivial note to file away.

All this adds up to the fact that this area of the Hudson is one of my favorite places in the world. I have said this before but it means more saying it here where I can appreciate so many things that I am away from at this time. This little nexus where the two sides of the river meet bridged by the product of the genius of the Army Corps of Engineers, and where the hills seem almost pinched together and decorated with beautiful foliage and an impressive and beautiful view also is a place which brilliantly collects my mind and body and spirit. I have never once driven through that stretch of valley without appreciating the beauty of nature at work there. Despite every odd weather occurrence, no matter what was on my mind, no matter how preoccupied I might have been or how tired I was I always have found something inspiring and refreshing about that area near Bear Mountain. I can say this definitively having driven it at almost every hour and in almost every type of weather (particular to the region). Its nice to be brought back there even while here, or to know that somewhere between the ears there inhabits all the wonders I enjoy so much and find so life giving. Thank you for joining me on this little written exercise in escapism and if you want to indulge in real escapism I encourage you to check out Bear Mountain, or Anthony's

Nose or "Mount Repenning" on your own or with some friends or family and see how blessed we truly are.

As Shannon had to say bye to Justin just yesterday, so he could return to us here, I remind her, "Remember when we were at Bear Mountain and West Point? Now you know why I was so excited about being there and showing you guys the area."

As for "Mt. Repenning" I have climbed it with Fr. Joe Fallon a few times, my father a few times, Fr. Ron once, and I want to say once with Fr. Frank Bassett (if not Frank you owe me). I hope I didn't forget anyone else. And this time I have challenged my mom to going, I told her to get those hiking boots out of storage cause we got work to do. I can't wait to take some digital photographs there. Bye for now. R

24 JUN 05 17:02 Combatative Inquiry
"The KKK Took MY Baby Away" by The Ramones

Saw a bit of the hearings yesterday on Iraq. What a comedy. Outrageous and undignified would be a good summary to an inquiry that had more drama than Godfather II's Senate hearing. The noble support of the soldiers expressed by some Senators proved to be mere lip service as they proceeded to berate our leaders and their lack of leadership. Two terms come to mind that express the hypocrisy and lack of integrity that angrily performed for the American people yesterday. The sanctimonious tone is a nice disguise for irrelevant talking heads that rarely deign to come here and are not up to speed on the situation, as it exists here. Is this paradise? Well if you look in my room you'd think so with my Scarface poster hanging there and Al Pacino saying, "I'm telling you man this is paradise." No, this isn't paradise. It's Iraq. A dangerous land. But a place where democracy is in its infancy and taking root each and every day here. I am here. Our senators are not.

(Somebody help me and I'll post the dates when either one of the two offending senators was here.)

I was once again surprised at the confident and dignified poise that the Secretary of Defense Donald Rumsfeld demonstrated at the Senate hearings yesterday. As a man in field, the Iraq our Senators profess to speak of with such authority is not the Iraq that I am in. The posturing on camera by our representatives is so disheartening.

I DO NOT WANT TO BE USED AS A POLITICAL ATTACK ON ANOTHER PERSON. I DO NOT WANT ANYONE STANDING UP FOR ME, DEFENDING ME, AND USING ME AS A PAWN IN A DELIBERATE POLITICAL ATTACK ON THE PRESIDENT!

I am a soldier. I am proud to serve my country. I am proud to serve under Mr. George W. Bush and Mr. Donald Rumsfeld. To hear anyone speak on the behalf of soldiers and then berate their leaders is duplicitous, insulting and disrespectful. I credit Mr. Rumsfeld for merely "smirking" any lesser man would have broke out in laughter at this charade of swagger and political ignorance. Even better would have been if Mr. Rumsfeld had told these Senators where to go.

24 JUN 05 19:43   The Main Event: Me vs. Tom Cruise
"Misery" by Soul Asylum
"Oops I Did It Again" by Britney Spears

Wow! It is pretty ironic that people think we are worse off then you folks back home. Mind you, I get a bit of the news and Mom she sends me the newspapers every few weeks and then I do a bit of reading to keep current, and I have to say I feel bad for all of you back home and the nonsense that you have to put up with on a daily basis.

26 JUN 05 20:06 Joy Revisited

The right order of love: J. Jesus (God) O. Others Y. Yourself

27 JUN 05 20:07 Disclaimer
"Waiting In Vain" by Bob Marley and the Wailers

The doctor is out. Am doing fine, but on a four day pass. Resting and recreating. If there is nothing new on here for the next few days fret not, I'll be back, and if there happens to be something so be it. Ciao, have a great few days and please keep me in your prayers.

28 JUN 05 14:17 Third day off in Iraq
"If I Can Dream" by Elvis Presley (for Irene and John Bailey)

So, this is my second day off in a row. The third altogether since I arrived here. I have been resting and relaxing. I have been officially banned from setting foot in the office (although, I snuck in last night to fire off a quick memo). So far, I have been catching up on sleep. Watching some videos. Today I was watching an Oliver Stone thing on Fidel Castro. Thanks to Mike I had some spaghetti for lunch. And thanks to Justin (who just returned this past weekend) I had a great cup of coffee. Justin had a great time at home, and though I feel bad that he had to come back here, I am very glad to see him and to hear his great stories. Thanks to Mom, I have been reading the papers (papers) and enjoying reading the Old Grey Lady. There is a new column that appears each Sunday in the Times called "Modern Love" which from what I have read is a neat look at love by a new writer each week. If for nothing else it is an interesting sociological take on love and family.

It is freaking hot. I just came back from a walk and my skin felt as hot as the sand at the beach. I could definitely go for seeing beach about now. To see the ocean would be great. Although, I don't want to see it in Tikrit or something would have to have gone terribly wrong.

Life is good. I hope the summer is beginning on the right foot for everyone. Try to make a point of enjoying it. Make sure you schedule mandatory fun. If you are a caretaker, make sure you also take care of yourself. Try to do something new that you have always wanted to do. (Mom and Oma are going to Pennsylvania Dutch country this week.) Look at what neat things there are to do where you live. (I am looking forward to doing one of those riverboat cruises on the Hudson, out of Newburg, when I come home (just so you know I follow my own advice)). Make good memories, and don't let the summer escape you. Good times to all. Blessings, R

28 JUN 05 20:18 Nestled (a sketch)

Ragged humanity ignores the rhythms as
green climbs limbs
leaves sprout
and packed tight between two branches
a basketed hemisphere of woven twigs rests

and a dove roosts there
nestled in pregnant vigil
still life flutes
while others breed clamor
in the evening's search and chirp.

29 JUN 05 13:31   The secret connection between 9/11 and Iraq revealed at last!

TERRORISM.

Why is it plain to me and not obvious to a people who claim to know so much about this country that they hold political office?

The facts are so basic: On 9/11 terrorists used planes to kill innocent people. On any given day, here in Iraq terrorists use cars to kill innocent people. What is the difference? It's the same modus operandi. Same disregard for human life. It's the same result - dead innocent people (who cares what nationality they are). It's the same result - dead terrorists. (The hoot is they don't even have regard for their own lives.) Iraqi's weren't involved with 9/11. Some Iraqi's are involved in this conflict. But many are foreign fighters hailing from the same countries as the 9/11 hijackers.

TERRORISM is the connection.

TERRORISM.

Repeat after me, TERRORISM.

Anyone who is willing to blow themselves up and innocent human beings is a terrorist. Obviously, something is going on in Iraq, which should be obvious to anyone with a pulse. There are terrorists here. Granted they are killing Iraqis for the most part but the fact is they are killing PEOPLE. They may not be Americans but is that all we should be about, saving our own and leaving the Iraqis to fend for themselves? It seems to me they have been asked to do that for far too long.

How on God's green earth can anyone with any intelligence and sense get up in front of the nation and say there is no connection between 9/11 and Iraq? Clearly, we need to vote people who can't add two and two together out of office. Their incompetence is starting to make my blood pressure rise.

The arrogance of idiocy. It swirls all around us and every so often it takes us on a ride that goes nowhere and means nothing. There are people still saying that we should have a timetable for our leaving Iraq.

All of the armchair warriors who sit at home and prognosticate on what the military SHOULD BE doing don't even know what the military IS doing. Gullibility is rampant in America. Of course exit plans have been drawn up. But what ticks people off the most is that it isn't being fed to us like an information "Happy Meal." We have become seduced by this idea that because the government is doing something we are entitled to know about it. What happened to national security, the past is prologue and secrecy? Should every bit of information just be put out to the American public so as to also ensure that our enemy knows everything we are doing?

Next topic: Gitmo. There's a lot I could say right now that I am not going to say except:

1. American toilets thanks to Mr. Al Gore (who spent his free time as Vice President, second term, defending pharmaceutical companies against the threat of cheaper drugs being manufactured in Africa to help fight AIDS (and the liberals gripe that condoms would save lives, why don't they try actual medicine, that is a real life saver)... timeout...rewind. American toilets, thanks to Al Gore who vigorously pursued a more environmentally responsible (not my sentiment but the gist of his), in 1995 saw a Federally mandated transition from 3.5 gallon tanks to 1.6 gallon tanks. So what?

Well, we use American toilets here and I can attest that they have the same stunning abilities as back home to flush. In all honesty, one would be lucky to flush what needs to be flushed, never mind a Koran or for that matter any other novel sized paperback book. That this was even taken seriously anywhere in the world only demonstrates the lack of practical knowledge floating around this world. You get the picture. Next.

2. Does anyone know where the folks at Gitmo were apprehended? Almost all (a few were turned over on the other side of the Afghan/Pakistan border) were apprehended or surrendered while in the midst of fighting the United States military in Afghanistan. By the way, it should be noted they were not wearing uniforms or commissioned officers of a particular military. There were a few, who perhaps were not fighters but were captured with fighters but it would be highly likely that they were co-operators. Time will tell. What is interesting is that criminals throughout the world speak the same language, they all can say, "I didn't do anything." Wonder what the 9/11 hijackers would have said if they had lived. More than likely they wouldn't have said a word just sang a few bars of that oldie but goldie jailhouse ditty "I didn't do anything."

Anyway, what bothers me is the miscarriage of common sense in our country and how few people actually point out the lies, inconsistencies, and fictions that abound in the public square and are being perpetuated by the left.

A year ago, I was a CNBC, CNN, FOX News, WABC 770AM, New York Times, Drudge Report junkie, consuming as much news as I could get a hold of, and now I am living in the midst of it. In all, I feel compelled to offer my perspective on things but I don't like it. I'd much rather talk about the weather or some nice story and think of pleasant things. I feel that it disturbs the flow of things but I don't see many folks trying to set the record straight, or presenting an alternate view to the status quo.

7

MIDWAY

1 JUL 05 23:07 Summer Wind
"Summer Wind" by Frank Sinatra

Hot summer days. Hot summer evenings. By 8:35 this evening it was still one hundred degrees, and it felt like it was eighty. The days have been hot but beautiful. Six days straight of beautiful weather. No rain, which at this point is obvious, but also no dust storms. It's almost like paradise. Except. This week, we have done battle with what looks to be a rat. The poor thing, stopped by the house, put a few people through the cardiac scare and then audaciously decided that the kitchen counter was somewhere he could find a meal or two. His sense of timing was off, and within a day he was caught in the cruel, yet kinder, traditional mousetrap (the regular snappy variety).

The mousetrap, I am talking about is a bit of a misnomer. This trap could have taken out a small puppy or a bulldog. I was asked by the Sergeant Major why I didn't save the trap but honestly I would have needed the Jaws of Life just to pry this device open. Unfortunately, as the resident cleric it falls to me to do the burials, so he got a Class A send off, although the tear was suppressed to impress the Chief that I could just dispose of rats without flinching. The numerous lizards that wiggle by with lightning speed and the dove, which is still in her nest, however made up for what the rat detracted from paradise. I give her a lot of credit. In the heat of the day, there she is so faithful to her duties, placid yet vigilant. There are now trees that have awakened and have sprung green leaves and it seems like nature needed a few months of the oppressive heat to get used to it and then or now it is time to get in gear. Kind of cool. I'll do a little

reading on this stuff and get back to you with better data.
Good night to all. R

3 JUL 05 09:31 "My Cross to Bear"
"It Is Accomplished" by Peter Gabriel

How many times have you heard this expression used in
ordinary everyday life? This expression concerning one's
own cross to bear is taken from Sacred Scripture. "Take up
your cross and follow me." Jesus uses this metaphor and
the cross is interpreted in different ways. The cross for me
is all of the hardships that we experience in our lives: the
uncertain hopes, fears, pains, difficulties and trials. These I
see as inseparable from doing the will of God. God's will
for Christ was to die on the Cross and be resurrected. God's
Will for us includes those negatives that I just mentioned. It
seems that where God's Will is involved we are going to
face testing and purification. I like to use the metaphor of
gold that's tested in fire to describe our plight in following
God's Will.

Today's Gospel then is a bit of a change in direction as
Jesus speaks of His yoke being easy and His burden light.
Making a pretty good presumption that our Lord would not
lie, one has to ask the question so as to reconcile these two
almost contradictory metaphors. Crosses are generally not
easy burdens, yet we are told that the yoke is easy and the
burden light. Recall, yokes are used in agricultural
communities even now. They are put on oxen, for example,
to pull carts and to guide these beasts of burden in farm
work. The yoke is also a tool for training a young ox along
side an older more trained ox. The younger learns from the
older.

Both the yoke and the crossbeam are put across one's neck.
In short, Jesus is teaching us the way to deal with our
Crosses. He shows us how to take up the cross in the
Garden of Gethsemane when He says, "Not my will, but

Thy will be done." A sentiment we utter each time we pray the Our Father. Thy will be done. This is the yoke. A "letting go letting God" attitude. When we demonstrate that living of God's Will the cross becomes one that is no longer impossible but one that we are willing and able to take. Guided by the constant presence of the Lord.

Blessings and peace, R

4 JUL 05   15:38   Article for Newsletter regarding Independence Day
"4th Of July" by U2

A belated Happy Fourth of July to all of you!

Two hundred and twenty nine years ago brave men declared their independence from England and began one of the most incredible historical legacies. The American experiment predated almost all of the other nations in its democratic aspirations. The ideas expressed by James Madison, and the signers of the Declaration of Independence were revolutionary and this document still is looked at as a watershed moment in the growth of democracy.

In a similar manner, the boots of American men and women trod through another watershed moment in history as liberty is now being offered to another nation. The war in Iraq has been controversial and in American discourse varying opinions are broadcast and printed and spoken, regardless what is undeniable is that our soldiers have been diligent in planting the seeds of liberty here in Iraq.

The road to liberty is a difficult one, but unsung heroes abound generously offering the Iraqi people a chance to not only survive but to survive as a free nation. From developing an infrastructure that meets the basic needs of the Iraqi people, to training men and women to defend and protect the peace in their homeland, to introducing Iraqis to new innovations and innovative thinking, our soldiers are changing the times. U.S. soldiers and the families that support us in our mission are living the legacy of James Madison's Declaration of Independence. This demonstrates vividly the ideals that took shape on the famous document two hundred and twenty nine years ago. The dream lives on.

The celebration of our nation's birthday was a rather subdued affair in Iraq. There wasn't a fireworks display or parades or the such but in a real sense we all celebrated the holiday in a most profound and commendable manner. All of us, here or at home, experienced the sacrifice that liberty demands, at times. We have supported the words we pledge with action.

Thank you to our soldiers for the great work you are doing. Every little bit counts. Given the mission our Battalion has, our contributions are most appreciated and commendable.

Thank you to our families. Thanks to your support and your hard work in our absence, we are able to fulfill our duties and carry out our mission.

And thank you to all of our friends who support us for your friendship and solidarity.

All of us are doing something great, may we never forget!

Some additional unrelated blog commentary:

"I Can't Help Myself (Sugar Pie, Honey Bunch)" by The Four Tops

This past week, we lost a legend with the death of Renaldo "Obie" Benson. Benson is most famous for being the bass vocalist for The Four Tops. In our family, the Four Tops lived up to their name and were the tops. Mom's favorite song in the whole world is "I Can't Help Myself (Sugar Pie, Honey Bunch)". I don't think there has ever been a time in my life where a copy of that song hasn't been accessible. At least twice a year the song receives deliberate airtime at home, on Mom's birthday (this year again, I intend to play it for her) and when we are on the way to the shore or on the New Jersey Turnpike. Years of visiting Grandmother Elaine would be accompanied with this song being played at least once on the Turnpike.

I am a pretty devout fan of Motown and this was made evident last spring when Danny O and I had a debate concerning the differentiation of songs between The Temptations and The Four Tops. To my ears it's like the difference of a lion roaring and a cat meowing. Out of the entire Motown stable, The Four Tops are and always will be my favorite. Interestingly enough, my favorite Marvin Gaye song "What's Going On" was written by Renaldo Benson.

By way of life here, it is horribly hot and dusty and dry. I can't wait to feel rain on my face, to smell rain, to see clouds and to see green trees all over the place. Bye for now, R

6 JUL 05 17:00 Living On A Prayer

"Oh we're half way there, oh oh living on a prayer."
   - Bon Jovi

Twenty weeks (ish) in country. And we have passed the half way mark. I will be updating my stats soon, but I am logging in some serious mileage with my assistant. Today we are about two hours away. Had a great flight. This one is a little long though. It is pretty neat to see the palm tree groves. Today there were some fires burning of dead leaves and trees, which have a real neat and exotic smell.

Someone asked me about the Fourth of July and if I enjoyed it and it dawned on me that the only time I thought about it all day was at the Prayer Breakfast that morning. It was a blessing not to hear any explosions here (you'd be surprised how some of the fireworks sound like explosive devices more than the explosions you hear in the movies). I do miss not seeing the fireworks, and believe it or not I didn't see any news coverage (I also didn't see a lick of the Live 8 concerts. I only heard on the news that it was pretty cool.)

Forgive me for being a little drab and less colorful today. Life is treating me well. Jerry, Mike, Justin, and my homies at FOB Danger are keeping me sane. The promotion is official soon. I will keep you posted when I get pinned on, but I have been told it should be by months end. And next month, hip-hop hurray I will be coming home for two weeks, which will rock.

Peace and blessings to all of you, R

P.S. Take a wild guess as to the weather today. If you guessed the same you are right. It is slightly cooler by five degrees or so though. Bye for now.

7 JUL 05 CLP poem

This close to dying
but even that's not on my mind
just a vague sense of nothingness
as sleep pulls me in
and mad delusional dreams
fill this dense hot space.

8 JUL 05 20:55 Thirty minutes of writing & then poof
"Astronomy Domine" by Pink Floyd

My blood pressure is now pretty high. I spent thirty minutes writing and then by accident I hit escape and poof there it all went. Justifiable anger at its best. So as to not push my limited patience anymore, I will just grin and bear it.

In all, I am saddened to hear about the terrorist attack in London. But it just is an affirmation, once again, of the importance of this mission. Democracy needs to take root in the Middle East. The list of reasons for this is large in my mind. But be that as it may. Things have been quiet here for the most part. Good things are happening in our area, judging by the news (seems one of Zarqawi's close confidants was captured a few days back). But we also had a little trouble; it involved Iraqis and not U.S. personnel. But still, we are working to forge peace here and there are still rivalries and tribal hatreds that precede anything Western here. Keep praying for peace and for the victims of this attack both proximate and remote.

Godspeed, R

12 JULY 05 18:27 A New Slant on the Rant Thing (Think For Yourself)
"Think" by Aretha Franklin

Think about all of the opinions that swirl about us and fill our ears, eyes and minds each day. It's a dysphoric tide that assaults us and the information overload poured out upon us leaves little room for us to do our reading and research and formation of independent opinions. Today, I proctored some college exams. This is one of the things that Chaplain's do. So I was grounded, sitting at a desk for several hours of reading, writing, and quiet. I finished The Stranger by Albert Camus, one of those novels that was on my high school reading list. I recall a time when I thoroughly enjoyed it and thought it was the greatest thing since French Bread Pizza. Time has not been kind to that estimation. This read around I was disappointed. I did not enjoy it as much as I did the first time. It is definitely one of those books that should be read at least once in a lifetime, but it may not be enjoyed.

I also read an article form the new issue of Esquire magazine on Donald Rumsfeld. Normally, I would have expected an article that would revile or caricature Mr. Rumsfeld into some twisted and evil power broker. Surprisingly, the author presented an interesting portrait of Mr. Rumsfeld that delved much deeper than the thumbnail sound bites that have corrupted public discourse. One hears enough in the media that something is such and from time to time one begins to believe it. Repetition is a pedagogical tool.

In reading the article, I considered how the author synthesized some pretty amazing ideas into a cogent article that assessed Mr. Rumsfeld's legacy as Secretary of Defense with an understanding as to the Secretary's role in government. Missing was the discriminatory tone that accompanies most characterizations of political personalities.

Discrimination. Who would think they are prejudiced? I wouldn't consider myself prejudiced, but if you look at my opinions there are times that I am very prejudiced. I have biases and I ashamed of them now that I see it. I am prejudiced against people who I perceive are defrauding our nation with bad information and ad hominum attacks. I lump into this group those who hold ideologies similar to them. So, a democrat is tainted in my perception since they are associated with a party that also embraces Howard Dean. Now I am being pretty open minded here. After reading this article, which had nothing to do with this subject, I will be re-examining how I lampoon and caricature some of the people with differing views from mine. (By the way, some of my best friends are democrats, so I hope no one holds it against me my opinion here).

In all, my credo has always been whether written or unwritten, "think for yourself." Don't just take my word for something, or anyone else's word for that. Check it out for yourself. Read up on subjects. Verify before you pass on bad information. For instance, the amount of forwards that we get with interesting stories, most of them are untrue or partial truths or complete fabrications. We need to be discriminatory not with people but with information.

Yesterday, I was head hunting for some quotes from Muslim scholars about the terror attacks last week. I had a bias. I wanted to prove a point. Bad Rob. What I found was some condemnations, without equivocation, of terrorism, Bin Laden, murder of civilians, etc. by a number of Muslim organizations and leaders. Believe it or not even I am wrong some times.

Another word of caution: be judicious in what you believe in the media. The other day there was a newspaper article saying that Muslims in England were equivocating the terrorist attacks with British foreign policy in Iraq and the Middle East. Notice how much the media is fanning the flames of hatred between the Western world and the Islamic world. There is definitely an agenda there. The media like conflict and it spares no expense at sowing seeds of discontent even if has to manufacture "truth".

Think for yourself. This is going to be a subject from time to time. I may provide links from time to time, but don't stop there. If something interests you, check out what is out there, but be discerning. Get a second opinion, and compare and contrast. I know everyone says they don't have the time, but is that true. We need to have time to eliminate error, and stop giving error a place to ferment. The first place is in your minds. Maybe in this way we can combat discrimination more and see things more the way they are than the way we are told it is.

Blessings and peace.

12 JUL 05 19:48 135 Degrees
"Hot In Here" by Nelly

This is the kind of heat that makes one feel as if there is something heavy pressing down on one's chest. The air is thick and hot and even the wind is hot. You can feel the heat crawl into the nostrils and down the windpipe and rob you of your strength. The notion of being to hot and the sweat will evaporate right off one's skin is still a myth for me. The other night though I washed my clothes and it took less than fifteen minutes on the line to dry them. When the sunsets it will still be a hundred very dry degrees. The blessing is that it is dry heat.

Now I said 135. Now marry that with the fact that wearing the IBA vest that we wear off the FOB makes one ten degrees hotter. Than sit in a Humvee with the windows closed and without air conditioning on and with the engine heat also being felt in the vehicle and a trip off the FOB is one hot prospect. I have never sweat so much in my life but believe it or not I'd rather be here than South Carolina.

13 JUL 05 22:07 Happy Anniversary
"These Are The Days" by The 10,000 Maniacs

Anthony and Carol,

As Paul McCartney once sang, "It was twenty years ago today..." All right stop the record and I'll take over from here. Happy Anniversary! Twenty years! Oh you thought I forgot, did you? Nah. But I figured you wouldn't be reading my words on the big two oh so here it is a little belated, but backdated nonetheless. Sadly, I missed a real awesome occasion with dear friends. Anthony and Carol please know that I was there in spirit and would rather have been celebrating with you guys then sweating it out over here (although the folks here are really good and need some support right now, but you get my drift.) Thank you for your friendship and the friendship of your family and for being a great presence in my life. I am most appreciative of the stellar job that you have done in keeping your eye on Mom and Oma (and the cats (I just have to include them since they are family)). In your way, you have brought much peace and ease knowing that they are not alone.

Happiness and joy to you and many more!
Please be assured of my prayers and blessings!
R

P.S. Can you save a Corona for me?

14 JUL 05 17:41 Sara
"Running On Empty" by Jackson Browne

A strange day indeed.

I had another lesson in humility today. Something must be going around (as these things do from time to time in these kind of places) because my stomach feels like I was in a fight with Mike Tyson (note I said stomach not ear). The heat doesn't help.

But in this world of balance discomfort is usually offset by comfort. Today I met Sara, a ten month old white and orange cat (who looks more like a two month old cat). I got to hold this little skinny kitten in my hands and she looks so absolutely tiny in them. Mind you this was my first interaction and contact with a feline since 2 January 2005, so needless to say I was delighted. The Commander took a few digitals of me and Sara, which was cool. (I think she knew that it was a big deal for me to see a cat). And soon, I will get to see my four angels, which will be awesome.

Well I got to run (pardon the pun). Pray I don't have dysentery. R

16 JUL 05 16:22 Untitled
"Wake Up" by The Arcade Fire

Greetings. It's Saturday, the heat continues. Went up to FOB Sumerall in Bayji today. Good run. I ride with great soldiers who know their game and are real pros. Also they are safe folks who don't do stupid things. I'm in one of those the days blend into each other mode. I got one thing on my mind, just in back of the immediate things and that's going home. I miss it much, the whole enchilada. But there's nothing to do now but get my business done and taken care of. A few weeks I should be breathing some cooler air, relaxing with the family and enjoy a few good meals. Then its back to here and finish up on a high note.

I found out today my unit back home, the 104th Military Police out of Kingston, is going to be gearing up for August 2006. It is hard to hear because they are great people. As weird as it may seem a part of me wishes I could come over with them. Loyalty is strange. But it just goes to show how much I enjoyed working with them. Similarly, the unit I am with right now, are also an enjoyable group and great people. I don't write about them as much as I'd like not because they are dis-interesting but because like everyone I write about I am concerned for their safety.

I was listening to a song the other day by a group called the Arcade Fire and it blew me away. I haven't heard something new like this in a one time that sounded so organic and natural. Most of the tunes nowadays sound like they were given birth in a lab or a clinic but these guys wow I am convinced that this is a band that twenty years from now will be very famous. So for my listening selection there it is. Also, I had heard the name and Mary Ellen told me one of her sons loved this band but I just listened to a song by Modest Mouse and they too blew me away. I thought their name sounded dumb and never bothered to listen to them. I guess I sound pretty dumb now saying I was wrong. These cats (note the ironic symmetry) are great and I am duly impressed. All right. I should be going. Well be that as it may. Keep those prayers coming, they mean a lot to us. I'm gearing up for a busy week ahead. Blessings and peace. R

17 JUL 05 22:28 Sandwiches, Mustard Seed, and Resisting Evil
"As Dreams Go By" by Harry Chapin

The faith life comes down to sandwiches. As I get older, sandwiches and faith are becoming more and more linked, to the point that sometimes when I even say, "Yeah that's nice but I 'm hungry." It's a gut thing. I know what I mean and for me it means that faith is married to the world. Look at the mission of Jesus Christ and you see one married this world to the heavenly kingdom.

> "Divine meet humanity. Humanity meet divinity."
> "Hello."
> "Oh, hi."

And so forth. Belief in the invisible requires a bit of visibility first. I need to see first before you start having me looking for something I can't see.

The sandwich? Well, it's like this. In Christian circles there's a lot of talk about love and compassion and mercy, but if I can't see it – it's words, just lifeless words. Keith Richards didn't coin the phrase but "Talk is cheap." Saint James said something similar talking about faith and works. So the message of Christ is made present when people do what he says to do. He said it already, why do I have to say it again? Instead of paraphrasing, why not just do it. He said feed the hungry, why not just give them sandwiches? Why all the words and why so little action?

What's got me thinking? Well, a couple of weeks ago, rock n roll stars got together around the world and used their talents and got people together and did something about a problem and brought attention to the problem. That's good, I suppose. But why them? Why are they doing the job that other people should be doing?

This is leading into my next question. If someone didn't go to church how would they hear the gospel message? God willing, through the works (walking advertisements) of those who go to church. Visibility is the issue. It is scandalous when pop stars take more seriously the work of Christians than Christians themselves. Where are we? We should be all over the place.

The recent bombings here in Iraq (Baghdad area) have awakened my Irish again after several months of being hypnotized into a pseudo-Groundhog Day malaise of heat and sun and lots of work. I have to confess when it comes to what is going on in Iraq I have been pretty much not reading or listening to it unless it involves Tikrit. Doesn't seem to make sense focusing on the badness when there is a job to do, and perhaps there is some concern about not wanting to add any bad juju thinking too much about that stuff. But then you here about children being killed by bomber and about Mosques being attacked and it just gets infuriating.

I keep thinking something needs to be done. I think about Daniel O'Connell, Gandhi and Martin Luther King Jr. who mobilized people and got them standing up against the adversary. I just wish there were more religious leaders taking it to the streets and demanding peace. This is the action, I as a believer thirst for.

I am finishing up Million Dollar Baby, which by the way I like very much. I did not like Mystic River, so I am happy that this is much better.

The whole military thing here is going reasonably well but we need something more. Forget peacekeepers we need peacemakers. We need to teach the Iraqis how to destroy the insurgency forever, and teach them the history that they are now a part of. All the masters learned from the generations before. O'Connell was the model for Gandhi and King. We need to teach the masses how to use this thing called democracy and how to use this *voce di popoli*.

They need to see those who have freedom exercise it for something valuable. We just need to show them with the intent of educating and not with any other intent. Let's put political rivalries to rest. Let's retire the chicken foot and the sixties retro wavy gravy groovy voice and put back on the mantle of greatness: let's look back to the man who set the standard in contemporary discourse Martin Luther King Jr. Check out the footage, look at his boldness, the forceful speech, the dignified manner, the inclusive dream, and his ability to knock down walls and build bridges. Look at the forces he mobilized in his mission.

That's what I'm talking about. It's time to get moving, resist evil at all costs and cease being mute witnesses.

And today's message: we are meant to extend the Kingdom of Heaven. It's not meant to be trapped in our imagination like the opening sequence to Highway to Heaven. It is meant to be brought here to this world. Jesus didn't build a rocket ship and tell the Apostles to climb aboard and away they went, off to the stars. Nor did he tell his Apostles to pack their bags and vacate the world. No he sent them into the world to proclaim his message. That proclamation demands action. It demands being the message, not just giving lip service.

Mustard seed. Small. In God's eyes, no good deed is too small or insignificant. They extend the Kingdom of Heaven here on Earth and claim a little more back for God.

21 JUL 05 13:37 Thanksgiving
"Into The Fire" by Bryan Adams

"Yesterday, all my troubles seemed so far away."
    – Lennon/McCartney

Thanks for your continued prayers and well wishing. Do I have to tell you how much it means to me? Yesterday, was definitely one of those occasions. Coming back from Kirkuk our patrol hit an IED (improvised explosive device). It went off just as our lead truck past it, and only about thirty feet ahead of us on the side of the road. The abrupt explosion was hardly the boom of the movies and more the dullard thud of explosives buried in the dirt. "Fire in the hole." The orange blast was haloed by a cement pallor cloud of dust (desert dirt is not brown per se) and with some dark chunks. We drove right into this sudden cloud of unknowing bewildered and rattled and anticipating a possible second blast to follow. Our vehicles were swallowed into this cloud of smoke and dust until we burped out the other side into the light and into the clear. Two miles down the road the lead vehicle could drive no more on its punctured passenger side tires. Strips of melted rubber peeled off the rims like the skin of a fruit.

What followed was a near three-hour wait for roadside assistance that required holding our position and maintaining a secure traffic free zone several clicks north of nowhere. The hot sun beat down us as we held our ground, maintained security, and lifted each our shaken spirits. The thrill pulsed through all of us that despite the aggressive nearness of danger we suffered no injuries or casualties. Thank God!

The crew that I travel with maintained such a professional attitude and demeanor that my safety never seemed an issue. I was impressed to see that under duress our soldiers have an extraordinary ability to push aside their own personal fears or anxieties and perform their duties as if this is a daily occurrence. Good stuff. The bomb had been set off by remote control, which means that someone waited for some time for us to show up and had us in their sights and made a deliberate decision to set it off. That is the wildness, to think that some total stranger and I are forever linked, I being one of the people he desired to kill and he being the one who had the determination. War is an odd and horrid event, but amid it all the goodness of the Lord can be felt.

Again, thanks for the prayers. Keep them going, not just for dear old me but keep them going for my soldiers and also for my commander, she is doing a kick butt job leading us and I know the day fell heavy on her shoulders knowing her soldiers were in such a tenuous position.

Bye for now, R

The day was capped off by something that just blew me away, and reminded me what "brotherhood means." On our return, there was quite a reception. Many people stuck around even though they could have spent there free time doing something else just so they could welcome us back to the FOB. Not only that, but a bunch of guys had gotten us food from the DFAC because we had missed our meal (and we were really hungry). What really touched me was when the Captain with whom I had a fairly serious disagreement with fairly recent to this incident, gave me a hug, and also gave me a tray of food. I was humbled and touched by the kindness and the practical expression of charity. Words might be good, but nothing compares to action.

21 JUL 05 22:30   Think For Yourself: Leonard Peltier
"Native Son" by Bryan Adams

Back when I was still training at Fort Drum, I read a touching book by Leonard Peltier entitled Prison Writings. I did a little more reading and research and I believe that there are way too many questions still swirling about the events of Pine Ridge. Check out what's out there. There is an informative documentary called "Incident at Oglala" that just has been released on DVD. It originally came out in the late Eighties. I highly recommend it as an introduction to his story. One thing that is interesting is the utter peace that surrounds this man when he speaks and his simplicity.   In his writing there are quite a few Christological references, although I am sure that was not his intent.

Just FYI if this seems to be from left field, I just finished a book called Lakota Woman by Mary Crow Dog. It is a neat autobiography, with quite a few neat insights. Now I am off reading News of a Kidnapping by Gabriel Garcia Marquez, which looks at Columbia in the early 90's and the Medellin drug cartel. The goal is to read his One Hundred Years of Solitude on the voyage home for rest and recreation. One of these days I will tally the stats and put the book list of things read on. I am averaging two books a week (ish, always the ish). In doing so, I am finding my ability to write and express my ideas is becoming more potent. To all the young ones out there, my message to you is this: Read, read and read. Turn off the television, put aside the video games and look up a topic and find some good books on it. This deployment, so far, has reinvigorated my deep love and respect for books and the great enjoyment and pleasure of reading. My mind has soared over these prison walls (well it feels like a prison, and I have been touched by fantastic ideas, and some great stories, and a few books that were awful but ornery old me I just kept reading our of spite. Blessings and peace. R

23 JULY 05 14:41 Another day
"Another Day" by Bryan Adams

So there is a nasty bug out there that I managed to catch and it has been playing havoc with my stomach and yesterday I broke down and went over to seek medical attention. They inserted an IV into my arm and put two bags of fluid in and a couple of shots of some drowse inducing medicine that sent me off to la la land for a bit. Waking from this malaise they then sent me back to the office. I went to bed only to be awakened a bit later with a THOONK (which sounds like a sock ball coming out of a wrapping paper tube) then about five or so seconds later a very loud explosion that woke me and I tumbled out of the bunk bed and hit the ground looking for my boots.

When I went outside all I saw was a crowd of our soldiers running over. We found where it landed and also saw from whence (hee hee) it had been launched, as there were still a slight contrail from the launch that bespake (hee hee) its trajectory (ish). These buggers are fastidious in their endeavors but quite a bunch of bunglers if you ask me. When they are lucky they are lucky but most of the time it's Spy vs. Spy ridiculous (which is most of the time). These are the folks that if they tried to kill themselves probably would end up giving birth.

So, with that said...all is well here. I am feeling better and back in the swing of things. Today we are enjoying (or not) the variety of a dusty day. It has been several months now since the last cloud passed by and I miss them. I'm off to say Mass in an hour.

Pray for me and be assured of my prayers, too, R.

Ricardo,

Thank you for your uplifting words. Last night I found myself in a position in which I felt anything but brave. I am visiting another FOB (Speicher) and the place I was staying at had a bed and a few military cots.

The bed was shot to hell, so in the middle of the night I switched to a cot. But as I was getting the cot, I heard a loud boom. I assumed at first that I was jittery and that I had jumped at the sound of my foot hitting a board. I kicked this board a few times but found I was unable to replicate the sound with any authenticity. When I proceeded to move this cot again the next "boom" happened.

Now drained of color and shaking I ran to the door and saw that in the distance about half a mile out there were bright flashes of red and a few more explosions. Needless to say, I reached for the cigarettes that I had purchased for situations such this (Following Robert's Rules of War #5 Don't quit smoking in a war zone.) Some other folks were around who explained the procedures at a make shift bunker (more like a concrete tube like you'd expect to see on a highway). I stood there and noticed in the dim glow that my hand was shaking. I decided the only way to deal with it was to drop pretense and admit to myself that I was petrified. In the darkness to know mortars are flying and have no idea where they will land is frightening. More so when you realize they are flying over your head, invisible to the eye in the darkness.

Soon we were given an all clear and told it was "controlled blasts" which would have been believable if they hadn't mobilized a large chopper group that flew over head for several hours and not to mention the inordinate amount of Humvee traffic going in one direction. I then considered the thing that frightens me more than bombs and mortars - lies.

Needless to say my dreams made for a fitful sleep of disturbing images in which my anger and aggression manifested relief in a variety of horrific and brutal images. Ah the brilliance of the mind that God has created for us. It even comes with its own pressure valves. This makes for three out of four days in which I have been confronted with those horrible reminders of where I am. I can't wait to feel the peace of R and R and feel genuine security and feel the warmth and peace of home. By the way: Never trust a place that clouds don't even go to. Hmmm. Stay tuned for another e-mail less egocentric and more conversational.

Many thanks for your friendship and good will and prayers, In Christ,

Rob

25 JUL 05 21:08   A Little Peace of Mind
"Only The Strong Survive" by Bryan Adams

Monday came early and found me tired and reluctant to get out of bed. A four-snooze alarm day begun all wrong as if to foreshadow a day made of tedium and dust (ah always some dust for drama's sake). But despite misreading a schedule of flights and missing a gig (as it were) the day unfolded delightfully into a successful, though measured, day.

In other words, it could have been the pits but it ended up being just what the doctor ordered. I knocked out a project that was terrorizing me, a paperweight of military writing, albeit brief only a two sided page. Paperwork is not something I have a keen appreciation of, especially if it is official and confined by the strictures of a form.

I also engaged in several mini-conferences with a few persons (what Jerry calls "making money") and I finished another gem of a book entitled "News of a Kidnapping" by

Gabriel Garcia Marquez. He is teaching me anew the joys of reading and the intricacies of writing, alas in translation. Another high recommendation despite the feat of juggling the various Spanish names (I do confuse easily (myself as much as others).

And somehow peace has decided to pay my mind a visit. The past few days had left me a little rattled and palely nervous. But through some of the mini conferencing I found some perspective and now am relaxing in the house listening to Morrissey (who incidentally I shook hands with in college at a concert supporting the Your Arsenal album. Joe Sultana, Michelle, and I saw him at Roseland Ballroom before Thanksgiving (1993?). I shook hands with him as I was being pulled out of the audience, in front of the stage, by security, as I was being pressed against the barrier. I looked up and there was Morrissey and I reached out my hand as he was singing "Last of the Famous International Playboys" I called Morrissey and he grabbed my hand and he wouldn't let go of it, and the security brutes were forcibly trying to pry me loose and then he let go and needless to say I thought it was the coolest thing.

Similarly, I shook hands with Vince Neil of Mötley Crüe fame when he was performing in Poughkeepsie two years ago, actually he slapped me five and I thought it was subversive as he probably would have freaked out that a priest had slapped him five, never mind knowing almost all of his songs by memory (which is humorous as that I do not know many songs by memory because I can't remember them too well).) Well that's it for today. Till tomorrow. Peace and joy.

26 JUL 05 22:32 Dusty
"In The Heat Of The Night" by Bryan Adams

Contrary to the subject line it was not dusty outside, but it was dusty in my office. Today I did a good cleaning of the shelves and threw out a lot of accumulated papers and junk. The office is pretty clean and looking good. However, I owe quite a few thank yous to a lot of you folks who have been doing some great things for our soldiers. Tomorrow I will attempt to chronicle the ones I can. Let me put into context the lack; I am seeing that I didn't segue into this topic well. In the course of cleaning up I saw that I had saved a bunch of packing slips from a bunch of you but that I had not properly listed you here. Mea culpa. This is what happens when one procrastinates doing simple tasks, for weeks at a time.

Things are going well. It's a bit lonelier here at the house with Chief heading home for his vacation (what the Army calls leave). I eagerly await my leave. Soon. Anyway, this is funny Chief always leaves his light on, sometimes all night long, and he's next door (not really a door, and the wall that we share has one or two feet on top by the ceiling that is open, to me. So sometimes I give him a hard time about it being on and keeping me up so he tries to cover it with a towel and then I complain that he is taking my reading light away. Then in the middle of the night I roll over and bang into the wall. The noise sometimes awakens me and then I go (say), "Hey Chief, did you hear that? (Sometimes I have thought in my delirious awakened state that it was the sound of bombs or something but it was just me running (rolling) into the wall. The wall I should add is made of plywood so we're not talking like gypsum or concrete or dry wall.

Oh yeah, I forgot to mention: This morning I was greeted with the news that my promotion finally hit completely. First, New York State promoted me but it was contingent on Federal recognition. Those two entities finally connected and my promotion orders were finally drawn up (but they say cut). In all that means that as soon as it can be done I will be pinned on (a little ceremony) and then I will wear Captain's rank. Should be by the end of the week or the beginning of next week. Funny though, Chief always teases me about my promotion and as soon as he leaves I get word, hmmm. I was hoping that he would be there for the ceremony but alas I guess his family is more important (I hope you all appreciate my humor as much as I do). Well, I'm off to bed now. Keep smiling and stay gold! That's an order!

P.S. The heat is infernally brutal in answer to Brian Murphy's question it is still pretty hot but for us its cool, about 95 at night. I also must confess that the 135 reading may be inaccurate in as much as the thermometer can absorb the ambient heat of that which it is affixed to and that sometimes throws the reading off a bit. But we are talking about five or ten degrees that can be offset by the clothing and the manner of exposure so I will not be quibbling much about the slight deviancy between fact and the perception. I did read a thermometer that read 135. I stand by that with both feet.

27 JULY 05 16:07 Travel: Another Newsletter Article
"Land Of Hope and Dreams" by Bruce Springsteen and the E-Street Band

A large part of my job here is traveling. In my time here, I have spent a lot of time on the road (and in the air) in support of the Division's Catholic coverage plan. But SSG Swain (my assistant) and I have also spent a great deal of time traveling as well in support of the 250th. It is always awesome to see our folks in the various exotic locales of our Area of Operations. Their easygoing manner, in the face of so many challenges, makes it easy to forget that we are in the midst of a war zone and they seem to be experts at breaking tension and dealing with tedium.

Wherever we have been in the Battalion's AO, I have been impressed with the caliber and ability that they possess. Plus, they are a whole lot of fun. But all you readers know this to be true because you know these people. Perhaps, though, this is not an appreciated reality.

It is not an easy task to adapt to so harsh a place as Iraq with its unforgiving heat and its knack for repetition. Variety is a precious commodity here, and that's where the personalities of our soldiers come shining forth. Why mention it, though? Well, as one deeply immersed in the lives of my soldiers, I have also great hopes for them. One of these hopes, after the obvious one of their continued safety here and as they return home for re-deployment is that they take stock of the lessons learned and bring home their experience and apply it to their life.

What I suggest is this, roll with the punches. Keep what you have gained. For instance, in the world I am a pretty impatient person. Here I have cultivated a bit more patience and have been practicing this art. For one, constantly saying, "I'm dying here" (in my best New Yorkese) is not the best thing to say in a war zone, but also because I have perspective there is little I can do about certain things.

So, look at what we have learned, think of the new ways we have handled problems and stresses and as we prepare to head home bring back the best of these skills. If there hasn't been much improvement, let's make the time that we do have left here count and worth the sweat we broke doing what we do.

Blessings and joy!

28 JUL 05 Notes for a report on the 250th Signal Battalion's Unit Ministry Team (UMT)

Shortly after (about two weeks prior) receiving Federal Recognition as a Chaplain in the United States Army I was assigned as Battalion Chaplain for the 250th Signal Battalion, 42ID. At Fort Drum, my assistant and I put together a religious coverage plan for the Battalion while we performed the necessary training for deployment.

In addition to Battalion responsibilities, I was responsible for all Catholic coverage for the 42ID division assets at Fort Drum, in addition to other units engaged in mobilization training. (There was a unit from Connecticut, that I did some things for before they deployed in early December).

At Fort Drum, I provided a variety of training briefings on: Suicide, Cultural and Religious Awareness in Iraq, Understanding Islam, Stress Reduction, and Drug and Alcohol Abuse and Awareness.

In Kuwait, further work was done in creating a religious coverage plan for the Battalion as well as coordinating coverage for Catholic soldiers.

At FOB Danger, I have been performing my duties as Battalion Chaplain, as well as maintaining visibility on the religious support of Battalion assets at approximately 12 other FOBs. This entails communication with the chaplains at other FOBs and is supplemented by visitations.

In the absence of the Battalion Chaplain for the 3-133 Field Artillery Battalion, Force Protection at FOB Danger, I have been responsible for and have provided coverage for 3-133 soldiers. To include delivering four Red Cross messages.

Additionally, I have provided Catholic coverage on the average of every fourteen days for six FOBs on a regular basis and 2 other FOBs as needed. This has resulted in, for the period of 30 Jan to 5 July over 70 convoy movements and almost 20 flights. In that time, I have prepared and preached at almost 150 Masses. I executed almost sixty percent of these convoy movements as driver.

As one of four Catholic priests in the 42ID AO, I have contributed to the creation of two FRAGOs dealing with the Catholic Coverage issue and have been a participant in drafting meetings.

In support of my assigned FOB coverage for Catholic services, I have arranged all of my transportation. Ordinarily, this is the responsibility of the receiving unit, but in the absence of support, I have arranged all of my transportation with the limited resources at my disposal. This would not be possible without my Battalion's support and assistance.

In May, I developed a slide presentation memorializing soldiers who have died in service of TF Liberty. The project complete for Memorial Day is also a work in progress ultimately commemorating TF Liberty's sacrifice in Iraq. Also, a similar project has been developed and produced for the 42ID Alumni's convention in Indianapolis, Indiana.

29 JUL 05 13:11 Promotional Item
"Do That To Me One More Time" by The Captain and Tenille

Well after much rigmarole and jumping through hoops and practically dancing on the ceiling, today is my promotion ceremony. I am definitely psyched. No more 1st Lieutenant now it will Captain. In lieu of the live comments I would like to say a few words:

Promotions are recognition of achievement in the Army but this is not a personal or private achievement. This is the achievement of a man blessed with a loving family, some great soldier role models, some dear friends, and an amazing unit(s). As a soldier I can think of no finer example in my life of the American soldier than my Opa (grandfather), Marion J. who was a tremendous NCO and veteran of World War II, Korea and Vietnam. I give thanks for his example of service, the blessing of my family: my Mom (Christel) who beams each time she can tell someone that I am a Chaplain in the United States Army and who is so supportive of my mission here in Iraq, my Oma (Elizabeth) whose pride for me mirrors her pride in our family's military tradition, and my father (David) who looks upon my spiritual support of my soldiers with the pride of a father and a minister (Methodist).

I am thankful for my friends whose kindness and encouragement enriches my ministry here. And I am grateful to all the soldiers that I work with, minister to, and whose company I enjoy so much. I recall the members of my home unit the 104th Military Police in Kingston, New York and I am grateful also to the soldiers of the 42ID that I have the privilege to serve with here and in a special way to my soldiers of this 250th Signal Battalion. You of the 250th have broken me in, and given me so much. I pray that I continue to be a source of spiritual strength for you and that the Lord continue to bless us all in our mission here in Iraq. Thanks for welcoming me into your fold and making me a better soldier by your guidance and leadership.

Additional thanks to three persons (on deployment) who could not be here today, Chief Salaun, Major Smith, and Chaplain Robinson thank you for helping me be the best officer I can be. (I do want to warn you that SSG Swain may not be receptive to his nickname or call sign being Tenille, so consider yourself warned).

Thank you to all my friends back home. This one's for you.

8

HERE THERE AND BACK AGAIN

1 AUG 05 13:56 Happy August!
"Round Here" by The Counting Crows

Today, I checked for the first time my countdown until I finish up here. 65% complete was its estimate. Thank God! The sameness is wearing on me; everyday is sunny save for when its sandy, no clouds unless they are smoke clouds or dust clouds, no rainfall expected this month again, just heat, heat and more heat. Talking to Mom the other day I pointed out that with the aforementioned commentary there are some other things about here that I haven't described. There is an absence of much sense stimuli and what there is usually is negative. Not that I am complaining.

For instance, the dominating sonic stimuli are the sounds of generators (outside), which sound like large lawn mowers or air conditioning (inside), also helicopters, and motors (vehicles). That's on a good day. On a bad day, mortars (loud booms) or car bombs (loud bombs). The car bombs are usually farther away, out in the city. Smells; the scents here are blah except when one passes the Porto-sans or the latrines. There is a peculiar smell, which is like a honey substance that they mix with the waste from the latrines, which is sour, and honey (ish) that sneaks up on you when you pass by. Other than that, there are no local scents like indigenous food, which would give the flavor of an exotic land.

Visually; the camouflage uniforms, the green right near the river and then bleak tan of the land, which highlights the austerity of the land. Very little color breaks through. Taste; the food after months of eating the same institutional fare is beginning to lack any appeal. Even the fun food, like popcorn is beginning to grate on my nerves. And texturally; sweat, sweat, sweat or dryness. The air is hot and the wind is hot. And I mean hot, not warm or cool/warm it is hot, like standing behind a jet on a runway except without the fuel smell, which would make it feel different.

Well, in a few days I am going on leave. About that; I am going to spend some quality family time, and get in a few triage trips to compensate for the privations that are here. I must see ocean! So that's on the list. I must see the cats! Another list item. I must avoid crowds, so I may refrain from public appearances like Mass where I know people. I also must see mountains with green foliage. And I am in desperate need of some good home cooking. Ideally, I would love to see everyone, but alas I can't. As Regis says, I am but one man. So, please do not be offended if you do not see me or hear from me while I am home. You may but I won't be able to see everyone I'd like to, but know that I will be home soon here after. The months are passing by quickly despite the Groundhog Day-esque quality of life here. Well I got to get back to work. Bye for now, blessings and joy, R

2 AUG 05 00:04 Goodbye "A Day In the Life"
"What's The Frequency, Kenneth?" by R.E.M.

Was perusing, in a moment in between moments, the net for "a day in the life" mention and saw a plethora of other blogs entitled "a day in the life". Ah, the perils of picking titles. I copped the title from one of my favorite Beatles songs of all time. (Am scared, as 1 am about to fall into a major Beatles mood thanks to my commander who was listening to them this afternoon). In retrospect it seemed as good as a title as any, but it just seems too icky and overdone seeing how many other blogs have the same title.

Ever the contrarian, I am retiring the title and adopting a

new title: Walking In My Shoes. I copped it from the title of a Depeche Mode song, but I like the reference it makes to the cliché/adage about walking in another's shoes. I guess that is what blogs are about. That certainly is what this is about, on a variety of levels.

Now I have to finish the laundry, so I bid you adieu, and then I have to wait till the odd hour of 0100 begins so I can take a shower. For the showers over by my building, males have the showers on the even hours and males on the odd hours, (which always cause Mike and I confusion as we try to ascertain whether ten is an odd or even hour. Look after a long day at work you begin to second guess yourself even with easy things like even and odd numbers).

Speaking of Mike...(has nothing to do with Mike but... Jerry left yesterday for his Rand R. I missed seeing him in the morning so I didn't have a chance to say bye, but I know for sure he has earned a well deserved rest, if for nothing else than keeping up with me and my propensity to vanish at the drop of a hat (I still pride myself in being able to appear to disappear. I call it the poof.) I also credit him for being able to keep track of my thoughts and not look completely frustrated. I can just see as he tries to anticipate what I am going to do next and being flabbergasted at times by my sudden shift. What can I say; unpredictability is ingrained in my genetic makeup. And finally, speaking of genetic makeup, I found a copy of "Big Fish" today. My dad just sent me an e-mail about the very same movie. As the Arabs would say it is kismet. (Kismet means that it was meant to be.) They had it at bazaar run by the locals here. I look forward to watching it if not tomorrow definitely while I am home.

2 AUG 05 20:52 FOB Caldwell
"Good Night" by The Beatles

Today I find myself stranded at FOB Caldwell. The most

noticeable thing here is the ever-present southern accent of Tennesseans all over the place. Wow! They are all y'allin' and yee ha-in' and make Texans look like Northerners with their Hazzard County twang. I said Mass and then have been hanging out for the rest of the day, not getting done what I wanted to get done back at Danger ""'Fo Ah Leave." Basically I was stranded for the day. Tomorrow is another day and I will be liberated from my temporary exile.

I am pretty tired having gone to bed last night around two in the morning. There is a primitive machine for washing clothes in our house, which is astounding. You put the clothes in, turn on the faucet fill up the machine and add detergent. Then it washes. When the cycle is done you drain the machine. Re-fill the machine with water and repeat. Then you take the clothes and you put it into the spin cycle part of the machine which is the unsafe kind of machine that makes it reasonable for someone to have their arm ripped off by a spin-cycle, despite this washer being pretty much all plastic. Then you go outside and hang the laundry out to dry and in ten minutes (if I exaggerate it probably takes less time) the clothes will be dry. Hot wind, remember?

Then I was folding the stuff. All my Army t-shirts are all messed up and look like I have had them twenty years. Unsalvageable. Iraq will have a huge amount of dust rags when I leave.

Well I finally went to sleep only to wake up at 0630 for another glorious day. Which reminds me of how much I'd like to turn in now. Adieu, till tomorrow.

3 AUG 05 14:46 Praise the Lord!
"Little Puffy Clouds" by The ORB

Well, I have been liberated from FOB Caldwell and now am back at FOB Danger. In the midst of packing some things to send home and getting ready to go on leave. The bestest present in the whole world aside from the obvious things like being home was given to me today. CLOUDS! Well, I am not that egotistical to think they were given to me, per se, but I look at as a gift. How cool it was to see to witness the first flotilla of clouds triumphantly returning from where ever it is clouds come from, sliding over the land today in isolated poofs. These clouds would ordinarily make the cut in terms of being noteworthy but after at least two months with out their presence in this land they sure are a sight for sore eyes. Welcome back boys, you sure have been missed!

4 AUG 05 14:35 With reservations

I am now on the journey back to home. It is a long trip and also there is significant uncertainty concerning flight times and arrangements. The beauty of it is: if it confuses soldiers and we are in the system and we don't understand how it works can you just imagine the confusion that it causes our enemies. Unpredictability is something I value and respect and more so now.

As I leave, my heart and mind are filled with elation but also I have the slight reserve. I am afraid for my soldiers. I feel ridiculous at times thinking that if I am there then they will be safe. Although, after my track record the past few weeks I think I better go home and recharge the good mojo. Yesterday, as I innocently was sending a package home, a mortar exploded near the building. (A mortar in case you don't know is a rocket fired usually from some distance away and is filled with explosives and shrapnel (either little ball bearings or metal bits) which pack a wallop and can do the killing job very easy. The explosions, I should be pointed out, are less dramatic looking compared to the movies but its deadliness, which is the concern not the visual. These things do lift up a cloud of dust and smoke and a flash when it explodes, but there are no balls of orange flame erupting up into the sky. Usually it is just followed by a blah dust colored mushroom cloud if it's flashy and hit something. If it just lands in a parking lot it may lift up some dust and punch a hole in the ground. Anyway. Well I should go now. I will be keeping in touch with this while I am home. Thank you to all my readers your support is much appreciated.

5 AUG 05 10:36 Searches
"Cry Me A River" by Justin Timberlake

Not for nothing but there is the familiar whining sound hitting my ears and it is coming from across the wide-open Sargasso Sea. It is the whine of people who are trapped in the mists of nostalgia recalling the good old days prior to 11 September. Might I say, that in the current climate of the world that if you are unwilling to open your bag or have a police officer search it you have serious problems and should not come to New York City? Illegal search and seizure freaks pay no notice that this has been happening at airports for how many years, and how many abuses of this enforcement technique have been made. If anything it is the failure to perform adequate and thorough searches by airport workers that directly caused the tragedies of 11 September. The job performance that day was comparable to the work of weathermen. Which makes me wonder why none of these security personnel were ever forced to testify to Congress on how these terrorists got through and why no one was ever punished for their dereliction of duty.

I understand the real taboo subject is racial profiling, but if anyone thinks law enforcement does not profile people in this country one must put down the has pipe and smell some coffee. It also is not racial profiling to see a trend in terrorism. If you are of the ilk that complained that we should have dealt with Saudi Arabia because most of the bombers were from Saudi Arabia, climb on board the Hypocrisy Express (after we search your bags) because you are guilty of guess what? PROFILING. You want privacy: stay at home. You want to take public transportation check your rigid black and white interpretation of the Constitution at the door, and go back to school (where incidentally you can't enjoy all the Constitutional rights you think you can.) As for the police and law enforcement, all I have is this to say: Do I get irked when I am searched? Yes, but I am also Timothy McVeigh had very similar complexion to me as well as a vaguely similar hairstyle, so I don't take it personal. It's business, not personal. And I am a law abiding American citizen, search my bag if you must, I have nothing to hide. And if you are a law abiding person what is the issue. Those that doth protesth too much...call the NYCLU.

5 AUG 05 19:39 Notes From Above (leaving for home)
"Eight Miles High" by The Byrds

(Written first on paper in a C-130, and later transcribed)

Iraq is thousands of feet below, while we are higher than kites. Somewhere deep down we are, at least, on the surface we are an exhausted, drained lot. The manner by which places us here is an elaborate process of discomfort, vigil, and an oppressive heat that leaves us even in this aircraft still moist with the sweat inflicted by its malevolent glare, culminating with us squeezed in on this massive, rumbling, stubby dinosaur of an aircraft known in military parlance as the C-130.

The best way to describe this demented aerial version of Jonah's big fish's interior is to say it is not dissimilar to a giant capsule shaped school janitor's boiler room. Save for the makeshift seats of red web netting that inflict cruel and deadening pain to one's buttocks, it is like flying in a boiler room. The ceiling is covered by a mess of ducts, tubes, pipes, beams, wires and dusty dehydrated lamps that convey neither warmth nor elegance. There also is a wealth of quilted cloth one usually finds in cargo elevators which slides down to the sidewalls. The walls and beams are remarkable only in as much as they bear a decayed turquoise shade long abandoned by contemporary tastes around the mid to late sixties. (Ironically, this very same shade abounded as "color" in the adversary nations of that era's Cold War conflict.)

And finally the windows, which resemble tuna cans of light that serve no other purpose than to dispel the rumors that we merely are waiting in the loudest boiler room in the Middle East.

So here we are, going, the ordeal of getting there is well underway.

6 AUG 05 04:02 Limbo

Today was spent in Limbo, Kuwaiti style. A joke often repeated by me is that Kuwait is actually pronounced with a silent k. Waiting is the name of the game in the Army but in Kuwait with the Army it is a way of life. Seeing as we were not given the cook's tour of the country I have only my experience to base the following reflection on Kuwait. Am I thrilled that they are an ally? Absolutely. But does this affect my experience? Not in the slightest. So forgive me for my biased entry. I can live with it, so I hope you can, too.

Kuwait is a hell of sorts. A simple cost/benefit analysis of Kuwait (from this observer's eyes) should be ample proof of Saddam Hussein's insanity. His harebrained scheme to invade Kuwait (whilst this writer was taking a summer school Math class at Clarkstown North) in 1990 may have been motivated by a greed for oil, but the negatives are so pronounced that it seems more a sin of folly than of greed.

135 degrees of misery. A searing white heat of oppression

as a brutish uncouth sun strides arrogantly across a sandblasted sky, heating everything and one under its vehement stare. Sweat accumulates in the oddest reservoirs of skin space collecting and clinging, persistently rebelling against the natural laws of evaporation.

The last time I was in Kuwait back in January I had experienced the torturous dullness of Kuwait. Endless miles of unforgiving sand; flatness and the occasional dunes alike. Then it was numbingly frigid. It is a harsh land outweighing the slight coastal vestiges of Kuwaiti civilization. Today is punishingly hot, overcast by sand and dust, which furtively invades the mouth and eyes (blink, don't rub). And yet from above at night there is a distinct Vegas/Chicago feel (whatever that means).

Well that's it for my reflections of Kuwait, straight out of my notebook. A hot taste of limbo. Bye for now.

7 AUG 05 13:31 Welcome Home!
"Home" by Depeche Mode

Newark, New Jersey never looked so good. Touched ground at Liberty International Airport around 1830 hours. Imagine my thrill to be greeted at the gate by Mom, Opa's words ringing through my mind, "There she is! Boy, are you a sight for sore eyes!" After recovering from a hug that nearly sent squeezed all traces of oxygen from my lungs, and exchanging the customary pleasantries appropriate for such an occasion, we walked out to where the rest of the entourage was. A wheel chaired Oma (no nothing serious, just a way to extricate some sympathy from the airport workers) was being chaperoned by the Wappingers Chapter of the Quaids (Anthony and Carol). As I began my greetings, from stage right appeared my father and the Milford Chapter of Repennings (Barbara, Danielle, and J.J.) After we all exchanged greetings and hugs an informal floor vote was taken regarding the motion to adjourn to a more gastronomical venue. The said venue was left unmentioned, but after going to the parking lot and moving out in our two vehicle logistical team, a location was decided by the fault of my very own exhausted sense of direction - the legendary and steeped in Wyatt/Repenning historical lore - Callahan's in Fort Lee. A good old hot dog, and cold beer was my sacred culinary welcome to the NY metropolitan area. Everyone had a good time! For me it was all a rush to the senses and I must admit I was considerably overwhelmed - so much to say - ah but why bother rushing.

8 AUG 05 19:12 Day One
"The Rain Song" by Led Zeppelin

A good night's sleep. In my room. In my own bed. At home. Sighs of relief. I am home, with Mom and Oma and the four blessed cats. In the afternoon, Mom and I head up to Newburg for a nice lunch at Cena 2000, on the river. How marvelous! A thunderstorm blew in, and we enjoyed it all under the canopy.

To hear the rain fall into a deafening whisper against the waters of the river is magical. What an absolute joy to look across the waters and see Beacon in the proximate distance with the magnificently compact set of mountains behind it. The contours of those mountains (albeit small mounts) are pleasing to the eye and keen reminder of the Hudson's sublime grandeur. The sense of peace is intoxicating and transmitted so deftly by this panorama of perfection.

From there we went to the Palisades Center where I did one of my monumental CD trades and procured a tidy sum of store credit to purchase more music.

9 AUG 05 13:55 Ruby Thursday
"Back From The Dead" by House of Pain

Yesterday evening got a call from Anthony inviting Mom and I out for a bite. We met up in Fishkill, at Ruby Thursday, with Anthony, Carol, Nicholas, Shannon and Anthony. It was great to see them and hear all the fun stories. It's weird being up in Dutchess again. Hard to believe I once lived here, and now I feel like a visitor. That will change but right now it still feels strange. It is good to see the Quaids. They are good friends. It has been especially comforting for me that they along with a few other friends have checked up on Mom and made sure things are going all right. With me half a world away it was good knowing that Mom and Oma were not forgotten.

The Quaids had an amazing story, which I learned more about from brother priests, and one that Mom and I had not heard about, at all - about when word was going around some circles in the Archdiocese that I was dead, around April 23rd.

9 AUG 05 18:35 Day Two
"Stranglehold" by Ted Nugent

This morning I drove Mom over to Pleasantville. While Mom was doing her thing, I ventured to a nearby bookstore, which was excellent. I found two books that look fantastic. Picked up a stellar cup of coffee at a coffee shop. I also spoke to Monsignor Bellew and was invited to say Sunday Mass at St. Mary's. I have to say he made my day. My departure from St. Mary's seemed so illicit the way I first said goodbye and then hung around for what seemed to be forever, so this seems a little more normal and legitimate. I also spoke to my guru, Bob. To say anything less than that he is my hero would be sacrilege. A great friend, a great priest and funny as hell. After the call, I say a prayer and hope he'll take up snowboarding. Bob's M.S.

worries me.

We then went to the Cabin Restaurant in White Plains. They have a few place mats from my ordination dinner, which Jodi and Mike put out anytime they see me, which is a hoot and a holler. The placemat was designed by me, Mom and the folks at Postmaster Limited in New City. Speaking of New City I sat in the yard, relishing the peace and serenity of the garden (as we call it). Barefoot, sipping a nice Peroni beer, and enjoying my soil. It's good to be home.

11 AUG 05 20:53 Sophie and a dog-centric pet roll call
"Pets" by Porno For Pyros

Today we got a new addition to the family. My uncle, Mike brought Sophie home. She's a beautiful five months old dachshund entered our family. She's a gift for Oma, who is still mourning the loss of Jordan, a few months back. This may surprise those of you. I hope that it does not cost me street cred, as a cat person, but Sophie is really cute and she is part of a proud line of canines that have graced our family with their spirit and joi de vivre.

As I drifted into consciousness as an infant, my family already had a dachshund named Mundie. Mundie was a longhaired dachshund, whom I loved very much. He was an excellent playmate, and there are many pictures of he and I playing in the yard and walking with Opa. I remember fondly, walking with Opa into the woods and down to the creek many a time with Mundie and later with Prinz. Mundie died on Saint Patrick's Day morning in the late seventies.

Prinz was a German Shepherd. Opa picked him up at Pathmark one day, while dropping Oma off at work. I remember he came into the house saying guess what I got here. There he was holding the small puppy and I answered innocently, "A raccoon." Prinz was also a great playmate. Being a bigger dog, he was a much more challenging playmate and many times he would challenge me to wrestle. Opa, Prinz and I also would go for frequent walks into the woods. Prinz, however, would sometimes run off and this eventually would lead Prinz to his demise. He slipped out the door and Prinz disappeared. After several fruitless hours of searching Prinz was found on Route 304. This was my first real experience with death. The following day, the County Animal Hospital cleaned him up for Mom and me to view. I met with Fr. Des later, being quite torn apart at losing my best friend, at the time. I remember how he said in response to my question if there were dogs in heaven, "If there aren't dogs in heaven, I don't know if I'd want to go there." This priest's humanity struck me then, and this probably was a significant reason for me to chose him as my Confirmation Sponsor, a year or so later.

Sasha joined our household not tool long before Prinz's passing. Sasha was our family's return to the dachshund fold. Brought home on Christmas Eve. I can't recall how many years Sasha was with us, but she really was such a delight. (Fill in dates later - will help me with memories). Around Sasha's reign, Toonces, the gateway cat arrived. The story of Toonces is one worthy of an entry all by herself, so I will come back to her at another time. She was preceded by a cat we found at the Marian Shrine that we dubbed Victor, who stayed in our yard forty eight hours max, but in that time this little cat got the jump start it needed to fight the good fight and strive to live. That's another story for another day, too.

Sasha was a little fireball and a blessing to our family. She passed away rather unexpectedly and shortly afterwards Jordan joined our family. Another dachshund and another delightfully sweet dog. Jordan had some health problems though. At one point she nearly passed away due to a kidney infection. For months, Mom had to give Jordan up to an IV of meds to help her fight the infection and to also help get her kidneys functioning properly again.

The cats' entered into our household at various times. Sportie and his twin Bucky lived outside appeared on our doorstep, as cats seem to do. There being two separate entities was a discovery only to be made after several weeks in our yard. Eventually, it became evident that these cats could not be the same being, made all the more apparent when they began appearing on the doorstep at the same time, for meals.

Smokey came into the yard a bit later, the poor little pitiful thing. But he would grow to rule the roost and bring us so much joy.

Bucky would disappear and never be seen again, after a week living in the pear tree. He would climb up each day and spend the entire day in a limb lying there looking at my window.

Much later, Fee Fee would come over for food. She had what looked like a mink around her neck. She would disappear also, never to be seen again.

Two years ago, Cee Cee appeared on our doorstep and has been living with us ever since. First in the garage and now up in my bedroom.

And the latest addition is Iggy. Iggy and I have not gotten off to a good start, as she is the first cat who has resisted my cat whispering skills.

In all, the gold fish I had don't really count worthy as getting mentioned. But it is weird that one of my two goldfish committed suicide and jumped out of the bowl, while the surviving one in despair ate himself to death. There are two good friends to our family named Hansel and Petey. Hansel was a parakeet but sadly I don't remember him. Too bad, because he used to call Opa and egg head in

German. Petey I remember from the time Mom walked into Nick and Dino's Beauty Salon in Pearl River to tell Oma that she had just bought him. He was a cool bird. Strangely enough, he spent the last years of his life unable to fly.

Well now that I have talked your eyes off. I will bid you adieu.

12 AUG 05 13:48 A Thought
"Lullaby For An Anxious Child" by Sting

I don't want to go back. I am afraid. I fear my fear.

We went to the Nanuet Restaurant for dinner. Pizza and beer, blessedly cold beer. On the way home, through a frightful thunderstorm we watched a transformer explode in a pale green blast three or four times at the corner of Middletown Road and Route 59. Sparks fled the smoky sphere and darkness swallowed all the lights in the vicinity.

14 AUG 05 14:07 Wappingers Falls
"It's A Sunshine Day" by The Brady Bunch

This morning had the 1030 and the 1200 Mass at St. Mary's Church. It was good to be home. To see my parishioners and to celebrate Mass in an actual Church and well just everything was really nice. Monsignor Bellew really made my day (actually the good feeling carried over a few days) in inviting me to say Mass. It also was great seeing all the familiar faces; it was as if I was never really gone. There were quite a few people I missed, but still it was good to be back.

From there a few of us went to the Dutchess Diner for a bit of lunch. This was nice. There was a classic Seinfeld moment regarding whether we actually landed on the moon or not (yeah, Mom was at it again with her conspiracy shenanigans, and now you know where I got it from - "I'm just a patsy." From there, Richard and Anthony joined us to pick up a couch, for the Family Room (two days at home, and I was already working on little projects to make life easier for the maternal unit and the grand maternal unit, as well) in Nanuet, helped me get it to New City and then we went back up to Wappingers where we had a nice dinner at the Quaids and special guest stars Elizabeth and Richard Smith.

15 AUG 05 23:05   Here I am (I'll be back soon)
"Do It Again" by Steely Dan

Hello friends! I am here, laying conspicuously low, despite a high profile appearance on Sunday. All is well. Am overwhelmed by the tremendous sound here at Wilton (Circle not town) of a hard earned and still being earned peace. The crickets are in concert, supported by a sonic backdrop of a soft metallic drone of insects. The simple pleasures of life are being indulged accompanied by a hearty dose of Catholic guilt at not being in ten other places and with everyone. At present the emotional triage requires the earthy freedom of the mundane and solitary. Today the scent of pine dust was thick in my nose as I pruned a few of the evergreens and also surveyed which ones will probably have to go soon or be choked out by the larger ones.

I have undertaken several of these projects as a nice way to occupy my mind and keep the thoughts focused in the now. Am also trying to avoid the questions: especially how is it over there. Oddly enough, and not in any distinct homage to the new TV show "Over There" I have been referring to Iraq as over there since I have been home. It is almost too much for these lips to utter "Iraq".

In a similar vein I find it hard to wrap my mind around the reality that I have friends there right now. I feel ashamed to say that I don't think about it, but then again I do pay close attention to cable news or the radio news as if my vigilance will ensure their protection. I have though learned to block out the talking head pundits for the most part, although the most idiotic statement has trickled into my ears, which I feel compelled to dismiss. It was said this weekend that women were better off in Saddam's regime then now in Iraq. This betrays an uninformed mind. The crimes committed against women by the regime are well documented and have even been commented on before on this blog. Before this silly notion is promulgated, please check out the facts.

Whoops, I was veering off. Rest and recreation is going well. I will fill in the blank days on the return. I am taking copious notes (ish). Have a few funny stories to tell (and as a teaser I will just say, one of the stories revolves around a rumor of my death and the ensuing drama amongst friends and fellow priests and involves two bishops and the Pentagon to find out I was alive and well). Wow! That is a teaser! It is however a story for another day. I'll be back soon enough. Peace be with you all. (And to appreciate it, tune in - stand at the door of your home with the noise turned off, and unless you are an urban dweller (then you need to improvise), check out the silence (or the ordinary ambient noise) give thanks for the lack of explosive sound or the feel of threat and then please say a prayer for those still "over there". It's a security they are missing right now.

Bye for now. R

17 AUG 05 23:18 Kayaking
"The Sounds Of Silence" by Simon and Garfunkle

Today went kayaking on the Delaware River with Dad. A very nice escape into the world of our beautiful wilderness in the Tri-State area (NY, NJ and PA). We left Milford, PA, which is near where the three states meet, and headed south a few miles. It was a warm day, but gorgeously cloudy. As we embarked on the couple hour sojourn a soft whisper of rain surrounded us. Along the way, we saw a large and impressive Bald Eagle, some neat water fowl (whose name eludes me at the moment) and Blue Herons (gawky stork looking birds). One of these Blue Herons played with me for quite a while as I attempted to pass by him in stealth. As a man who loves nature it is always nice to share that with someone who appreciates these things as well. My father has a genuine, almost reverential love for the outdoors that is palpable especially in his appreciative silence. That leads into just a concept that I will reflect on again sometime, silence. The beauty of silence. And also, my deeper love of silence. All for another day, though.

18 AUG 05 21:43   Time Stands Still
"Time Stands Still" by Rush

I am in the process of reading a book entitled, "Ghost Rider: Travels on the Healing Road" by Neil Peart. If you are a biker or a motorcycle aficionado you will most definitely enjoy this book, and although he might argue against this observation I find it a deeply spiritual account as he describes a journey he took as part of healing from the double tragedies of the death of his only daughter and his wife.

Neil is also the drummer and lyricist for the band Rush. One of their songs has been going through my mind the past few days and features guest vocals by Aimee Mann. The song is "Time Stands Still". It's an absolutely beautiful song and it rocks. Thought I'd share this with you as it sort of captures the sentiment I feel being home and preparing to go back.

19 AUG 05 20:36 John and the Smiths
"Friends" by Michael W. Smith

Today saw me go up to Wappingers twice. In the morning, I played a nice round of golf with John. Nine holes up at College Hill in Poughkeepsie. Thanks to Herb Owens I have played there before. Herb also had given me some pointers that now ensure that my drives, at least, are nice. I used Christopher's clubs and they were very good. The drives were good; my short game is little messy. John and I had a great time. Plus what a joy to be home in the Hudson Valley. After a quick bite at the Southside Cafe, I headed home to get Mom.

Then it was back up to Wappingers for dinner with the Smiths. Went to Outback where I indulged in a nice cold glass or two of Budweiser and had the marvelous Alice Springs Chicken, oh yes and should I forget we had the Blooming Onion, too, followed by coffee and deserts at the Smith's house. I can never say enough about the Smiths. This says it all about them: they saved, from April, their 50th Anniversary cake top so that they could share it with me when I was home. Plus they had a picture of it at their party. That gesture says the type of friends they are to me and I hope I am to them.

21 AUG 05 19:25 West Point
"Sunny Side Of The Street" by The Pogues

Another nice memorable Sunday. Thanks to Father Jerry Deponai I was able to say Mass at the Catholic Chapel at West Point. It was a tremendous honor to celebrate Mass with the cadets and the families stationed at West Point. As an added bonus, Paulette and Jim and their son Jeffrey were there as was Danny O'Gallagher and Brian Murphy. After the Mass, we went over to the Hotel Thayer for a nice brunch (thank you to the Maggiacomo's for treating). Mom then did a quick bit of food shopping whilst the CDB troika had a few beers in the Cocktail Lounge discussing old time, present endeavors, and future prospects. In the mix was a bunch of "war" stories, which left me feeling like I dominated the conversation with my vignettes (I get very self conscious about talking so much). In all, what a beautiful afternoon, another Sunday spent with some good friends.

23 AUG 05 14:15 Bye (Part One)

The hardest part of saying bye for a pragmatist is the cold hard heart possibility. Though a victim often to chance, I leave nothing to chance. Bye for me anticipates any number of possibilities and implications even those that are horrific and absurd. Bye is a gaddang horrendous word. When you've said it like you mean it, you know and understand exactly what I mean. You also move up a notch from the innocent naiveté of a fledgling to a hardened soul with a much tougher ethos.

I did it again today...another peril of breaking the ice once, you repeat it too many times. The worst part is the pretense that one has not wrestled with the possibilities. That one is ignorant of the unsaid danger. Usually we wear the mask of denial to protect ourselves or we wear the mask of mercy to preserve the sense of security of our loved ones. I have done both at times and at times concurrently (ah the confession of an ignoble creature).

I once trivialized these things, jokingly saying ridiculous things like, "When it comes to flying, I make my peace with God every time I get on a plane." It was all just good fun until I dealt in matters of true life and death. Now I just feel like an idiot. A lonely idiot. The bye thing is one of the most isolating experiences one can face. It's just you, your life (viewed from the outside in) and your Maker. Oddly, He seems to step out of the way, I guess to make room for our wounded egos and the tidal wave of sentiment and memories that comes to unrest the beach of life.

A shallow hearted farewell is sometimes all we know. We believe it is endowed with some supernatural sense of meaning and candor but usually this is just a put on, until one day it finally just happens. For some it happens in an imaginary world expressed only in regret and remorse. Generally it is something we all face. Part of growing up human (yeech).

So today I ask myself the question (in all its inquiring Germanic concern): Did I do it right this morning?

23 AUG 05 14:16 Bye (Part Two)

On the plane at Newark Airport, seat 1D of a B-737-200. First class, baby! And yet I don't enjoy it that much. Said a tearful bye bye (pronounced bu-bye) to Mom and the Smiths. I sat down in my chair and the tears came down for a minute or two and then the old tough guy came back. "Neutral thoughts kid, nothing personal or memorable, disposable thoughts, plastic and meaningless. C'mon tough it out," said like a real coach. He's a hard man, my interior self. He tolerates little in the area of weakness. He hates dependency. Loathes needing, and he believes that I should be tough as nails, all the time. From time to time, he pops in and kicks out the jams like a high school football coach. This is my detached, pragmatic, self reliant, stubborn, dedicated, driven, resistant core. Without this core I would be completely swept away by emotional, tender self and would be absolutely defenseless.

While I'm at it, the answer to how was leave is thus: "It was a hiccup of rushed normalcy in an anything but peace of my life."

27 AUG 05 22:06   Back in Tikrit
"The Long And Winding Road" by The Beatles

So. Tuesday I leave New York and I arrive back at FOB sweet FOB today. Holy Moley, as Father Pat would say. It was a long and arduous journey and it is great to be back. Not that I wanted to leave home, but now I am mission focused and ready to get this tour done and get home safe.

For security measures, I obviously won't go into details about where I flew from but I did end up in Kuwait and spent three infernal days there. It was there that I lost my ability to sleep and found myself in a real genuine state (ish) of insomnia. Wowzers. The past three days I have "slept" a total of six hours max. And yet, I feel so alert and awake and well now I am starting to wane. It's 1030 at night, but I have been up since 2 this morning.

Kuwait is silly hot, but when we got to Iraq last night I was met by a beautiful and blessedly cool evening. Where we stayed *at FOB Speicher* the stars were visible in all their Middle Eastern glory and it was truly magical to see. Saw the moonrise into the heavens and then this morning watched the dawn erupt and the sun rise. Way cool. We finally convoyed over here this afternoon. The anxiety was heavy and I was not thrilled to have to convoy but it was good to get that out of the way right a way and break the ice, so to speak, again.

It was great to be home. Sadly, I did not get everything I wanted to get done, and I didn't get to see everyone I wanted to see (Bob and Joe especially), but there will be plenty of time for that later when the job is done and I return to NY. I am blessed that I got to spend some quality time with Mom, the cats, Oma, Dad, and some friends. It also was nice to see the folks of Saint Mary's (although I didn't see everyone) and be able to say Mass there.

I also was blessed with a great opportunity to celebrate

Mass at Most Holy Trinity Church at West Point. That was cool. I loved the fact that I could do something for the cadets and left feeling very inspired by their example. (FYI, if you want to check out a cool Mass sometime, a Mass at West Point is really neat (hot in the summer) and it's so cool seeing the cadets at Mass (they also sing in the choir)). Talked to them about learning about oneself through relationship and interaction with God (and I ended up fitting in that most sublime passage of Genesis 1:27 (If you have to ask, look it up). Also, it was nice to feel safe and not have to worry about hearing things blow up or worry about that kind of thing. Ah, how much I took for granted before.

I am beat, as you can imagine so allow me to bid you adieu and wish you all blessings and peace and joy. Bye for now, R

28 AUG 05 20:04 Wild!
"Summertime" by The Sundays

What a nice day. Things started slowly as I indulged in Super Sunday Sleep In. A rare treat indeed for a Chaplain and a priest. Evidently, the best laid plans of mice and men...I don't know the rest of the quote but...I was greeted by one of the chaplains who claimed he was unsure of my plans for Sunday. A minor annoyance, considering the plans had been made (one of the things that gets under my skin) but I have learned that if you roll with the punches, sometimes, unexpected blessings may be just around the corner. So to make a short story long, I slept in and had a lighter day with two Masses. It was a nice pace to come back to work.

The heat is still epic but the temperature is almost at the point of breaking for cooler. (It is amusing to think of how the heat at home was nothing compared to the heat here.) If you recall my comments awhile back on Tikrit. It is worthy to note that the little dim city of the past is yielding to a brighter and more vibrant feeling. I am amazed how the dimness is giving way to a real life filled glow. There also seems to be a large increase in improvements. There is some construction taking place and things are looking much better here (the city) than only a few months ago. I don't remember mentioning it previously, but the Iraqi Police presence on the street is much more professional looking and they seem to have a real growth in pride in their organization. When I first arrived they had a more guerrilla look and a lot of them wore mismatched uniforms and ski masks. There are still some who wear ski masks even in the mid-day heat, in order to conceal their identity and prevent reprisals, but that is a minority of the police now. The police here have suffered many attacks and assassinations and yet there is a continual line of recruits stepping forward. This is a great sign of taking ownership of their country. The cynic would scoff and say that it is because they need the money and there is no other work. But I recall that back home the police don't work for free and they don't seem to complain about their nice.

And then there are the soldiers here. Spirits are high. There is a light at the end of the tunnel. There is still a lot of work to do, but we are a highly motivated Division. Believe it or not, but many of us are already packing gear up and personal things. My schedule for the week already is looking a little busy but there aren't too many weeks left of work here before we come home. The rosy picture though has its shades; our persistent yet anonymous opposition still has a penchant for firing mortar rockets at our FOB, which cause quite a jolt when they explode. This afternoon one such mortar shook me up a bit and interrupted my reading of "Last of the Mohicans" which is a stellar book. Just FYI if you ever feel compelled to see the Michael Mann movie, please do not. I watched it a few weeks ago, and it is pretty good, but it has almost nothing in common with the book. The book is quite awesome and is regarded as the real birth of American Literature predating all the great American writers, there may be an exception to my observation but I still stand my assertion. Hollywood though, did not find Cooper competent enough to write a compelling drama, so they invent a new story, interject new plot points and introduce a romance from whence there was none and rewrite the ending (I peeked). Sad, sad, sad as Mick once sang.

So anyway what is so wild to warrant that as the subject line? This afternoon after Mass, as I was leaving headquarters I looked out at the Tigris for a few minutes and I thought how wild it was to be back. Not a week ago, I was sitting barefoot in the yard back home enjoying a warm (German style) Perroni (splendid Italian beer) enjoying the frigid (90's) balminess of an August in New York and drinking in the quiet and serenity and now here I am in Iraq looking at an ancient river and drinking in the virtual serenity of a Sunday afternoon warmth (110's). Pretty neat. I have to say I am a very lucky man to be able to see this kind of stuff. An unparalleled learning experience plus I also get to work with excellent people. I was also really touched by the outpouring of welcome for me. Everybody keeps telling me that they are glad to see me back and that I was missed. As Mom would say, "tya," which really doesn't have a translation but more of an amorphous utility phrase of agreement. But I am sure she is agreeing with the sentiments of my being missed.

Well. I am sure I have talked your eyes off so I will call it a night. God love you and bye for now. Oh by the way: I did get some real sleep last night, finally. Ah, life is good.

29 AUG 05 21:35 Monday, Monday
"I Don't Like Mondays" by The Boomtown Rats

Monday...and I am back in the ring. Today came charging in like a truckload of cinderblocks, no thanks to my alarm clock. Once in the office, the hits just kept rolling as word trickled out that Chappy was back. Talked with some soldiers and once more marvel at the many pressures and burdens that weigh heavy on their shoulders and yet they persevere. These Guardsmen (and Guardswomen) impress me so much with their devotion and dedication. True heroism, unsung, but present nonetheless. Men and women who struggle and juggle their duties and their lives with so little support out there. I feel sometimes so useless and yet I know that I am doing what I can to at least make their lives easier. Even if it's just listening. Sometimes it's the matter of a kind word (which sadly comes in short supply at times. Yes, even here mean spiritedness can be found by people who should know better).

So another day goes by and a request is made from me to you...Please pray for the soldiers and their families for their safety, and also for their strength. This is the last lap around the track, everyone is feeling it, but we still got a lot more to do, and we all want to finish up on a high note. We definitely can use all the help we can get, and right now that help is best supplied through the power of prayer. Blessings and peace!

30 AUG 05 22:35 Hurricane Katrina

I am sure that like me, you can't really fathom the scenes on television. How terrible. I don't have a clear understanding yet of the extent of the damage, but it is evident that this is a catastrophic tragedy to befall our nation. In light of the disaster, I'd just ask for your prayers for everyone who has suffered loss of property and for those who have died in the hurricane. As a man of action, I'd also encourage all of you reading to research what charities will be reaching out to this devastated region and please consider making a donation. These are the times when Christian charity and genuine concern for our fellow man is so vital and makes so much sense. As Americans we are so often the ones who give to other nations this time it is our own nation in need,

God willing we can attend to the tremendous need with outpourings of love and goodwill.

God bless you. R

9

A LIGHT AT THE END OF THE TUNNEL

2 SEP 05 17:30 Tragic

There really are no words to describe what we are all witnessing on television and in the papers. It is heartbreaking to see the vast swathe of destruction that has ripped apart the lives of those in New Orleans and the affected regions of the Gulf. Sadly, we also witness during this deep tragedy the cruelty and heartlessness of so many people. It makes one angry to see the way people have exploited this tragedy to perpetrate acts of wanton lawlessness.

This should disturb us as Americans and cause us to ponder what can be done. The initial response is to send money and just the other day I advocated something to that effect by asking you to research what charities need assistance at this time. Might I also suggest that everyone who reads this also do something else? We need to ask our elected officials to take heed to this tragedy and explore ways in which we can prevent this lawlessness in the future. We need to be proactive in defending our nation from the enemy within, who will exploit disasters and tragedies for their own personal gain and as an opportunity to exercise their misanthropic tendencies. Provisions need to be in place in our communities to defend the defenseless, to protect our citizens and to protect those in most need, and also mechanisms need to be in place to protect the transportation of much needed supplies.

We should be wise enough to learn many lessons from this

terrible disaster. America is under a microscope now and many eyes are watching our nation and its response to this event. Our enemies are watching us and we should beware that they may take advantage of us, especially in light of the evil our own are perpetrating against our own.

Please make use of your voice and call your Senators and Congressmen/women, Governors, etc. and ask the question, "How can we ensure that this anarchy will not happen in our communities?" This is not a time for us to delay; this is a time for action and on multiple fronts. That is all. Let's remember the poor people of the affected regions in our prayers and in our deeds. May God protect us all.

4 SEP 05 09:51 Lighter

The past day and a half was quite an adventure. Oh nothing exciting, just the mundane insensitivity of people. At first, I was quite angry. Furious. Ah, the Irish blood in me was boiling. But time has a way of cooling tempers. So here I am, very tired, and a bit perplexed at how such a high concentration of incompetent people can so closely affect my mission. Its funny, all I want to do is help people and bring them closer to God and I find my enemy most time is dumbness. Like that marvelous bumper sticker reads, "I see stupid people." So thanks to the senseless I met quite a bit of frustration.

There is however a thought that brings a smile to my lips, "This too must end." One of these days, this will look like quite an adventure. Six Masses in two days. I could probably deliver my homily in my sleep at this point. Holy Moley. And then I had the privilege to say the prayer/thought of the day that began a briefing for the general. Thought y'all might find it interesting:

Consider the great peaks of the world: Mount Everest, K2, Machu Pichu, Mount McKinley, Kilamjaro, and Mount

Cook. These heights have been conquered by many a brave and adventurous spirit. But the mountain climber's accomplishments are often overlooked and not often appreciated. Their resolve, skill and merits are only half praised. They receive accolades and are remembered for the ascent and yet their prize is the climb in its entirety.

To reach the peak is but one part of the journey. The most difficult challenge still lies before them. For they must face the downward challenge, their descent must be met just as vigorously with skill and resolve despite their tired and exhausted state. There is no room for error and careless, there is still a task to complete.

Lord, look upon Task Force Liberty with your loving gaze and invigorate us with your Spirit and continue to fill our hearts with your gifts of patience, perseverance and diligent care as we face the downward climb of our deployment. And remind us that our work still requires all the skill and resolve we have invested in our labor thus far, until our challenges are finally met.

And we make this prayer in your Holy Name.
- Amen

5 SEP 05 20:19 Labor Day
"Working Class Hero" by John Lennon

Happy Labor Day to all of you. There is no holiday for us here, but I am not complaining. Cooler weather is coming in. It's still hot but not oppressive, like before. The wind also has coolness to it, and no longer feels heartless. Busy days are here, and there is much more than my words can say. Today I went to get my laundry and uniforms cleaned at the laundry point, and I am in the midst of boxing things up and consolidating stuff. Anticipation is in the air of our eventual return, which should be in the next few months. Have a great day.

Bye for now. R

7 SEP 05 08:09 Busy busy busy
"Watching The World Go By" by Glen Burtnik

Things are going really well here. Mission is going well.
Busy is the buzzword, more so than usual in my sphere of
influence, but I am really charged and working hard. In the
process, I am also having a lot of fun. There is a disconnect
with what I am writing and the full scope of what I am
doing but that is to be expected. Needless to say, someday I
will have a lot more to say, and be able to tell more of the
story, but as for now I have to avoid certain subjects and
thus the pre-dominance of op-ed pieces. Know that when
that happens I at least want to write something, and
somewhere in there is the experience of an American
soldier looking in at his country from the same lens as the
rest of the world. I understand a lot more why the world
looks at us as weird, at times, especially with our major
export product - "culture". Our cultural ambassadors,
though, really make us seem so plastic.

Enough about that. The weather here has broke. Mornings
now are genuinely cooler and the days are dramatically
cooler. Temperatures still peek into the low 100s but that is
downshifting. A sense of autumn is palatable, and even the
light is beginning to shine a little different. The coming
equinox is evident. This brings a twinge of sadness to me as
I know that in the coming weeks my favorite season will be
visibly crawling down the Hudson Valley in all its splendor
and grandeur. Hopefully, some of you will take pictures, so
I will not miss much.

Well as it is morning, for me. Have a great day. If I can I
will write a little something later.

Bye for now. R

9 SEP 05 08:36 Back to School
"They Can't Take That Away From Me" by Artie Shaw and His Orchestra

It's that time of year again. Back in the parish, this is kind of like New Years, as the calendar kicks off another year. Though quite a distance away, know that my thoughts are with all of you students and all of you teachers. Have a great school year and make a point of making this one as great as possible. Even here, the legacy of my education has been right there in the forefront of my mind. Several books that I have read this year were part of my high school reading list, a few of which I either re-read (Camus' The Stranger) or read for the first time (Last of the Mohicans).

The greatest influence this deployment has been that of my tenth grade Spanish teacher, Geiner Bruno (El Unico) who lauded frequently the great literary tradition of Latin America. Inspired by his words, across the span of 15 or 16 years, I finally started tackling Gabriel Garcia Marquez. He is a true literary gold mine that has opened my heart once again to the power and glory of literature. Also, the magical words of the poet, Pablo Neruda. About now, I am packing up books and quite a few of these two authors books are finding permanent homes in my library when I return home. The point: never take the gifts of learning we are offered for granted. It may take years to sink in, if we are open to it, but untold treasures are just a lesson away.

Blessings and peace. R

11 SEP 05 22:12 Remember. Four years ago...

In a sense, on this day, four years ago, the "War on Terror" began. At times, even I wonder if this is not a very ambitious term but nevertheless, it is what it is. The enemy that lurks in the shadows of Iraq is of the same cowardly ilk that slipped into those airplanes and with no mercy or decency murdered so many innocent people. While our minds may be focused on so many things, and as our nation is focused on so much this day, it would be a grievous error to forget that now as it was then our enemy is terrorism.

We need to remember the hard learned lessons of September 11th. Amid all the political clamoring we need to apply those lessons to our current situations.

The aftermath of Katrina has revealed much to us that is lacking. There are things that need to be fixed seriously. It is important because the world's eyes are on us. The eyes of terrorists are on us. My prayer this day is that we can engage in positive discourse; that we can fight the temptations of shrill arguments and issuing inflammatory rhetoric. We need to come together as a nation as was done four years ago. This is vital. We need to have a united front against the real enemies of our nation. They wish to exploit our vulnerabilities and the greatest vulnerability I see in our nation is ideological. We need to get beyond the politics and look at the problems that we face sensibly.

It would be terrible if we were to forget the significance of September 11th. Our enemies hate America. They make no distinctions between red states and blue states, they hate us without prejudice. It might behoove us to acknowledge that and to adopt a similar view of America too. Let's love America, but without distinction and without prejudice.

14 SEP 05 21:20   My Top Twenty Under-rated Guitarists

"Let's Go Crazy" by Prince and the Revolution

1. Alex Lifeson - Rush
2. Phil Collen - Def Leppard
3. Robert Smith - The Cure
4. Dave Davies - The Kinks

5. Peter Buck - R.E.M. or Peter Frampton
6. Brad Whitford - Aerosmith
7. Prince
8. Neil Finn - Crowded House
9. Jeff Beck or Keith Scott (Bryan Adams)
10. Mick Mars - Mötley Crüe
11. Bruce Springsteen
12. Dominic Miller or Lou Reed
13. Malcolm Young - AC/DC
14. Glenn Frey - The Eagles
15. Mick Taylor - The Rolling Stones
16. Robbie Robertson - The Band
17. Neil Young
18. Nancy Wilson - Heart
19. Johnny Marr - The Smiths
20. Andy Summers - The Police

15 SEP 05 19:34 Escape
"Jailbreak" by AC/DC

Today is one of the days I call prison days. I feel like a prisoner. One of the negative parts of the job is I am never given time alone. I have to steal it. Having now come to terms with my need of solitude to survive long bouts with people, I agonize over my lack of solitude. Being constantly "on" is very difficult for me. Today I managed to steal a few hours and watch "Nixon". I am also now hooked on the new "Battlestar Galactica". Not the seventies show in the least, but a very clever reinvention. Well keep me in your prayers, that I remain sane.

15 SEP 05 23:56 Stranded again.
"Disintegration" by The Cure

Well it is midnight and I found out late in the evening, for no intelligible reason, that I am stranded once again at another FOB. In the past weeks since I returned I have spent several sleepless or very painful sleepless nights at different FOBs, invariably without the creature comforts that can at least allow for a better rest. I have my little pillow and a sleeping bag and now no clean clothes. On top of it all, not an ounce of privacy and I have to explain every time I walk to a door where I am going and usually it means accompaniment. Sartre's maxim about other people has a vague ringing sense of truth right about now.

So much for trying to be a happy camper. Well, this all I can muster right now for an entry. The tone may not be the best, but it adds another dimension, one that I have not spoken of before in these pages, of the all around experience.

Bye for now. R

16 SEP 05 19:03   Blueberry Pie and Ice Cream
"Savoy Truffle" by The Beatles

Better spirits have arrived. Yesterday was yesterday and today I recall fondly one bit of goodness from yesterday. Blueberry pie and ice cream. If I said it was a spiritual experience, having the cookies and cream ice cream and the blue berry pie, I would not be exaggerating. That and a nice cup of black coffee. Hmmm Hmmm. You talkin' about good. Except the coffee was awful. But one out of two ain't bad. When I get home I am going to have to have blueberry pie a la mode. That and the great coffee of America will hit the spot.

Pie a la mode reminds me of the Dutchess Diner and my many futile attempts to satisfy a craving of apple pie a la mode with less than stellar results. One particular time, perhaps instinctively detecting the waiter's incomprehension, I explained in detail how the pie a la mode was to be made. I was tweaked by my friend for being a little obnoxious (by explaining what I wanted), however, I was vindicated, as only a vindictive German could be, when the waiter arrived with the pie a la mode improperly made. I felt the pie and it was cold as a grave marker in February so I sent it back. He returned shortly with the pie still cold to the touch like the carrot nose of a snowman. I acquiesced, and gave up, only to fight this subtle battle in other campaigns at the aforementioned diner. Needless to say, I enjoy the diner much, and even though ordering pie a la mode there has always been a crapshoot, in favor of the house, I know that whatever outcome results I will still have a little entertainment even if I lose the pie.

Well folks, that's it for me. The weekend is about to begin and that means busyness. Peace and blessings, R

16 SEP 05 21:06 Books
"In The Garden" by Van Morrison

One of the things that has been great about my time here in Iraq is that I have been reacquainted with the art of reading. I have always been an avid reader but during this deployment I have made it a priority to read each day. I had a few dry periods while I was here when I couldn't do as much as I would have liked to do and while I was home reading slowed to a snails pace but still it has been great. We have a place where there is a gym and we had a coffee shop and I also say Mass there and there are thousands of books there. I have spent countless hours scouring those bookshelves for good books and things that interest me.

One of my first discoveries here was Small Vices a book by Robert B. Parker. I picked up because I had read a Parker book several years back called Gunman's Rhapsody, which was a retelling of the Wyatt Earp story. I had enjoyed that book tremendously. I was also interested in finally reading a Spenser novel. Spenser was made famous as the lead character in the Robert Urich ABC Television show

"Spenser: For Hire". As a kid this was one of my favorite Saturday evening shows. This book was interesting and enjoyable and so from that point on, I sought out the various books that make up the series. I think I have read all thirty books in the series (though out of order) and one of his other books from the Jess Stone series called Night Passage. Interspersed in there are a variety of other books.

One of my other pleasant discoveries is the great Gabriel Garcia Marquez. He is probably one of the greatest writers in the history of writing. Marquez makes Hemingway look like a crackpot. Mind you I am a huge Hemingway fan but Marquez his books are right there after the Bible in terms of greatness. A few of you have commented on the development and improvement of my writing from when I first began this blog to now (although I have been slacking on spelling and editing for the sake of time and speed) and I can only attribute this to my near constant exposure to good writing. Heck even bad writing can teach you something but good writing pulls you in and challenges you.

Anyway. The point of all this is to say, I highly recommend and suggest that you treat yourself to a good book. Pick something that interests you and enjoy. Also, don't be afraid to challenge your mind with something new and different. The book "Brunelleschi's Dome" by Ross King was a book that really is out of my normal oeuvre and yet I thought why not and found in it a real enjoyable exposition into Renaissance architecture and life. Well, that is all for now. TGIF. Have a great weekend!

Dates indicate dates books were completed:

04 FEB 05 – Small Vices by Robert B. Parker
08 FEB 05 – Sudden Mischief by Robert B. Parker
16 FEB 05 – Walking Shadow by Robert B. Parker
20 FEB 05 – Thin Air by Robert B. Parker
22 FEB 05 – Hush Money by Robert B. Parker
24 FEB 05 – Widow's Walk by Robert B. Parker

01 MAR 05 – Backstory by Robert B. Parker

07 MAR 05 – Metallica: This Monster Lives by Joe Berlinger with Greg Milner

14 MAR 05 – The Switch by Elmore Leonard

17 MAR 05 – God Save the Child by Robert B. Parker

20 MAR 05 – Ceremony by Robert B. Parker

25 MAR 05 – Potshot by Robert B. Parker

28 MAR 05 – Promised Land by Robert B. Parker

29 MAR 05 – Pastime by Robert B. Parker

31 MAR 05 – Double Deuce by Robert B. Parker

04 APR 05 – Hugger Mugger by Robert B. Parker

09 APR 05 – Chance by Robert B. Parker

09 APR 05 – Pale Kings and Princes by Robert B. Parker

15 APR 05 – Stardust by Robert B. Parker

17 APR 05– Crimson Joy by Robert B. Parker

22 APR 05 – I'm Not Scared by Niccolo Ammaniti

27 APR 05 – Now Watch Him Die by Henry Rollins

30 APR 05 – Bono In Conversation by Michka Assayas

03 MAY 05 – Night Passage by Robert B. Parker

11 MAY 05 – Playmates by Robert B. Parker

24 MAY 05 – Taming A Sea Horse by Robert B. Parker

26 MAY 05 – Mortal Stakes by Robert B. Parker

03 JUN 05 – Walk This Way by Aerosmith/Stephen Davis

07 JUN 05 – The Judas Goat by Robert B. Parker

09 JUN 05 – Fahrenheit 451 by Ray Bradbury

11 JUN 05 – Looking For Rachel Wallace by Robert B. Parker

18 JUN 05 – Brunelleschi's Dome by Ross King

21 JUN 05 – Early Autumn by Robert B. Parker

25 JUN 05 – A Savage Place by Robert B. Parker

29 JUN 05 – The Widening Gyre by Robert B. Parker

02 JUL 05 – Valediction by Robert B. Parker

06 JUL 05 – A Catskill Eagle by Robert B. Parker

08 JUL 05 – Bad Business by Robert B. Parker

11 JUL 05 – The Stranger by Albert Camus

14 JUL 05 – Of Love and Other Demons by Gabriel Garcia
Marquez
17 JUL 05 – Dog Eat Dog by Edward Bunker
21 JUL 05 – Lakota Woman by Mary Crow Dog
25 JUL 05 – News of the Kidnapping by Gabriel Garcia
Marquez
28 JUL 05 – Gabriel Garcia Marquez by Sean Dolan

07 AUG 05 – One Hundred Years of Solitude by Gabriel
Garcia Marquez
24 AUG 05 – Ghost Rider by Neil Peart

03 SEP 05 – Last of the Mohicans by James Fennimore
Cooper
09 SEP 05 – Cold Service by Robert B. Parker
14 SEP 05 – 9 Stories by J.D. Salinger

19 SEP 05 19:35 Laundry
"Dirty Laundry" by Don Henley

Confession time. So put on your stoles everyone. Are you
ready? Well, in recent weeks I have not been doing my
laundry...I have been using the laundry service here. Ah, I
feel better having shared that with you, not that you think
that I diligently do my laundry each week. I mention this to
you, again, so you get a hint of the day-to-day life, but also
so I can tell you the following anecdote. I just picked up
laundry on Friday and yet today I have two full bags (there
is a twenty item per bag rule). I don't know how it is
possible to go through laundry like I do, but I do. The
uniforms are tougher. There is a place I go, like from an
episode of M*A*S*H. I go there and they are ready the
next day - washed, dried and ironed. When I hit the fourth
uniform, I know that the other three better get laundered
quickly.

When I go to bring my laundry to the service I usually have
one problem. You have to count out all your clothes at a

table and you tell them how many shirts and socks and underwear and as you give them a number you put the items in the bag. Invariably, I end up with an odd number of socks. Each pair counts as one item, so my laundry ticket seems to always have 19 1/2 or 12 1/2 items. It's pretty funny that the numbers rarely even out and when they do the laundry people look at me incredulously. I must add that the worker's attitudes have been fermented by the constant propaganda machine I call Mike. Yes, the great Warrant Officer delights in humiliating me in front of these innocent bystanders inciting amusement by asking why I never have the right number of socks. Ah, the blessing of being in a war zone with friends.

20 SEP 05 22:03 Sundown
"Sundown," "The Wreck Of The Edmond Fitzgerald," and "If You Could Read My Mind" by Gordon Lightfoot

Watched the sun begin its descent into the western sky, keenly aware of the end of another summer. This was the summer that WAS in so many ways. No rain (here, at least), lots of sun, and heat beyond belief. It also was the summer that wasn't. No family (here at least), friends (the old set), barbeques (here, again), swimming, ocean, etc. The way the weather has been here, I can't imagine an end being in sight to the heat. Granted there has been a slight degradation in temperatures but they still are in the triple digits. Everyone (here) told me that it would cool off in September. Um, not! What do they know? And there it is...What do they know? Think of all the people who have offered advice or stated facts and it is as if they are immune to their own words of wisdom. I am thinking as I write so I might not make sense but allow me to elucidate on this train of thought.

Folks, who I came in with, offer their expertise on the weather here. Now why would I take their prognostications with any more credibility than my own research abilities, after all we both arrived at the same time. However, what I have noted is that we sometimes parrot what others have told us. And we parrot without filtering the information. We take it on face value and we don't look deeper. As I seek to become a more tolerant and discerning person, I take things less and less on face value. Even people we trust sometimes pass on bad information or less informed hearsay. In regards to personal interaction with people, I have also tried to be more discerning, and I am now less likely to believe hearsay. Rumors are a potent enemy. Hearsay, too. Also, it is good to base decisions on knowledge that is reliable and rooted in truth.

Just for the record, I am flinging no stones or arrows at anyone. This is just something curious I thought I'd mention. A lesson learned, you could say.

I used the word tolerant before. I have a funny story about tolerance. Back in the day, when Mom was driving her red Camaro and getting speeding tickets galore, she had a groovy device called an 8-Track. Kids if you thought records are a strange term, 8-Tracks are a primitive forebear to the tape cassette (and back in college, a type of 8-track was still a studio norm at the radio stations). Anyway, one of the 8-tracks in her keeping, stored in the glove compartment (ironically, I have rarely ever seen gloves in a glove compartment (comboxment in my childhood/family's parlance), was an 8-track with a fellow on the label, sitting cross-legged with an acoustic guitar and the shocker for the young eyes of Robert Repenning - HE WAS BAREFOOT!!! YEECH!!! It was a real thing with me, perhaps I have mentioned this before here, but I hated seeing bare feet when I was a kid. So much so was this distaste for all things feet that I would wear socks when I was forced to wear sandals (ach, the only negative to being raised in a German household, it was socially acceptable in German culture for boys to wear sandals, alas also one could wear dark socks, too). Dorky? Yes! But dorky in a so uncool it becomes cool manner (I call this the Coolness

Magellan Theory or CMT).

For this reason I despised the fellow that graced the label of the 8-Track bearing the name - Gordon Lightfoot (Argggghhh! More feet!!!!). Well the last year in the seminary, I reconnected accidentally with some of his work and wouldn't you know it, I had it all wrong...Gordon Lightfoot not only kicks butt - check out "Sundown" or "Wreck of the Edmund Fitzgerald" or "If You Could Read My Mind" and you will agree with me, this guy is amazing. I only really know these three songs but when you've written those, so what, you don't need to have written anything else. Making surface judgments based on personal prejudices can sometimes leave you wanting for more. The lesson is learned, as are the chords to "Sundown" thankfully, Gordon and I share a similar key for delivering the song. Bye for now, R

21 SEP 05 14:34   Recommended Reading
"Silver and Gold" by U2

> *As Gregor Samsa awoke one morning from uneasy dreams he found himself transformed into a gigantic insect. He was lying on his hard, as it were armor-plated, back and when he lifted his head a little he could see dome-like brown belly divided into stiff arched segments on top of which the bed quilt could hardly keep in position and was about to slide off completely. His numerous legs, which were pitifully thin compared to the rest of his bulk, waved helplessly before his eyes.*

This is the opening paragraph to Franz Kafka's most excellent novella, "The Metamorphosis". Sounds interesting? Go to your local bookstore or library; it is a classic. I read this book prior to deployment and enjoyed in tremendously. Not only is it great storytelling but it is a rather quick read.

This reminds me of four other books read between Fort Drum and FOB Danger, all of which were great reads and that I highly recommend:

1. Bob Dylan's "Chronicle: Volume One"
2. Gabriel Garcia Marquez's "Chronicle of a Death Foretold"
3. Greg Critser's "Fatland"
4. Malachy McCourt's "Danny Boy"

25 SEP 05 14:43 Another message for the Division
"Everyday" by Bon Jovi

Had another meeting in which I represented the Division Chaplain and offered a few words for the Command and the General. Well here's the message I had for the boss:

Have you ever had days where nothing seemed to go right? Where things just seemed to go from bad to worse? Have you ever been confounded by inefficiency? Vexed by miscommunication? Seen our plans frustrated by the unexpected? Or been annoyed at how easily things can go wrong?

With this bit of human experience in our thoughts might I suggest that we use this as fodder for our prayers, as we ask God to bless our enemies with these same inconveniences. From our work stations in Theater to our lives back in the States a simple request can be uttered like this:

O' God frustrate the designs of our enemy,
confound their evil deeds,
and may their efforts of ill will bear no success.
Would you join me in prayer?
Lord continue to bless Task Force Liberty, give us strength we need to persevere and overcome all obstacles an may

the work we do bear fruit in this life and in the world to come. – Amen. Rainbow, Sir! Never Forget!

26 SEP 05 19:13   Another Monday
"The Code Of Handsome Lake" by Robbie Robertson

"The days run away like horses over the hills"
    - Charles Bukowski

Here I am in the office. It's evening, and I came back from dinner a little while ago. The I-Pod is on and I am listening to "Close to the Edge" by Yes, one of the great musical discoveries Fr. Ron introduced me to. Today was a significant day. Sent out five packages home. One box is filled with books that I hope to delve into once I have reached stateside. I have a stack next to my bed that I hope will be just the right amount needed. There is still much to do, but joyfully I have a date in sight. The day that I come home is --/--/--. Sorry folks but operational security. I'd love to tell you, but I also enjoy teasing you. As Jesus said, "You will not know the time nor the hour." Anyway, I think you can appreciate my delight in having an end date in sight.

"Other than that Mrs. Lincoln how was the play?" Other than that, things are going well. I am working on the latest update of the slide show presentation in memory of the soldiers who have died in service of Task Force Liberty. It is a little heartbreaking to see how many have died in service of our mission. It is, also, awe inspiring, and it does encourage you to do what you have to do and see that the work these people did be brought to completion. Seeing it through to the end. This may seem like jingoism but it was exactly what I was thinking when one of the waitresses at Mariella's asked me if I had to go back to Iraq, while I was on leave. I looked at her incredulously, and responded, "I still have a job to finish." Where did it all go wrong? When did we stop having pride in our work and caring to see it through to its completion? Seems this attitude is pretty prevalent but it is not realistic or responsible.

In other news, I just finished Crow Dog: Four Generations of Sioux Medicine Men. Neat book. He is the husband of Mary Crow Dog whose story is told in Lakota Woman.

28 SEP 05 20:34   Good stuff
"I Walk Beside You" by Dream Theater

In the midst of the day, I found nice a sliver of time to get some good reading in. Found a marvelous book of essays from a Funeral Director/Poet by the name of Thomas Lynch entitled "Bodies In Motion And At Rest". His views may vary from mine, but his command of the language is brilliant and challenging. It is amazing how certain authors can breath freshness into our English and make it crackle with excitement.

I heard today was the new Depeche Mode single "Precious". This is an absolute hit single. A gem of a song. Beautiful and fresh and unobtrusive. Depeche Mode has hit a home run and re-created themselves into band that is neither self conscious nor bound to the trends of their peers. This is a must have for other eighties bands to learn how to write good music the right way, where it sounds real. Well that's it for the day. Stay gold folks. R

28 SEP 05 14:19   What does the Chaplain really do?
"Show Me How To live" by Audioslave

Oh, hi! This is a little article I was working on. I was asked to write a job description for our 250th Signal Battalion yearbook. No one told me that they only needed a few lines, and so when I turned it in they were a little shocked. Whether it makes the cut or not, allow me to share with you a little reflection of what my job here has been about. I figured that the obvious thinking is that I say Masses here, and much more.

What does the Chaplain really do?

Before I begin to tell you the marvy and exciting things that a Chaplain does, what I say should reflect what my job is about. Others. So, instead of saying I bear with me as I say he. I can only hope that I have lived up to this job description to the best of my ability.

The Chaplain has an interesting role in the Army. His job is pretty intangible, despite the times his feet get mired in the mud of administrative paperwork. For the most part, there is little that he can quantify (it's not like he can say, I rescued three people from despair and sadness today), and less he can show for his work. And yet, he does work – with and for the most important responsibility around – his soldiers. His concern knows no preference between a General to a Private. Every soldier is the most important person in the world, and their concerns are his concerns.

He is a soldier who puts his life in his soldier's hands. He relies on them for his safety and well being and in return he offers the same. He hears it all from the complaints about the section Sergeant (or higher) to concerns about the family. He shares the laughter and the tears. More often than not, he understands the problems. A little less often, only a little, does he understand the solutions. He knows when he needs to be soft spoken and when to give a swift kick. He can joke and play with his soldiers but he also must bear difficult messages. He may nod his head but he always feels the weight of what is said. He prays with and for his soldiers, in word and action.

It's about them, he says. And it is. Despite all the pulling to and fro, despite how busy he may look, his concern is always about them. From an explosion in the night, to word of a Red Cross message, from the convoy that is a bit late to the simple response, "I'm doing to well," he is always concerned. When he is away doing what he does, as a priest, he prays his soldiers are okay, and that they are safe.

His is a job of presence, of being there, of giving a damn, and of letting it show. In his humanity, he prays that the divine is recalled. He hopes that he can be a sign of the Other that cares even more than he. He works for God and he works for Country and they both demand from him his best. They expect this, because entrusted in his spiritual care are souls more precious than diamonds or and earthly treasure. In his care our precious souls, brothers and sisters, soldiers he takes pride in serving and serving with. Blessings and peace.

29 SEP 05 16:13 Clouds
"Careful With That Axe Eugene" by Pink Floyd

That summer seemed to last forever. It wasn't the summer of '69, it was the summer of '90, and there I was caught in the limbo between 11th and 12th grade that educators call SUMMER SCHOOL. (Note to the wise High School students - don't get stuck having to do summer school, it isn't pretty.) It was one of the few years I recall not being at Camp Don Bosco and all due to a freak outbreak diagnosed later as an early stage of Senioritis which hampered my ability to do the right thing and do my school work and paralyzed me into the form of an uncool dork. Luckily, I only bore that mantle of dorkiness three hours a day.

As far as I can remember that summer I had to tackle Math at Clarkstown North and Spanish via the mail. And in between these academic pursuits, I searched for a job and rode many miles on the bike, just for the heck of it. The job search consisted of a fruitless three days at the hellish Dellwood Country Club in New York hearing a constant refrain of the Lord's name pronounced with anger by poor skilled golfers who sliced and hacked themselves into a self esteem bursting stupor. The only consolation was that they were members and they had the perfect foil - the seventeen year old kid hired to be their lackey who had no skill at finding their golf balls in the wooded borders of the club. Even when the Caddy Master invoked the benevolence of my uncle to train me the arcane arts of being a caddy, I was lost to the point of serving a bunch of spoiled rotten, irreverent, snobs who had to live with the reality that all the money in the world could not give them a skill in golf. Ironically, my driving skills now - playing every now or never - far exceeds any of them. A little tired from to 18 hole loops, I recall being liberated from their presence, walking home, and stopping at the United Artist Theater asking if they had a job. Dawn said they didn't have a job but after seeing my disappointment added that I could come Saturday evening and they would see what they could do.

The point of this was not that, it was the bike rides that I took through out New City. I don't recall a day of rain that summer as each day I put on my Walkman and went for an extensive ride. I did several rides to Germonds Pool in Bardonia, taking all back roads, mind you. I did a whole circuit of northern New City, too, quite a few afternoons spent at the Dutch Gardens enjoying Orangina and just enjoying nature around me. Religiously listening to a collection of older (fronted then by Syd Barrett) Pink Floyd tunes, the most recent of which was "Set Controls for the Heart of the Sun". Pink Floyd, weeping willow trees, impossibly green lawns, a very bad habit of crashing the bike into the ground (all accidentally, usually getting my foot caught in the wheel) and hurting my knees, and a thousand different poem ideas all under a beautiful blue sky with towering white clouds floating across it all come to mind today, looking up at this sky. That summer was a blur. But it was the birth year of my writing, the year I became determined to put the pen to the paper, with true sincerity.

Clouds then and praise the Lord clouds now. I am happy seeing the seasons are gradually changing here, the heat is tempering, the breeze slightly cooler, the clouds have returned (saw a splattering of them yesterday, and quite a few majestic panoramas as the sun broke through this morning). The times are changing. But some things never do. I still love those clouds and I still have a soft spot in my heart for the place of my youth, my home sweet home. The countdown is on!

30 SEP 05 15:59 Gratitude
"Thank U" by Alanis Morissette

It has been a long time and coming for some more words of thanks and gratitude. The supporters are many. There is a whole host of folks who have been major supporters doing what I consider very valuable work: praying for me and my soldiers. Others have spiritually adopted soldiers and many of you have prayed incessantly for peace in the world.

Sister Francis Jerome sent me a really neat, handwritten letter. She's "ninety-two years old - retired and suffering - from progressive arthritis. I offer my suffering for all your brave sisters and brothers. My rosaries and chaplets of Divine Mercy are prayed every day, for your safety." I know that for every declared sentiment like this, there are many unknown pray-ers out there covering similar spiritual ground, and for all of your prayers I am indebted.

There are also many people who have put together packages and sent them. It is humbling to open these packages and see the love, care and thoughtful concern that you have for my soldiers.

It seems appropriate that you catch a glimpse of how it is I could become so careless in saying thanks for so long a time. I have a "the left hand shouldn't know what the right hand is doing" ethic at distributing the bountiful booty sent my way. As soon as Jerry's "knife" (more like a machete) has broken through the bounds of tape (and the packages do look like mummified parcels often enough) I scan for a few items of absolute necessity (razors (for sensitive skin), shaving cream) - and then whatever I genuinely can use. Recall Catholic guilt keeps me from just being a pack rat and not sharing. When I have done the quick scavenge of the loot, I bring the box to the end of my hall (which is a corridor of pressed wood walls in a small building) and I put the stuff down. It is a help yourself arrangement for the most part. Sometimes the items are presented to people if I know there is a particular need. Everyday you see soldiers going through these boxes and finding all sorts of treasures. In the process, you save them a bunch of money (razors can be like $3.75 for a small bag, and not sensitive skin razors either (ouch)). You also have provided items that we couldn't find on the outside.

Our Post Exchange is just about to close, and thanks to your generosity we will have some things to get us through. That's great stuff.

So thank yous and shout outs time now. To the folks at Telefax (a religious goods store) in Hopewell Junction, and particularly Deacon Stan, Annette, Lorraine, and Joann - many thanks for your several awesome boxes of goodies, toiletries, sports pages, and letters from the school kids. Your giving spirit is a great testimony.

Brian and Laura Murphy for their box of individual care items (including a pair of clean socks (new) in each gift bag). We have an air terminal locally and these were given for the soldiers who come through there and usually are delayed a day or two and most of the time they did not plan for an overnight. So, needless to say, something so little is very appreciated.

David and Molly Dziena sent a few boxes of knickknacks, snacks and goodies that found there way to the end of my hall after I raided the box for the cd's (great spiritual listening stuff). (No Dave, it didn't seem like a garage sale!)

The next one is a biggie! St. Mary's Girl Scouts and Brownies sent a huge box of kids' clothing. Thank you to all of them and to their liaison officer Kim Vidulich. These clothes are going to the school our unit sponsored. (I can't get into more detail, out of concern for their security - the bad guys hate this kind of thing, a lot). In addition to the beautiful clothes from the Girl Scouts and Brownies, we have been sent a lot of office supplies and pens and notebooks and paper and whatever our soldiers couldn't use we also sent to the school.

I couldn't forget to mention my gratitude to the maternal unit, Ma Repenning for her great attempts at bringing a taste of home to me here in Tikrit. The cat items were a huge hit, the posters, door stop, magnets (yes I even had an "I LOVE MY CAT" sticker on my Humvee when I'd go on convoy (I added an s though, and the love was a heart graphic), postcards, and the inspirational cards brought many people a lot of joy and disarmed them if the day was hanging over them like a metaphorical dark cloud. And the food, popcorn, cleaning supplies, and Sunday New York Times' made this a bit less painful.

Our Family Readiness Group in Westfield, New Jersey did a pretty good job with sending goodie boxes to all the soldiers in our Battalion. Many thanks to all of who made it possible, several times during the year, especially SGT Nevarez.

Finally, for this entry, many thanks to the Marine Corps League, Tristate Gung-Ho Detachment #909 and the Knights of Columbus, Council 12571 both of whom are from Lords Valley, PA. Through Peter Gangarossa, their liaison, I have received easily ten boxes during the year, filled with all sorts of coolness.

One more thank you: to George and Jean Quaid for the great little prayer book I received the other day from them. Many thanks, and alas how perfect - it is pocket sized!

Well, this is it for the entry cause I am getting tired. Let me say this about that before I go. Gratitude is a funny thing, and one of the greatest lessons of this deployment. Be grateful, always! There is always cause to, no matter how bad things seem. Watch sunsets and sunrises and look up at the clouds from time to time. Yesterday I noted the clouds and today I am happy to say that after a bit of red/gold lightning in the distance last night, rain finally fell here. The smell of rain this morning from the night was more a stench that infected the cooler air. It was two notches less pungent than a rusty dumpster behind a super market which Jerry described vividly this afternoon, how those garbage containers also always seemed to have a "primordial ooze coming from it as well. Yeah, the fragrance of sewage, clay, and wet dust wafted about but it grabbed one's attention and reminded me "Hey, notice that it did rain last night after months of your complaining about no rain." All I could say was, "Yeah I hear you. Many thanks God. This is a welcome sign, to say the least."

What a sign it is indeed. A brand new day is coming, and I can't wait.

Blessings and peace, happiness and health to all of you. R

10

WRAPPING UP OPERATIONS

1 OCT 05 12:33 Right Here, Right Now
"Right Now" by Van Halen

Right now, where ever you are is exactly where God needs you.

This is the basic premise of my homily this week. How often do we place ourselves in the fantasy of world of elsewhere and forget that where we are and what we are doing right now has purpose? Let's not look to be anywhere but in the present. Present in the present. In this way, we can stay focused the past is gone, never to return. And the future is just beyond our grasp. And we can't reach for that beyond unless we are fixed to a point - the present.

This has been a major survival tool for me here, a bit of something I heard on the desert wind.

2 OCT 05 13:04 Expectation
"Bittersweet Symphony" by The Verve

Good morning, afternoon, or evening; where ever you are. Another Sunday bustle here In scenic Tikrit. Since the rainfall the other night, it is becoming more evident that summer is leaving. There is still sweating, and heat but something else is in the air. A refreshing coolness is loitering more and more in these parts. That is good.

This morning, I heard an interesting 'rumor' in which a date I would be home, home as back in New City was given to me. Obviously, I like any other soldier jumped at the definitive sound of this date, and yet I am not at liberty to discuss it or hint at it or to allude to it in any depth. Operational security is one issue and healthy pessimism is the other. One of my maxims has been for a long time, "Expect the worst, and be pleasantly surprised." Monsignor Bellew once commented when I said this, that this particular philosophical outlook seems a little Irish. Well there is a bit of the Irish in my blood, albeit Orange (not that there's anything wrong with it, in my book). So, there is a nice expectation in there somewhere that the date could be the date and praise the Lord a little substance can go along way.

As I gear up for the homeward push, the farewells have increased. My footprint of ministerial responsibilities is rapidly shrinking. A bittersweet presence appeared yesterday at one location in the form of a priest - my replacement at one of my assignments. It is bitter knowing that my time is winding down, and yet definitely sweet as well to know that I will be returning home in the near future. In anticipation of this blessed occasion I am already looking ahead to the future of this blog and considering when I will be shutting this down.

Yes, the truth be told that once I have returned home, I will be shutting the lights out on this location. It has served well but I don't think I will be maintaining it beyond the New Year. Until then there are more stories to tell and blanks to fill in. Who knows I may end up changing my mind, but I will definitely be kicking something else off.

2 OCT 05 12:41 Sunday
"Waitin' On A Sunny Day" by Bruce Springsteen and The E-Street Band

Nice day spent with my soldiers over at FOB Speicher. Presented briefs on Suicide Prevention and also on Reintegration. Did some odds and ends business and hung out with one of my buddies Dave King, who previously worked with us over at Danger. Friday night we did the daylight savings thing, so now it is only seven hours difference. The U.S. will be doing it soon enough and then we will be back on an eight hour difference, again. But it really won't matter much for me because the time difference will soon be reconciled the good old fashioned way, going home.

03 OCT 05 12:58 Kirkuk
"Stranger In A Strange Land" by Iron Maiden

My travels find me in the scenic city of Kirkuk. Oh, to do some sight seeing. That would hit the spot.

Unfortunately, this war is not a war friendly to those who enjoy cultural immersion. I am the kind of traveler that enjoys letting go a bit and seeing if I could blend at all. In Germany and Italy this somewhat easy to do. Granted my command for the languages cannot compare with a very slow-witted domestic animal - but I can eek out what's being said (very -ishy) and I know how to keep my mouth closed. It should be noted that I did pass German in the seventh grade and I did hear it growing up, and I can say very well, "Ich weis nich!" or "I don't know!" This is a great phrase to know in any language. My cultural immersion idea sometimes violates the prime directive of the Starfleet and I end up getting the indigenous personnel perturbed because they wish I would just speak English. I believe, though, it is uncouth to make people in other countries obliged to speak my language.

It may seem strange to take such glee in such a silly thing, but it is cool to be mistaken for someone from another place. In Berlin, I was mistaken, in a shop, for a German and after indicating that I was not German, the same person then mistook me for a Russian. That was pretty cool. I don't have to worry about that in Iraq, however, even if we were able to mingle with the citizenry of the nation, no one would mistaken me for an Arab or a Kurd.

Someone said that in twenty years, we would probably be tourists here in Iraq. Who knows, but it sure would be neat to come back and see the land as a tourist. I have too many questions.

4 OCT 05 13:51 Reactionary
"Rhythm of the Night" by DeBarge

It has been a year and two days since I began this endeavor with the "Sound of Might." The Grateful Dead could write songs about the trip it's been (long and strange, indeed). The evolution of this medium has also been long and strange. We have traversed a lot of territory. As I consider what to write each day a wrestling match takes place. I wrestle with what I can say (without jeopardizing OPSEC), what has been happening (again, OPSEC and also what I would feel comfortable having all of you know - i.e. It is not Club Med or Tigris here), what funny things should I mention (some of the stories would amaze you - human nature, and the ridiculousness of human behavior, also some people would be shocked and think I am being mean spirited), what is happening in the world, what are personal views, what am I preaching about, etc. There is a great amount of material to present, but much editorializing also. I am glad, I have managed to curb my human impulses and air too much negativity.

As a priest, this has been an eye opening experience to how human beings treat each other and the viciousness that can occur in the work environment. I am probably more amazed at the viciousness with which people can attack each other, which makes the terrorists look like small potatoes. I clarify by saying "as a priest" because most people think that we are oblivious to what regular people go through each day. Consider me attuned to what is considered normal by most of you. I can almost hear some of you say, "Thank God, you understand." Yes, I understand. The office politic is more savage than I could ever have imagined. Also, striking is the lack of inhibition people have even in the presence of a priest. Some people don't care, and they will say it, and they will act that way, also. What a shame. Anyway, what has become an enduring quality of this deployment experience is the sense I have of reacting to events, personalities and this experience. This reaction has been one that is analyzed each day and then expressed in words and ideas. Whether we have touched on personal, artistic, theological, philosophical, historical or political realms this has been a fairly reactive environment. More so than I imagined that it would be. Well I probably have said more than I thought I would but that's just what's on my mind.

5 OCT 05 14:25 What's New

Well, now that the news is reporting it and now that it is being publicized I can freely say that the U.S. forces will be turning this complex over to the Iraqis when we leave. This has been a major part of my experience here the past few months. I read an article today in USA Today that described accurately what we at FOB Danger have been witnessing, and you can see also how frustrating it can be not being able to say anything about it. It also flies in the face of what detractors claim to be a prolonged occupation.

While people have been calling for a time table for withdrawing U.S. forces this clearly demonstrates that such an exit plan exists and has been being implemented. I am glad that this President has decided to put soldier's safety above his own popularity and kept this quiet for quite awhile.

6 OCT 05 22:12 Humbled
"Welcome To Wherever You Are" by Bon Jovi

This is an exercise in humility and confidence. Most of the time, to get it done, and to not be discouraged I come out roaring like a lion (or at least it feels that way from my point of view). The confidence is comparable to the confidence one needs as a soldier - the attitude that gets you through. And yet, if that confidence is not matched up to some genuine humility, what you get is a pretty ugly sight. Again, this is just my point of view.

As I grow older, I see humility as a must have ingredient in living a successful life. I am constantly telling myself to stay grounded and remain true to who I am, to not forget from where I have come, and that I have no right to gloat about anything.

When all is said and done I am a simple man. The reminders are many. For instance, I am listening to the new Bon Jovi album "Have A Nice Day" and nice song called "Welcome to Wherever You Are" just was playing and I heard the homily I just preached (my nutshell description from Sunday - ISH) being sung. Pretty cool, pretty funny, considering I just got the album, and heard the song today for the first time. Perhaps God's sense of humor is greater than we think (not for nothing, but we sure take ourselves so seriously when we relate to Him (kind of like how upset my uncle used to get watching Mystery Science 3000 "with those little jerks making fun of some really good movies")). Here I think I had a great idea for a homily when I could have written a song and made a bundle of cash. (lol) Or not.

> *Welcome to wherever you are*
> *This is your life; you made it this far*
> *Welcome, you got to believe*
> *That right here, right now*
> *you're exactly where you're supposed to be*
> *Welcome to wherever you are.*
>   - Bon Jovi

7 OCT 05 09:40 Special Guest Blogger - My Mom

I think I have found a new talent for the blogging community, here she is making her debut: (DRUM ROLL PLEASE) Mom:

I just got back from the book signing...got the dishes going, kitties settled, table set and now I'm writing to fill you in on the book signing.

IT WAS GREAT! HE WAS GREAT. He's younger than I expected (72) and even looks younger than that! He came in, on time, and as soon as the applause died down, he started in a conversational style, telling us that he's going to try to speak without the microphone and he was off and going, telling us about himself, his wife Joan and marriage of 49 years, the writing process and a lot about Hollywood projects, both past and in the works with I think, his company, CCA and that he's got 5 more books done that are coming out and by the time the next one comes out, he'll have another done. This week (I think) he said that he's #3 on the New York Times Bestseller List.

His anecdotal style was full of humor and was quite dry and wry. Then he opened up the floor for questions, and of course, there were some that I didn't get because I hadn't read his stuff yet, but you would appreciate. I was the last person that he called on, I simply mentioned to him a little about my son, the Chaplain Army priest in Iraq and what his books meant to you this deployment. You could tell that this was the most unique situation that he had ever heard of in a fan. He then said, "That's interesting! Good luck to you both!"

When I went up for the actual signing, I had the new book opened and as he was signing it, he says to me, "When's Fr, coming home?" I answered that it would be within the month and he answered, "Good, very good." I took out the letter (in a sealed enveloped addressed to him from you) and told him that you had written him a letter, could I leave it with him? He pulled it close to him and then I asked if he could possibly sign your other two books. He said 'absolutely" and then asked the title of the thinner book. He reads the title Mortal States and then jokingly said, "I never saw that one!" I think that he meant the cover proper.

When I arrived, at 6 on the dot and got parking directly in front of the store, I went in and the young man that you spoke to recognized me immediately and showed me where the books were. I got yours. (I sat in the second row, the signing was downstairs in the children's' room, and when it was time for the signing, the young man that you spoke to announced that we would be going up row by row. He asked me how you wanted to be addressed by Robert Parker when he autographed your book. Then he wrote Father Robert on a sticky note opposite where Parker signed your book. Parker signed your book "Father Robert, All Best and Take Care" His signature is an RB circled.

Parker lives in Cambridge, MA. When he talked, he walked back and forth; He gives his wife credit for a lot. She has a lot of input in his writing, example how/where Susan puts her makeup on. He says that he doesn't know anyone like Hawk, that he made him up. He says that he doesn't know where a book will go when he's writing it; it just goes chapter to chapter. He has a PH D from Boston U. AND THEY WILL BE REMAKING THE SPENSER TV SERIES.

AND, HIS LIMO WITH THE DRIVER WAITING WAS PARKED DIRECTLY IN FRONT OF YOURS!

I'm glad I could go for you. Thanks for asking me to go. I really enjoyed it.

8 OCT 05   17:31   A few more new chaplains & sermonizing
"Is There Anybody Out There?" by Pink Floyd

Today found me saying another last Mass at one of the FOBs. I also met a few more new chaplains who will be taking over once we head out of here. One of the ones I met today was actually one of my instructors back at Chaplain School. So this weekend's message from the homiletic point of view is courtesy of Def Leppard...no really, that was just a joke...here I'll start a new paragraph for the nutshell sermon.

The past few weeks, the lexio continua (ish) have been from Matthew's Gospel. Each Sunday's Gospel has been picking up where the last one left off. Lexio continua is just fancy talk for a continuous reading. Now recall there has been a subtle progression happening.

04 SEP 05 - Matthew 18:15-20 - If your brother sins
         against you.
11 SEP 05 - Matthew 18:21-35 - How many times must I
         forgive my brother?
18 SEP 05 - Matthew 20:1-16a - Parable of Vineyard
         generous owner hiring all day
25 SEP 05 - Matthew 21: 28-32 - Vineyard
02 OCT 05- Matthew 21: 33-43 - Parable of the Vineyard
         and the Tenants
This Sunday Matthew 22:1-14 - Wedding Feast Parable"

The progression has been moving from one's relationship with others to one's relationship with God. It is a brilliant progression and really makes us now step back and look at the big picture our Lord has been painting for us. What we are seeing is that these two relational aspects of our lives are tied together: others and God. We find other examples of this sprinkled throughout our faith life. You cannot separate the two: others and God. In the "Our Father" this is relationship is pronounced on our lips; quite dangerously as we invoke the Lord to forgive our sins as we forgive the sins of others. Man, how many times do we utter those words and have not a single clue what it is we are asking? Ergo, my assessment of this prayer - it is very dangerous.

The skinny is this: How we deal with others is a reflection of how we deal with God. We cannot be all nice nice with God and be bastions of misery to our neighbor (anyone you encounter or know). There is no "Hell is other people" in relation to God. Actually, the converse is true. In a sense, the mystery of the Trinity illustrates this in some way, "God is other people". This is jingoistic sounding, but that is the implication of Christ's words and deeds, "What you do to the least of my brothers, that you do unto me." How we treat others is a direct expression of love and respect for God.

Now before you all say, "It can not be done." Recall that "can't" is the foulest of all four letter words. "Can't" is also profoundly an un-American concept. This nation was founded on the principles that things can get done. There is a vein in the national consciousness, slowly being ignored, of the great possibility and potential that we have. This is especially evident in our own brother and sister Americans who have found themselves in the dregs of poverty. When you lose the tangible, the intangibles of hope and dreams aren't too far behind. Generalizations? Perhaps. But I have great faith in hopes and dreams and their pursuit. I believe that things can be done. As Yoda said, "Try not, do." We need to be men and women of faith, and we need hopes and dreams in our faith life.

It can be done. In fact, the beauty of it is we don't have to invent an it (for it can be done) we need only say, "Thy Will Be Done". And say it we do, more than we consciously can recall, but now we need to internalize it and believe what we say. Thy will be done.

Let's never be afraid. And let us never be afraid to do. And let's always do for others. This is tough stuff, but tough stuff strengthens us. We become spiritual athletes, we become fitter, we become better, we defy limitations and thus we become freer. In doing so we achieve our destiny - to be built to last - made in the image and likeness of our God. We will never recognize that treasure of our own life, if we can't see it around us. God is there. God is here. Emmanuel - God is with us. Blessings and Peace!

9 OCT 05 21:47 Nutshell
"Dirty Work" by Steely Dan

Slept in, went to lunch (yuck), Mass (great!), office work (yuck!) Dinner (more yuck - weight watchers got nothing on the Army mess), more office work (not as bad), typing in the entry, send an e-mail home, head back to my room, do a little reading 1/3 of the way through "The Catcher in the Rye". Hope this finds everyone doing well.

10 OCT 05 23:06 Columbus Day
"The Man Who Sold the World" by David Bowie

Happy Columbus Day! I am an avid admirer of Native Americans and a firm believer that the treatment they received from our Nation and the preceding visitors and explorers has been far from humane, but I also do not see the practicality of demonizing Christopher Columbus. I will be the first to admit that the history taught to me was devoid of the moral absolutism of today's history. Folks my age are just on the cusp of the new history, so we didn't learn about the tuberculosis blankets or what not.

I think the explorers suffered from an overzealous ego, but aren't they just safe targets? What about the overzealous egos of this era that are shrouded in respectability, now? All those folks who work on Wall Street, who knows in two hundred years they might make you the equivalent of Joseph Stalin for participating in an evil enterprise.

Legitimacy is a shady piece of ground. In one instant, you might be a hero and the next you might be Satan. Anyway, Columbus' achievement was stellar regardless of the details...he traversed a sea and went where few Europeans had (save for a couple thousand (pulling it out of a hat, but who cares) Norseman and a few other folks. Columbus was hardly perfect, and he may have been a horrible person, but still if that meant everything we wouldn't have Ty Cobb in the Baseball Hall of Fame.

In today's world we try to sanitize history and it can't be, and there is little black and white and much gray. Today's mentality would have scratched Judas from the Twelve and shuffled his deeds under the rug. They might consider him "misunderstood" or telescoped his deeds to being a mass murderer. Who knows? Most of the folks we demonize are really just like us, and probably we in their position might have faired no better or been any more humane. Again who knows, but let's be honest...if we were all so darn perfect we wouldn't be hanging around here, now would we? Hmmm. I feel like Holden Caulfield is rubbing off on me. Just kidding. Although, what a character.

By the way, his creator, J.D. Salinger has a very funny line that I was reading today and "it killed me" because it is a critique of some military types that only someone who was in the military could make and only someone in the military could completely appreciate. It made me laugh, and it did remind me of a few people that my work brings me in contact with. It goes like this, "He (D.B., Holden's brother) once told Allie (Holden's other brother) that if he'd had to shoot anybody, he wouldn't've known which direction to shoot in. He said the Army was practically as full of bastards as the Nazi's were." I am still giggling from that line. Spoken like someone who served.

What is cool, and few people really know this, is that Salinger actually did serve in the Army, during D-Day at that. He was there, Hemingway was there but not as a soldier, Fr. Charlie Szivos' dad (a shout out to the new vocation director for NY) and Sam Fuller. Fuller was the director of "The Big Red One" which I just saw in its reconstructed form. Fuller is the director that not only depicted D-Day on film but also actually was there. I still am loath to say anything good about "Saving Private Ryan" save for the invasion sequence, and yet the clichés just astounded me. Seems a lot of genres of film need to learn a new vocabulary of imagery. We really need an influx of some originality. Unfortunately the only originality Hollywood appreciates is injecting more sin, debauchery, or vulgarity into movies or music or what not, instead of being truly artistic.

It's pretty wild; Salinger really blew me away back when I was fourteen. Then I thought he was a vulgar pig. By senior year, he seemed a bit less so, and now compared with an hour of network television he'd be seen as downright tame. Well, I guess all this rambling means one thing...perhaps I should hit the bed. You might be amused to know that I awoke this morning at 4:45 completely rested and unable to fall back asleep, and I have been up ever since. Peace and blessings!

11 OCT 05 13:54 Tuesday Afternoon
"Show Me The Way" by Peter Frampton

Tomorrow is our final Prayer Breakfast. These have been excellent opportunities to share with our soldiers in fellowship and prayer. It is awesome when you have men and women of such diverse religious backgrounds able to come together and share some spiritual time together. It is also an amazing thing that we go to great lengths to include everyone in a genuine manner. Usually, at inter-religious events in the civilian world, ministers seem to feel it necessary to show off their individuality and uniqueness as opposed to trying to establish commonalities. What happens then is more of an ecclesiastical fashion show/performance rather than a coming together of hearts and minds in prayer.

One of the great leaveners here is that we all dress alike, Desert Camouflage Uniform (DCU), so right away all the silly accoutrements that might spark comments or create impressions is out of the way. We also are focused on bringing the participants into some kind of prayerful union. This focus weeds out some of the alienating elements such as gender language experiments (like praying Our Mother or Parent instead of Our Father). We just jump right into the mix and hit the things that really matter. As I mention the Our Father, I should note that we have to constantly be conscious of how much explicitly Christian focus our prayer breakfasts take, seeing as all the Chaplains here at FOB Danger are Christians. We do pretty well, though, while not denying our own faith backgrounds. Here is the delicacy of Chaplaincy, but where some may see this as watering down one's faith, I see it as an extension of my own faith. To be able to show respect and kindness to another of a different faith, I see as a Christ-like quality.

Too many people try to shove their own views down the throats of others and it seems so agenda based. The God I believe in is not expecting me to be converting souls by force or prostelyzation and keeping a running tally of my successes. I think God, though, is very conscious of how I treat other people. We got a cat here that insists on talking religion and about conversion and yet he doesn't value letting it flow through his actions. That's what it is about for me. I can talk theology till I am blue in the face but unless you see it in me, unless you see me walking the walk, I am just a gong (that's the basic concept of Paul saying you have got to do all you do with love). Love means relating to others. I might add to Paul and say love is not a parrot. Well, now I must get back to work. I am working on the memorial slide show for this Prayer Breakfast and I am almost done. Just a few more final touches and it will be ready to show. Blessings and peace!

This morning, the 42nd Infantry Division had its final Prayer Breakfast of Operation Iraqi Freedom III. It was a nice way to bring to a close one of our big events as a team (the several UMTs (Unit Ministry Teams - consisting of six Chaplains and their Chaplain Assistants) on the FOB. General Taludo, our Commanding General once again offered some inspiring insights that put into context what exactly we have done here in Iraq. He spoke of the sincere compliments General Casey proffered to him regarding our "great" work we have accomplished in Task Force Liberty. He made a statement that ordinarily would have me annoyed, about the soldiers of the military being the best that our country has to offer. (Usually I would be annoyed because I am not a fan of speeches and what can sound like empty platitudes. On further reflection, I couldn't help but agree with him, though.

Our soldiers really are the best; they are proficient in so many wide and varied areas. They strive to achieve success and yet are not driven by financial compensation or by what they can get from the world, but they are driven by a spirit of generosity. They take the talents they have and contribute to a greater whole, and serve a higher purpose. Our soldiers then, are the best, in that they represent the sacred legacy of our nation, and carry on in its rich traditions. Our soldiers make the Army something that is awesome "An Army of One" - a genuine "melting pot".)

His thoughts then turned to the next few days and the historic moment the people of Iraq will face as they vote on the referendum, and his continuing concerns for our safety and well being.

Today, I also saw our Alpha Company receive some of their awards. In the coming weeks, this will be a familiar exercise of gratitude from the Army and our leadership for jobs well done. It was sure nice to see so many deserving men and women rewarded for their excellent service. Blessings and peace!

13 OCT 05 09:08 Surprise
"Wonderwall" by Oasis

This morning, I had a lot of trouble getting up. It was a long night, punctuated by several rude explosions in the city. Each time I'd wake up, the old heart was beating like a tom tom. Honestly, perhaps the terrorists need to realize that their gig is up. This little fad of destruction is hanging on with the tenacity of bellbottoms. Anyway, I knew I had to get up and make sure Mike was up too, because this morning was another awards ceremony. I was told yesterday, but I had no idea what it was, but I did know that Mike was getting his Bronze Star Medal. Well to make a short story long, we get there, everyone forms up, I have no idea where I am supposed to go, each soldier was called up individually and there personal citation was read, and suddenly, "Captain Robert Repenning, post!" I had to make it look as if I had been in formation, I posted (at least I think I posted (whatever that means)) and I came to the front, where I saluted LTC Thomas and stood at attention while the citation was read. Today, I received my first Army Achievement Medal for my work at Fort Drum prior to the deployment.

So that was cool, and really a surprise. Each award also comes with the write up and I was impressed reading it. It just described what I did, but after a bit of thought I was impressed that I did all that I did do. That's something I kind of don't deal with enough, ownership of achievements. The Army has taught me, though, that we should be proud of a job well done, and take possession of our successes.

Awards are cool, but the coolest thing is when someone tells you that you did something for them and you didn't realize that you did. A fellow the other day, thanked me after Mass for my work and said, "You got me going back to Mass Chaplain. Thank you." That just about blew me away. Well that's that. Have a good one, till tomorrow.

13 OCT 05 21:51 Here Comes the Rain
"Rain" by The Cult

Perspective. So, I see that my beloved New York is awash in a seemingly endless deluge of precipitation. I must confess my pallor is tinged with a shade of emerald that betrays my envious heart and mind. One of the things I cannot wait to experience is the precious and delightful fall of rain. I might have said it before (but that has not stopped me from saying things again) but I was born on a misty, overcast day, one Wednesday soon to be thirty-three years ago. Perhaps this might explain my affinity for rainy overcast days, or maybe it merely a matter of coincidence. Whatever the case may be, I have so many pleasant memories that accompany the rain. I adore the way rain affects acoustics. I adore the way light is defused on rainy days. I adore the way other visual elements are altered by a rainy day. I can think of a thousand marvelous things that make me happy about rain. One of my favorite things about rainy days is the way that it polishes autumn days. How I wish I could see the blur of golds and fiery oranges of the Hudson foliage burn across my rain-soaked windshield.

Right now, it is still hot here, a sun piercing through a stained overcast veil of oil burnt clouds, and a fetid mélange devoid of flavor or mystique. Pray for peace.

14 OCT 05 13:37 Presence - Philosophical and Theological
"Achilles' Last Stand" by Led Zeppelin

Talked to Mom the other day and she had me in stitches.

Seems that someone had decided that she needed an instruction into which this enlightened person called, "The Theology of Presence." Pardon the sarcasm, but it is rich, in that, whereas some people find it necessary to speak without knowing their audience, and then offer their wisdom, which is founded on bywords and catch phrases then actually lived and experienced. It is rich to imagine a person being so lightweight of intellect to wing that cumbersome concept to one who doesn't need to wear the pretense of spiritual enlightenment but actually practices it. The presumptuousness of the speaker was hardly surprising to me, yet I have encountered many such "authorities" in my walk of life.

Before this term was in vogue, and since it is I might have to adopt something less in vogue, I had come into contact with it in the person of then Msgr. Gerald Walsh. (I've mentioned this term months ago.) In fact, the first time I had heard the expression coined was by him at a dinner table in Washington Heights. He taught many things about presence and the importance of such as a priest. I gleaned from his example and the words he said that it was and should be troublesome if a priest isn't visible each day in the school or for religious education classes.

I agreed with this so much that at St. Mary's I tried to follow this line of thought, though I must confess I did so less than I would have preferred for Religious Ed. Alas, the theory is being present may bring others into contact with Christ.

In a similar manner, I have learned in my own life the value of presence. Here in Iraq, it has been a hallmark of my ministry, but it also reveals the age old lesson learned back home - presence means something.

The unspoken hours I could spend at home with family members was key in realizing that my love for them could be expressed just as loudly in silence than by blabbering a whole lot of words. Pleasant quiet time spent with my grandfather or grandmother or my Mom was absolutely precious to me. In their presence, I learned that being present with someone is a very special thing.

Over the years, I have grown somewhat protective of that, almost to the point of being a curmudgeon (at least in my mind) about who and how I spend my person time. I realize that one cannot always be in the presence of others, but we must be selective and protective and also we must treasure that time. The gift of presence is a gift learned and then shared. In my opinion here, that is one of the greatest gifts I can offer another person. At times, that is all I have. At times "wisdom" departs, the words lose their flavor, the mind tires, but being is the easiest (and for those who like personal recoup time - the hardest) thing to do.

As I discern annoyance at the lack of perception of my Mom's interlocutor, and as I also contemplate my resentments of those who inflict their presence on me (at times) I can not help but see the beauty of that genuine theology or philosophy of presence and the rich gift we have and possess in just being there. Blessings and peace!

15 OCT 05 15:14 Referendum Day
"Desire" by U2

Today is another great day in the history of Iraq. A significant segment of Iraqi people are involved in democratic process and at great risk. They are putting it all on the line. A good question we can ask ourselves today as we consider the news here is "Have I been involved in the democratic process as an American?" There is no worthwhile excuse. Now before the news hands you a load of horse manure by interpreting the news for you as they report it, consider this: What matters is not if they vote for the constitution or against the constitution. The significance rests in whether they voted. That they voted is the revolutionary event. We will then need to scrub the stats with the participation of voters in the U.S. and then assess what has happened. Hopefully, the Iraqi people jump at this chance to vote what they believe, and hopefully this will be followed by many more displays of democracy taking root in the Middle East.

Had to make a comment about King Abdullah of Saudi Arabia prognosticating the eventuality of women driving in Saudi Arabia. Get this; he sees it as possible, sometime in the future, but not in the immediate future as Saudi Arabia is still very conservative. Conservative is not the word...extremist would be more like it. The fragile male ego of the Saudis is astounding. Even more astounding is that Allah would give two hoots whether a woman was driving a car or not. A perfect example of micro-management on a cosmic scale. Puuu-llllll-eeeeee-aaaaaaaa---ssssss---eeeeeee! And we wonder how almost all of the 9/11 terrorists happened to be from Saudi Arabia. Heck, they probably were reeling with the fact that women can walk side by side with men in the civilized world. Note this is not annoyance with religious belief it is annoyance with idiot humans.

"Extremes mean borders beyond which life ends, and a passion for extremism, in art and in politics, is a veiled longing for death"
    - Milan Kundera

15 OCT 05 14:46   The ACLU - Love 'em Or Hate 'em
"Loser" by Beck

Brian sent me an article entitled, "NFL Fan Sues Buccaneers Over Searches at Stadium"

Thanks to Murph for pointing out this idiocy. The lunatic fringe is so out of control with shrill (Gosh I need to find new vocabulary to adequately (and with out boring my readers) describe these hysterical idiots) scenarios that predict our plummeting into a fascist regime. Please note they never worry that we may collapse into a socialist regime. Also note, this leftist cabal love to point towards Nazi Germany but they refuse to examine the manner in which Nazi Germany developed and the subtle assaults to human life that found its climax in the Concentration Camps and the wholesale extermination of those deemed unworthy by that regime. Who were those you may ask? The unborn, the aged, the terminally ill, the mentally handicapped, and the usual suspects (such as Jewish people).

Are we so ignorant of what it means to lose rights that we site being searched going into a football game as a decline in our constitutional rights? This is ludicrous. In our litigation happy society, people will sue for any reason - especially if money is involved. This jerk is the same type to sue if a terrorist were to strike for the NFL not doing enough to protect game goers. There is no satisfying them. But watch the NFL that bastion of moral integrity will waffle and capitulate and apologize for any undue stress caused by this policy, and once again safety is placed second to the right in the United States to be stupid.

And speaking of Nazis - I'd encourage my faithful readers to check out to investigate the connections between Nazi Germany with the PLO, Yassar Arafat, and Muslim extremism. This is chilling stuff that they don't teach you in school.

While on topic I have a strange anti-Semitic story. In Kuwait, on the way home from leave, I did a bit of shopping at the PX. I bought a map of Iraq. One of the graphics showed Iraq in relation to the Middle East. Apparently the cartographers have a vision that denies reality and history. In place of Israel it was written Palestine. No mention of Israel. The lack of logic is that Palestine consisted originally of what is now Israel and what is now Jordan. Jordan however was labeled as Jordan. Strange. Appalling that this kind of subtle prejudice is sold on U.S. Government property.

16 OCT 05 22:30 Give to Live
"Give To Live" by Sammy Hagar

"Give to Caesar what is Caesar's and give to God what is God's." Often enough I have heard the words of the Lord used referring to taxes, which I think was of the least of the Lord's concerns. What matters most to him, love. His words have nothing to do with anything else than his love for us. To understand the response we need to remember the question Jesus asks, "Whose image and inscription is on this coin?" They answer - "Caesar's"

The unspoken question that gives draws the answer to relevancy and also makes for a nice parallel argument should be obvious - Whose image do we bear? God's. Consult Genesis 1:27. And there in lies the message. Give to God what is God's. That is the secret to life. Giving to God our very selves. Uttering the prophetic words, "Here I am. I come to do your will."

17 OCT 05 08:20 Prayer Requests

Another request for my powerful prayer posse out there. One of your number back home, Irene Bailey is going to be operated on today. It's a pretty serious operation, and I just ask that you all say a prayer for her and the success of this operation. She and John, her husband, are real wonderful people. Back at St. Mary's they were really encouraging and supportive. Since my deployment they have had to deal with quite a few health problems. I'd be most appreciative if you would remember Irene and John in your prayers.

17 OCT 05 20:30   The Dust Storm
"The Song Remains The Same" by Led Zeppelin

Another day closer to getting home. That was my though this morning when I walked out my door. Everything was hidden in a fog of dust. Thankfully, though, it was cool. All day, the sun was hidden by the blankness of dust. For the most part it was quiet. Today saw (through the dust) one of the best buds I have over here head out. Justin left this morning and my assumption is once the dust clears his journey's pace will pick up. All I know is that I can see a light at the end of the tunnel and that has been a great aid in keeping me mission focused.

I have seen little in the news about the referendum so my presumption is that it went well. I have read a few scraps of reporting with a mixture of dire predictions and optimism. From this vantage point, I can say that we had a quiet day, and having seen the roads where we are empty of traffic save for police vehicles - it must have been a great day for the Iraqi Police and Army in that they held the country together and they were able to enforce the traffic ban. That is a pretty significant step. Also, it is great that violence was for the most part curbed. This is a major story, in that the Iraqis were able to vote virtually unmolested.

Speaking of perception. I was looking at the collection of photos from various Chaplains in Task Force Liberty today. I am a bit jealous as some of them had quite a bit of interaction with Iraqis. I had virtually nil. Anyway, a lot of these candids show a side of the story about this "war" that is rarely reported or presented: Iraqis interacting with Americans and visibly joy filled. For every disgruntled jerk that is quoted in our newspapers wishing the United States would pack it in and go home, the media never balances it with a decent person saying that they are glad we are here.

(Next paragraph is a bit of a harangue so feel free to ignore it)

The cynics would say that's because there are no people that share this opinion, but I think it is more that the media seeks out proof for their agenda and refuses to present truth. Recall the words of the late Peter Jennings, "My job is to interpret the news." I refuse to bow to the altar of his memory like everyone else, I thought he was a seriously flawed journalist and my reason for that assessment is his own description of his job (in addition he was Canadian). That is the heart of it, and the heart of what is wrong in the media today; not the Canadian bit, but that the media would rather interpret the news, rather than report the news. Some reporters, I think go as far as to re-interpret it. Show and tell the truth is what the media should do. I am still saying it; the media in the United States is more interested in cultivating an image of themselves and their version of truth rather than presenting the facts as they are. Note, I have seen very little press while I have been here, and its not because the military doesn't welcome them. I think there is a general disinterest in the real story. Bye for now. Blessings and peace.

18 OCT 05 20:45 Just A Perfect Day
"Perfect Day" by Lou Reed

What do beautiful blue skies, cool air and a pleasant non-aggressive sun equal? A perfect day in Iraq. Today was one of the most human days weather-wise in months. This would be the kind of great day to go golfing. I did some walking today, but I am not really all there physically. On Saturday, I did a diagnostic Physical Training Test and pulled something in my stomach. I have been sore ever since. I am not sure I mentioned it, but I improved my run again and did 2 miles in 16:01, which is a Rob record. I am hoping to maintain that or improve on it but the legs too have been hurting me since the run. Saturday I also did a huge amount of walking and that may have contributed to my bone on bone pain. All I can say is that I will try my best. No retreat, no surrender. Huah!

19 OCT 05 16:41 Perseverance
"Get Up" by Van Halen

Hola sports fans. Morning came early to FOB Danger with the Physical Training test. In this military exercise (pardon the pun) I learned something quite interesting, once again. Today I learned that heart is about 90% of getting something done. I also learned that my heart could overcome my mind.

So here I am. A confessed non-traditional exerciser. For me, push-ups and sit ups and running is bogus. It means little to me, other than it being a requirement as an Officer. I also, am not the most cooperative person with my body. I eat pretty poorly here in Iraq. I have in the past not taken the best care of myself, and even at one time I was stupid enough to smoke. And so, here I am faced with that PT test and what do you think I was worried about the most? The run. Well I probably should have been more concerned about the sit-ups, which beat me up pretty bad and which spelt a certain need to retake the test in the near future. But I'll get back to that in a second. First event was pushups. I did the minimum on that although I honestly put all my heart into trying to surpass the 36 I did do. As I was hitting pushup number 15 I felt the pull in my abdomen that signaled a forthcoming problem.

Next event was the sit-ups. I had to hit 42. I made it to 34 and that is where yours truly was unable to muster another one courtesy of that ten minute prior pulling feeling in the abdomen. At this point, I am dispirited, because I have now failed the test and no matter what I do for the next event I am a failure. Or am I? Next event is the two mile run. Non-runner Rob (though the progeny of an athletic runner of a father) has been seeing subtle improvement having invested the barest minimum of effort (meaning in a year I have run five times).

But recall it is not all about physical, nor is it a mental

game; this is a matter of the heart. Normally, I would have thrown the run and been weak and given into my failure, but not this time. I sucked up the defeat. I stood up straight. I recalled the efforts Justin put into my performance today. And so I lined up. The start command was given and I shot out with the crowd. True to form, I blocked everyone out, and did my thing. I focused on a strength; I work well alone. I then set a pace for myself, and pushed it. The pains came here and there.

For the past few days my right knee felt like it was going to fall out but I kept pushing. I ran, looking down at the ground immediately in front of me. Several times the thought came to slow down or give in to the pain (bite the bullet, it's only pain, as Fr. Rich would say), I pushed on. Shake the arms a bit, stop running so stiff, no drama Robbie baby, keep on trucking - darn I think as I see the half mile sign - why am I doing this, what the heck does this mean - everything - I keep pushing, I hit the half way mark 7:15 keep pushing, I am running!!!

Holy cow. Best half time yet, maybe I can slow down - Hey, no sense beating yourself up Rob its not going to matter anyway - YES IT IS - do it for someone else - fight it, maybe someone will be inspired seeing you push it - keep going - I can see the finish line ahead 100 yards...75 yards...50 yards - Hey Rob I say to myself, push it out, and I start sprinting - I am going to beat it I am going to win 15:12, 15:13, 15:14, 15:15, 15:16!!!!!!!! I made it. I'm here; I'm passed the finish line. I did it!!! 15:16!!!!

Saturday morning, Justin woke up at 0500 to run with me. He was thrilled to see that his coaching paid off with a solid 16:01. This morning, I beat my goal, and I can't wait to tell him that I crushed that 16:01. This was perseverance. Telling the "I can't" to take a hike. The heart is in charge. I may not have passed the test today, but I can honestly say I did my absolute best. I didn't cave in. I didn't take the easy way. I took the pain and made something of it.

I am better now. I have faced it, and it has nothing on me. The thought that kept going through my head was this run wouldn't kill me so why should I be afraid. The heart has a lot of power, and it can overcome so much, if only we are willing to exercise it, or in the case of fear and discouragement if we are willing to exorcise it. Blessings and peace.

19 OCT 05 14:17 Sad news from NY

I got word today that my classmate, Fr. James P. has died. I'd ask that you pray for the repose of his soul, and also for his parents, friends and parishioners in their time of mourning.

20 OCT 05 20:14 A note from the management
"Enjoy The Silence" by Depeche Mode

Well sports fans, the operation tempo is increasing at such a rate that I may not be able to publish an entry each day for the next week or so. Please know all is well, and I am doing well, too. Blessings and peace.

21 OCT 05 16:19 Ramadan from a distance, and a word on the referendum

Well it's Friday again. Last Friday, Justin and I walked over to dinner greeted by a serenade of gunfire erupting in the city. Friday is known as the 'Eed. The basic idea of the 'Eed observance is:

The Friday congregational prayer is compulsory for every Muslim who is required to observe the prayers and has no reasonable excuses to abstain. It falls on Friday of every week and is especially important because:

(1) it is the occasion earmarked by God for the Muslims to express their collective devotion;

(2) it is an appointment to review our spiritual accounts of the   week gone by and get ready for the following week just as people do in any other business or enterprise;

(3) it is a convention for the Muslims to reassure themselves and confirm their religious bonds and social solidarity on moral and spiritual foundations; and (4) it shows how the Muslims give preference to the call of God over and above any other concern in their lives.

Most of my readers are not Muslim but these same principles could very well have a correspondence in a Christian's Sunday observance with some obvious differences.

Now, I am not clear as to the why, but during Ramadan I have observed a more boisterous use of celebratory gunfire then during the rest of the week (save for Wednesdays, again I do not know the whys to this observation either). So, what we have been hearing is gunfire - guns pointed to the sky (which is a rather unsafe practice, but certainly safer than aiming at someone, and firing them. The closest approximation I could make is like how back home we use fireworks to celebrate a holiday. Now this is not a typical practice throughout the year, but is done during Ramadan and after certain celebrations. So, at weddings in this part of the world it is quite common to fire off a banana clip from your Kalashnikov AK-47, up in the air, to celebrate the health of the newly wed couple. A little different, but never dull.

So, in about an hour, as the sun sets here in Tikrit and the call of prayer is issued forth from the minarets, a steady volley of gunfire will erupt throughout the city signaling the end of the day's fast and this will carry on for a good half hour and from our perspective sounds quite similar to the sound of fireworks.

And there you have it. Now, just a comment on the Referendum. The votes are still being tallied. Projected results show that the Constitution most probably passed, however, there have been rumors of possible voting irregularities and also allegations of fraud. These issues are being investigated by the Iraqi authorities and hopefully will be resolved. God willing, any fraudulence will be rectified and the perpetrators brought to justice. It would be ashamed to see such good work be invalidated by the machinations of a few.

Regardless of these issues the fact remains that the Iraqi people demonstrated the ability to keep the peace on a day with substantial risk, hopefully those who expect perfection in a short amount of time will not ignore this indicator. Also, hopefully it is appreciated that the political process is necessary for the Iraqi people to have not only peace but also their basic needs met. In all, this vote was a major step in the self-determination of the Iraqi people. This was a sign to the world of their eagerness to take hold of their own future. Let us pray that they may achieve this and the security they deserve so much.

21 OCT 05 16:04 Cooler
"Get Right With Me" by Depeche Mode

The sky is impossibly blue. The air is crisp and cool. In fact, the change of climate is drastic enough that I am now chilled. It was literally an overnight thing. The vibe of autumn's arrival has reached even here. No leave changes or nice smell of burning leaves nor the warm cozy feeling that comes with seeing the blazing waves of fallen golds and oranges, but that should be in my sensory perception in a matter of...

As I said, last week, things are picking up at a furious pace.

Read: not combatively, just a lot of scheduling things and deadlines and stuff to get done. So, the entries may get a bit sporadic; know, though, that all is well.

One of the big agenda items is getting the last load of boxes sent home of personal stuff. Books, cds and DVDs and the collection of assorted articles. Which reminds me, I have to go get some boxes. Bye for now.

24 OCT 05 12:26 Last Dispatch
"Last Dance" by Donna Summer

So here it is Monday. The availability of computers is very limited. I turned in mine last evening. The office is stripped bare. The room is pretty much stripped, too. There are some boxes that I have to mail out and then it is just biding time until we head out. As I said previously, I will be taking notes and fill in the missing dates if it is warranted.

Yesterday was my last Mass here in Iraq. As I am apt to get a little sentimental I kept the comments short at the end, but I did have trouble landing the plane at the homily. It has been a good run. It was great seeing the regulars there. We really made a spiritual journey while we were here. It is something I want to bring home with me, that kind of thinking. We are all on a journey, priest and people - together. It's not an "us vs. them" dichotomy, it's a "we're all in this together" perspective that this experience has taught me to value and cherish.

As I looked out at the Tigris, after Mass, it hit me - this is it. The moment I have waited nine months for is rapidly approaching. Soon I will be back in my beloved New York. Praise the Lord. So, thank you for the prayers and the kindness and I look forward to alerting you all directly that I am back and safe. Keep up the prayers; I will still need them and my soldiers, as well.

Though, we are soon going to be home, the re-integration process will take a considerable amount of time. The experts say about six to nine months depending how long we have been away. I plan to follow the advice of the experts and the advice I have parlayed to my soldiers and take it slow as I ease back into the world. Blessings and peace, bye for now, from Tikrit, Iraq,
Chappy

26 OCT 05 Another UMT Report

The Unit Ministry Team (UMT) provided comprehensive religious support throughout all phases of Operation Iraqi Freedom III from pre-deployment activities to reunion/reintegration. The UMT worked to meet the emotional, spiritual, and relational preparation needs of soldiers and their family members.

Battalion coverage:

a. While in pre-deployment, the UMT developed a comprehensive Religious Support plan for Battalion coverage.

b. UMT provided briefs on Suicide Prevention, Cultural and Religious Awareness in Iraq, Understanding Islam, Stress Awareness and Reduction, and Drug and Alcohol Abuse and Awareness.

c. Maintained visibility on the religious support of Battalion assets throughout the Area of Operation. This entailed communication with the chaplains at other FOBs and was supplemented by visitations.

d. The UMT performed a Ministry of Presence to over 450 soldiers, in addition to soldiers who were OPCONed to the battalion and spread throughout the AO on 13 FOBs.

e. Advised Command on matters of moral and morale in the Battalion.

f. Conducted over 450 counseling sessions with soldiers on an as needed basis dealing with a wide range of morale and spiritual issues.

g. Provided Reunion and Reintegration briefs to 100% of unit soldiers assigned to FOB DANGER prior to R&R. Provided briefs for 100% of the Battalion soldiers for Redeployment.

Division coverage:

a. Conducted Bible Studies on a weekly basis during pre-deployment.

b. Represented the Battalion at weekly Chaplain meetings on FOB, and at MSC Chaplain Conferences.

c. Performed additional Chaplain duties for other units in the absence their Chaplains. This included delivering Red Cross messages, counseling and advising Command as needed.

d. Conducted and/or participated in one prayer breakfast each month of deployment beginning with a joint breakfast with 1ID. Each breakfast had a different emphasis depending on the closest holiday.

e. Created and presented a Memorial Day Video honoring the soldiers who had died during the tenure of Task Force Liberty. Although developed for a prayer breakfast, this video was later expanded and used at a 42 ID alumni banquet in Indianapolis, Indiana.

f. Was available for counseling and ministry of presence after traumatic incidents.

Denominational coverage:

a. As a Catholic chaplain, the UMT had further responsibility at the DIV level for Roman Catholic coverage throughout the Area of Operation (AO). Coverage consisted of providing Catholic Coverage every 14 days to soldiers on six FOBs and 2 other FOBs on an "as needed" basis.

b. Contributed in the creation of two FRAGOs dealing with Catholic Coverage. UMT also participated in the drafting meetings for those FRAGOs

c. Arranged for all of the transportation in support of the Catholic Coverage mission on assigned FOBs. This responsibility is normally the responsibility of the receiving unit. This was done with limited resources.

d. Prepared for and conducted over 250 Catholic Masses. Additionally, this entailed preparation of and delivery of a homily (sermon) for each service conducted.

e. Offered sacraments to practicing Catholics and administered sacraments as needed including the sacrament of Reconciliation (Confession) Catholic throughout the deployment and the AO.

Through the above, the UMT continually improved the morale of the soldiers in their care. Much of the above was only accomplished by movement between FOBs by more than 100 Combat Patrols and 25 flights through dangerous territory and difficult situations.

28 OCT 05 06:55 Sunrise
"Homeward Bound" by Simon and Garfunkle

Woke early to the sound of the call to prayer. Took a hot shower. Got dressed. Brought my bags over to get picked

up. Walked over to where there are still a few computers working and connected. Watched the sunrise.
No I will go get Mike for breakfast. And then read until our flight arrives. And then the homeward journey begins.

Blessings and peace!

28 OCT 05 21:44 Combat Action Badge

This afternoon there was another award ceremony. SSG Swain and I were awarded our Combat Action Badge stemming from the incident back in July when our convoy was hit by an IED. A few Chaplains have already received them, but it is still a bit of a novelty as the award was authorized this past June. I teased SSG Swain that he may be the first Chaplain Assistant to get one, actually doing his job, since other teams seemed to not have followed the doctrine all the time and sometimes would travel separately. Ain't no way I'd travel without my bodyguard. I have to say this was a big honor, but not one that we came to Iraq hoping to get.

So what is the Combat Action Badge? Here is a little of the official military-ese to explain what and who qualifies:

Specific eligibility requirements.

(a) May be awarded to any Soldier.

(b) Soldier must be performing assigned duties in an area where hostile fire pay or imminent danger pay is authorized.

(c) Soldier must be personally present and actively engaging or being engaged by the enemy, and performing satisfactorily in accordance with the prescribed rules of engagement.

(d) Soldier must not be assigned/attached to a unit that would qualify the Soldier for the CIB/CMB. (For example, an 11B assigned to Corps staff is eligible for award of the CAB. However, an 11B assigned to an infantry battalion is not eligible for award of the CAB.)

29 OCT 05 22:35 Army Commendation Medal

I hope you know that I am not bragging, but I have had several surprises in recent weeks. Yesterday, prior to leaving FOB Danger I was awarded the Army Commendation Medal. Needless to say, I was a little moved especially as that was the punctuation to what has been an amazing deployment. Some of you may know that for whatever reason I was adamant in not going to my college graduation. At the time, a clearly defined personal belief existed and which motivated this boycott, however, as time has progressed I have forgotten what that principle was. Anyways, this has been a bit like college - a huge learning experience. But whereas back in the day I didn't own the experience and appreciate it (in the moment) now I have learned to do just that. God is so good. The deployment has been excellent, and many prayers were answered. Here I am in Kuwait so grateful for the joy to be going home within a few days, and for having been kept safe while in a pretty dangerous place.

Blessings and peace!

29 OCT 05 22:48 Kuwait
"I'm So Excited" by The Pointer Sisters

Several hours ago, I left Iraq! Hallelujah! Am now in Kuwait, and doing just that (recall the K is silent in Army speak). Am reading Albert Speer's memoirs and eagerly awaiting my return to CONUS. Blessings and peace!

11

HOME SWEET HOME

1 NOV 05 14:41   Home Sweet Home '05
"Home Sweet Home" by Mötley Crüe

Well, around 10 a.m., arrived back in the United States of America. Landed at an undisclosed location, and is whiling away an undisclosed amount of time in the demobilization process. At that point, plans include slowly entering back into the life of normalcy as a civilian. In around three months I will enter back into the parish life at a location to be determined (not being coy, this is one of those things to be settled during this re-integration period, and to dispel any rumors there is not a plan to return to my previous assignment (just fyi)). There is a one monthish guest appearance of yours truly in the works, assisting a friend while his pastor is away. For now, with as little pressure as possible am just quietly re-entering the non-combat world and after this temporary military gig will re-acquaint myself with my family, mis gatos, mis amigos and some much needed solitude (sans stress and pressure).

Faithful readers, friends, fellow journeymen (persons) thank you for making this day what it is - a reality. I am home alive and well and praise the Lord. Some days I had a lot of doubts whether it would all work out, and many days I was scared senseless. It is such a relief to know that faith can conquer fear. Thank you all for your kind support. Please know that all is well and that I am taking this, like my advice to my soldiers, I am taking this very slowly. If you don't hear from me right away just know there is no ill will just a soldier who has to learn how to be a civilian again. Blessings and peace! Robert

Appendix A: Poem fragment

This was my attempt at examining the birth of language. The idea was to write a history of writing from the first expression to the birth of the typed page. This was written in one, uninterrupted session in a Humvee, caught in the grips of a Gabriel García Márquez inspired writing frenzy.

The manila enveloped snugly the hard cover novel
and that form it drives him wild with excitement
the anticipation of thrills that await
pleasures promised
and for a moment one could say that something
vaguely resembling guilt penetrates his conscience
as his fingers fondle the tight package
eager but delicate to feel his fingertips
touch the sensuous skin beneath
and finally like a child at Christmas
he enthusiastically rips off the garments of paper
and address ink embroidery
to see the virgin cover below
miraculously embossed in rich colours and an irresistible gloss
the author's name prominent below a title telegraphing
unimaginable joys soon to be fulfilled
as the cover is opened invisible spirits soar and spiral out and
above and about and then down grabbing hold of the reader
and vibrations are conceived as the fingers push the first pages
aside
exposing that first magical page
that begins the sacred spell
and the heartbeat accelerates
as the words steal into his eager reader eyes.

The wind roared across the expanse of the snow heavy tundra
daylight was a white blur
that drew no distinction between ground and sky
the crunch of footsteps
swallowed by the hushed whirling vacuum
and then they arrived
a volley of crushing roars
through the empty space

thunderous thunks that shook the world
and all around a blizzard of characters converged
misshapen twists and curves and emphatic edges
collecting together in small groups
[pieced together and knit to each other and words are born
a little something for everything
and sometimes more for less more or less]
and the words conspired and colluded and formed up
lines in the cold harsh barren wasteland
and sentences were molded in arbitrary precision
and the sentences joined together into paragraphs
and vast armies grew filled with images and ideas
bringing the blank desolation to life
and thoughts became matter became thoughts
and the pounding flurry of letters continued
and the emptiness melted away
{transition}
but the thunder continued
as the image dissolves into darkness
fade out/fade in

(the jungle vibed poem is next)
[] = added while typing this out in other words improvisation
that may need to be improved upon.
fade into darkness]

High above spinning in uncontrolled excess the
Star points like fire flies swarm and stab the tar pitch sky

Drum beat thunder pounds into the reptile night and
Dense pulsing nocturnes hollow through the sweaty jungle
A surrounding plethora of organic primal arias
Clarion calls and responses, threats and chatter
Telegraph the invisible jeopardy that lies beneath the flora skin

And deep within, buried in the obscurity of the untamed valley
A fire crackles glowering orange against and beneath the
towering siege of
Shadows and leaves and branches and vines and an impenetrable
darkness
The drumbeat tempo boils to a frenetic pace
Song and rhythm smother the night songs

And dancers strangle the bouncing flames
Tightening their writhing grip clad in leaves and blood, skins and mud,
Feathers and antiquity caked upon their bodies

And the moans and groans of the epoch punch out over the din
It is the anguished destiny of a species the demand to break
The bounds that keep this race tied to the earth
The rage of confinement forms into syllables
Lips open and tongues unite in a solidarity of intent
A pronouncement is uttered and mimicked and
A consensus is tacitly reached by imitation and repetition
And the voices grow louder in unison and
They celebrate their newfound freedom
Until night surrenders to the encroaching dawn
And the sun steals over a distant ridge like a thief

Appendix B: Travel

Here is a compilation of my travels in the AO. This is a fairly accurate record, however there are a couple of uncertain trips, which are indicated by an asterisk. The dates and mode of transport are accurate, the destination is uncertain.

12 JAN 05 - Left Ft. Drum for Kuwait
13 JAN 05 - Arrive in Kuwait.
29 JAN 05 - Leave Kuwait. Arrive FOB Speicher (Tikrit).
30 JAN 05 - Leave FOB Speicher, arrive FOB Danger (Tikrit).
05 FEB 05 - 1st Combat Logistics Patrol (CLP) to FOB Speicher.
07 FEB 05 - CLP to FOB Danger.
19 FEB 05 - CLP to FOB Speicher.
20 FEB 05 - CLP to FOB Danger.
22 FEB 05 - CLP to FOB Summerall (Bayji). CLP to FOB Danger.
01 MAR 05 - CLP to Midland. CLP to FOB Danger.
05 MAR 05 - 1st Blackhawk flight (BH) to FOB Speicher.
06 MAR 05 - CLP to FOB Danger.
12 MAR 05 - CLP to FOB.* CLP to FOB.*
16 MAR 05 - CLP to FOB Speicher. CLP to FOB Danger.
18 MAR 05 - BH to FOB Summerall. BH to FOB Danger.
19 MAR 05 - CLP to FOB Speicher.
20 MAR 05 - CLP to FOB Danger.
27 MAR 05 - CLP to FOB Dagger (Tikrit). CLP to FOB Danger.
28 MAR 05 - CLP to FOB Wilson (Ad Dawr). CLP to FOB Danger.
29 MAR 05 - CLP to FOB Warrior (Kirkuk). CLP to. CLP to FOB Warrior.
30 MAR 05 - CLP to.* CLP to FOB Danger.
01 APR 05 - BH to FOB Summerall. BH to FOB Danger.
02 APR 05 - CLP to FOB Speicher.
03 APR 05 - CLP to FOB Dagger. CLP to FOB Danger.
05 APR 05 - CLP to Midland. CLP to FOB Danger.

09 APR 05 - CLP to FOB Summerall. CLP to FOB Danger.

16 APR 05 - CLP to FOB Speicher.

17 APR 05 - CLP to FOB Dagger. CLP to FOB Danger.

19 APR 05 - CLP to FOB Warrior.

20 APR 05 - CLP to FOB Kalsu (As Sulaymaniyah).
CLP to FOB Warrior.

21 APR 05 - CLP to FOB Bernstein (Tuz).
CLP to FOB Danger.

23 APR 05 - CLP to FOB Summerall. CLP to FOB Danger.

25 APR 05 - BH to FOB Wilson. BH to FOB Danger.

30 APR 05 - CLP to FOB Speicher.

01 MAY 05 - CLP to FOB Dagger. CLP to FOB Danger.

09 MAY 05 - BH to FOB Wilson. BH to FOB Danger.

12 MAY 05 - CLP to Midland. CLP to FOB Danger.

14 MAY 05 - BH to FOB Speicher. BH to FOB Danger.

21 MAY 05 - BH to FOB Summerall. BH to FOB Danger.

23 MAY 05 - BH to FOB Wilson. BH to FOB Danger.

25 MAY 05 - CLP to FOB Warrior.
CLP to BNOC (Kirkuk).
CLP to FOB Warrior.

26 MAY 05 - CLP to FOB Gaines Mills (Yachi).
CLP to FOB McHenry (Al-Hawijah).
CLP to FOB Danger.

28 MAY 05 - BH to FOB Speicher.

29 MAY 05 - CLP to FOB Danger.

02 JUN 05 - BH to FOB Caldwell (Kirkush).

03 JUN 05 - BH to FOB Danger.

06 JUN 05 - CLP to FOB Wilson. CLP to FOB Danger.

07 JUN 05 - CLP to Midland. CLP to FOB Danger.

10 JUN 05 - CLP to FOB Dagger. CLP to FOB Danger.

11 JUN 05 - CLP to FOB Speicher.

12 JUN 05 - CLP to FOB Danger.

13 JUN 05 - CLP to FOB Bernstein. CLP to FOB Danger.

18 JUN 05 - CLP to FOB Summerall.
CLP to FOB Speicher.
CLP to FOB Danger (night mission).

20 JUN 05 - CLP to FOB Wilson. BH to FOB Danger.

24 JUN 05 - CLP to FOB Dagger. CLP to FOB Danger.

25 JUN 05 - CLP to FOB Speicher.

26 JUN 05 - CLP to FOB Danger.

04 JUL 05 - CLP to FOB Wilson. CLP to FOB Danger.

06 JUL 05 - BH to FOB Caldwell. BH to FOB Danger.

08 JUL 05 - CLP to FOB Dagger. CLP to FOB Danger.

09 JUL 05 - CLP to FOB Speicher.

10 JUL 05 - CLP to FOB Danger.

14 JUL 05 - CLP to FOB Speicher. CLP to FOB Danger.

16 JUL 05 - CLP to FOB Summerall. CLP to FOB Danger.

18 JUL 05 - CLP to FOB Wilson. CLP to FOB Danger.

20 JUL 05 - CLP to FOB Warrior. CLP to FOB Danger.

23 JUN 05 - BH to FOB Speicher.

24 JUN 05 - BH to FOB Danger.

28 JUL 05 - CLP to FOB Wilson. CLP to FOB Danger.

30 JUL 05 - CLP to FOB Summerall. CLP to FOB Danger.

02 AUG 05 - BH to FOB Caldwell.

03 AUG 05 - BH to FOB Danger.

04 AUG 05 - BH to FOB Speicher (Leave begins).

28 AUG 05 - CLP to FOB Danger (Leave ends).

31 AUG 05 - BH to FOB Caldwell.

01 SEP 05 - BH to FOB Danger.

03 SEP 05 - BH to FOB Speicher.

04 SEP 05 - CLP to FOB Danger.

10 SEP 05 - BH to FOB Summerall.

11 SEP 05 - BH to FOB Danger.

14 SEP 05 - BH to FOB Caldwell.

16 SEP 05 - BH to FOB Danger.

17 SEP 05 - BH to FOB Speicher.

18 SEP 05 - BH to FOB Danger.

21 SEP 05 - BH to FOB.*

22 SEP 05 - BH to FOB Danger.

24 SEP 05 - BH to FOB Summerall. BH to FOB Danger.

30 SEP 05 - BH to FOB Bernstein. BH to FOB Danger.

01 OCT 05 - CLP to FOB Speicher.

03 OCT 05 - BH to FOB Warrior.

06 OCT 05 - BH to FOB Danger.

08 OCT 05 - BH to FOB Summerall. BH to FOB Danger.

10 OCT 05 - CLP to FOB Wilson. CLP to FOB Danger.

29 OCT 05 - Depart from FOB Danger to FOB Speicher.
Depart from FOB Speicher to Kuwait.

31 OCT 05 - Depart from Kuwait to New York.
01 NOV 05 - Arrive back at Fort Drum, NY.

Appendix C: Thoughts of the Day

Here are some of the thoughts of the day that I prepared for daily briefings. I am grateful to my Chaplain Assistant, SSG Jerry Swain for his research and his input truly making this a team effort. All attempts were made to ensure the accuracy of the quotes and their proper attribution.

28 FEB 05

According to William Menninger, there are six qualities that are the key to success: sincerity, personal integrity, humility, courtesy, wisdom, and charity. Let us take advantage of this opportunity to be successful in our work. If we do it right we will not only get the job done here, successfully but we will be able to bring home with us a mature character which will enable us to get the job done there too, successfully.

1 MAR 05

Believe it or not, we are lifesavers. We are in the life saving business. The work we do, and the effort we put in it ensures that lives are saved. Each time a soldier is able to transmit information they place their lives in our hands. They trust us, or if they don't realize who is doing it, they trust the system to work. In essence, they have faith in our work. May we always accept that responsibility gratefully and may we work, to the best of our ability to reflect that reality.

Invocation for Combat Patch Ceremony 1 MAR 05:

Would you join me as we pray:

Almighty God,

We thank you for your abiding presence in our lives. We stand before you this day, and ask your blessings upon us. As we receive our patch today, we continue a legacy established many years ago, when the 42nd Infantry Division first took up arms in defense of our nation and the principles of justice and freedom. We now embrace the proud yet humble symbol of this division. May all those who look upon it see a symbol of hope and all who look upon us see in our mission the fact that hope endures forever. Guide us in our duties, keep us faithful to our mission, and encourage us always to persevere. Help us be the soldiers you desire and bear witness always to the goodness of freedom in all that we do and say and may our service here in Iraq, bear fruit in eternal life for we ask this through your holy name, AMEN!

2 MAR 05

"The only thing you should do behind a person's back is pat it."
     -Unknown

Teamwork is not achieved tearing another person down. Teamwork is achieved when we encourage another person. Let us not take delight in individual defeats but let us spur each other on to victory by our encouragement.

3 MAR 05

We can learn from mistakes. Mistakes have the potential of teaching us valuable lessons. Don't get me wrong, we shouldn't strive to err. But when we do make mistakes we need to own up to them, and seek to repair them. The energy spent denying a mistake or making excuses for a mistake could be used for much more productive causes.

4 MAR 05

"Be of good cheer."
         -John 16:33

5 MAR 05

"Kind words do not cost much. Yet they accomplish much."
         -Blaise Paschal

7 MAR 05

Don't be fooled. Everyday may seem like Monday, but there is only one actual Monday in the week. And here it is again, another opportunity to begin anew. Take advantage of Mondays. The beginning of a new week presents a new challenge to us, a challenge to change for the better, to improve. Consider the words of Lord Alfred Tennyson, "That which we are, we are, and if we are ever to be any better, now is the time to begin." May we constantly strive to become better individually, so that we can become better as a collectively. God bless us, and the all the work we do.

8 MAR 05

"Don't worry about anything. Worrying never solved anything. All it does is distort the mind."
         - Milton Garland (at 103)

9 MAR 05

"What we ever hope to do with ease; we must learn first to do with diligence."
         -Samuel Johnson

10 MAR 05

"Try not. Do. "
    -Yoda

13 MAR 05

"The more elaborate our means of communication, the less we communicate."
    - Joseph Priestley

Sadly, this is an observation that still is true today. Our mission needs to be to make this observation false. Communicating is the best way to resolve conflict, problems, and misunderstandings. But we also need to ensure we are speaking to the people we need to speak with and not around them.

If we are not communicating in times of calm, what will happen in times of crisis? A miracle? Or a tragedy?

15 MAR 05

"Solidarity is not a matter of sentiment but a fact, cold and impassive as the granite foundations of a skyscraper. If the basic elements, identity of interest, clarity of vision, honest of intent, and oneness of purpose, or any of these is lacking, all sentimental pleas for solidarity, and all other efforts to achieve it will be barren of results."
    - Eugene V. Debs

16 MAR 05

If you were in a firefight, would you be there for your fellow soldier? God willing the answer is yes. That same level of responsibility and trust is not confined to the dramatic moments of military service. This responsibility and trust must be translated to all aspects of our military life. If we are willing to not care for our soldier in an office, or a workstation, or in the simple moments of service, it does not bode well to how we would act in times of jeopardy.

"Whoever can be trusted with very little can be trusted with much, whoever is dishonest with very little will also be dishonest with much."
    – Luke 16:10

17 MAR 05

Let us always remain vigilant not only for the threats that we face but for the miracles that surround us. Today let us give thanks for the safety of our injured and let us not grow complacent in praying for our safety daily.

18 MAR 05

Guess what today is? FRIDAY!!!

Let's be a little wild and crazy and turn to that great font of wisdom, Steven Wright for our thoughts of the day:

"A cop stopped me for speeding. He said, "Why were you going so fast?" I said, "See this thing my foot is on? It's called an accelerator. When you push down on it, it sends more gas to the engine. The whole car just takes right off. And see this thing? This steers it."

and

I was going 70 miles an hour and got stopped by a cop who said, "Do you know the speed limit is fifty miles per hour?" "Yes, officer, but I wasn't going to be out that long."

The moral of the stories: Keep smiling.

19 MAR 05

Happy Saint Joseph's Day! Saint Joseph teaches us a valuable lesson in the New Testament. If you peruse the New Testament you will not find him quoted even once, yet he is always described as a just and upright man.

We may not always be remembered by what we say, but undoubtedly we will be remembered by what we do. And no, he is not the inventor of the aspirin.

22 MAR 05

It is part of human nature to judge. But do we do so fairly? A wise man once said, "When we judge others, we judge ourselves." In all honesty, does it help being judgmental or to criticize unfairly, are problems solved or only exacerbated? Perhaps we need to be solution oriented, and start by being fair to others and also to ourselves.

23 MAR 05

Attitude is everything. What is our attitude? Perhaps, John Lennon had the right idea, "I tell them 'There are no problems, only solutions.'"

24 MAR 05

The phrase, "United we stand, divided we fall," is often repeated but it is also very true.

A team is made up of individuals. If we are a team, then what have we done for the team? That means we need to regard each person we work with as a member of our team. If we look around this room, can we honestly say we have respected each person as a member of our team? Let's make this a priority, to respect each other, to support each other and to assist each other. Is it easy? Not necessarily, teamwork by definition means we need to work at it. When we work at building unity the team becomes stronger. A strong team means many things but most importantly a strong team will save lives.

25 MAR 05

What have we done to erase disunity today? What have we done to establish unity amongst ourselves today? It is essential that we each day work to build unity and promote it and allow it to flourish in our ranks. It is a lived decision made daily. Each day offers us a multitude of opportunities to be uniters or dividers. What will we choose to be today?

26 MAR 05

Two for one day:

"I want to share something with you – the three sentences that will get you through life. Number one, 'cover for me.' Number two, 'oh, good idea boss.' Number three, 'it was like that when I got here.'"
- H. Simpson

"Never put socks in the toaster."
- Eddie Izzard

For me, one of the most difficult things to do, at times, is to place myself in a place of vulnerability where I am looking directly into a person's eyes and being honest and clearly and calmly telling them how I feel about something. It takes trust to live that way. A lot of trust. It means risking being yelled at, laughed at, or being blown off. But the benefits outweigh the risks. What I gain each time I do this is a better sense of confidence in myself, personal growth, and the ability to forge bonds of camaraderie and trust.

As professionals we all need to do this. Look around the room, if there is someone we cannot do this with, then we must challenge ourselves to take the risk. For a team to function it needs openness. We need to know what we are doing. Imagine the Chicago Bulls ever winning (I'm talking back in their glory days with my favorite coach this side of Pat Reilly, Phil Jackson, along with Michael Jordan, Scottie Pippen, and the prince of rebounds and body piercing – Dennis Rodman) had they not known each other and really communicated with each other. They became the best by being open with each other. Then without the walls between them, they made magic happen (especially that money year 1996).

29 MAR 05

Don't be afraid to ask for help, and certainly don't be afraid to help.

30 MAR 05

We must always do our job with care. We need to care. We need to care about each other. We need to care about the quality of our work.

We can never forget that all of this translates into how much we care about our soldiers, both inside the wire and outside the wire.

31 MAR 05

Complacency is as dangerous an enemy as the insurgency. Maybe it is even more dangerous.

1 APRIL 05

Balance separates the wise from the foolish.

Are you making sure there is balance in your life? Work is good. But when you aren't working are you meeting your needs? Are you attending to your spiritual needs? Are you eating your meals? Are you getting enough rest? Are you exercising? Are you socializing? Have you called home lately? Are you maintaining your relationships with those back home?

If the answer is no to any of these questions you more than likely are not working as well as you could be working. In order to do this day in and day out for extended periods of time we need balance. That is the sensible approach to being successful. Let's support each other in our efforts.

5 APR 05

Do you know where the flowers are here? Have you smelt the flowers?

16 MAY 05

"Take the world as it is, not as it ought to be."
- German Proverb

17 MAY 05

A quiet few days, can lull us into a false sense of security. Vigilance and preparation are our tools for success.

"Don't think there are no crocodiles because the water is calm."
      - Malayan Proverb

19 MAY 05

Question: How often do you receive a call saying, "Thank you, for a job well done"?

Answer: How many people are making calls each day? Their trust is the surest sign of their gratitude. Keep up the great work! (By the way, if you want to look wise, answer questions with questions.)

24 MAY 05

"Being busy does not always mean real work. The object of all work is production or accomplishment and to either of these ends there must be forethought, system, planning, intelligence, as well as perspiration. Seeming to do is not doing."
      - Thomas Alva Edison

I got this prayer is from a little book.

Almighty Father,
Watch over my family,
Encourage them while we are separated during this deployment
And give them health of mind and body
That they may serve you with perfect love
Until the day when we,

With all who have served you,
Will rejoice in your presence forever.
*   - Amen*

27 MAY 05

"Sometimes your joy is the source of your smile, but sometimes your smile can be the source of your joy."
        - Thich Nhat Hanh

31 MAY 05

This is an Iraqi poem:

Condition

When the city becomes a vast prison
You ought to be
        Cautious like a sharpened sword
        Simple like a grain of wheat
        And patient like a camel.

    - Mahdi Muhammed Ali, 1979.

1 JUN 05

Let us share a smile today with someone. Search the person out, the soldier who needs to be assured, consoled, or encouraged. They may need just that, something so simple as a smile.

2 JUN 05

"Whenever work is done, victory is attained."
        - Ralph Waldo Emerson

6 JUN 05

Let us give thanks to the soldiers who so valiantly gave their lives on this day in 1944. Their service will never be forgotten.

"But we in it shall be remember'd
We few, we happy few, we band of brothers;
For he to-day that sheds his blood with me
Shall be my brother; be he never so vile,
This day shall gentle his condition."
        - Shakespeare, Henry V

7 JUN 05

"Tell me and I forget, show me and I remember, involve me and I understand."
        - Unknown

8 JUN 05

"Real integrity is doing the right thing, knowing that nobody's going to know whether you did it or not."
        - Oprah Winfrey

9 JUN 05

"It is better to offer no excuse, than a bad one."
        - George Washington

10 JUN 05

"We are what we repeatedly do."
        - Homer

11 JUN 05

"It is cruel to discover one's mediocrity only when it is too late."
> - W. Somerset Maugham

13 JUN 05

"A person's true wealth is the good he or she does in the world."
> - Mohammed

14 JUN 05

"We should seize every opportunity to give encouragement. Encouragement is oxygen to the soul."
> -Anonymous

15 JUN 05

"Reflect on your present blessings, of which every [person] has many, not on your past misfortunes, of which all [persons] have some."
> -   Charles Dickens

16 JUN 05

"If the going is real easy, beware, you may be headed downhill."
> -Unknown

17 JUN 05

"What you see and hear depends a great deal on where you are standing; it also depends on what sort of person you are."
- C.S. Lewis

18 JUN 05

"To reach a port we must sail, sometimes with the wind and sometimes against it. But we must not drift or lie at anchor."
- Oliver Wendell Holmes

19 JUN 05

"Smile: If you can't lift the corners let the middle sag."
- Unknown

20 JUN 05

"A coward gets scared and quits. A hero gets scared, but still goes on."
- Unknown

21 JUN 05

"The real [person] is one who always finds excuses for others, but never excuses [themselves]."
- Henry Ward Beecher

22 JUN 05

"There are two types of people – those who come into a room and say, 'Well, here I am!' and those who come in and say, 'Ah, there you are.'"
      - Frederick L. Collins

23 JUN 05

"The willow knows what the storm does not that the power to endure harm outlives the power to inflict it."
      - Blood of the Martyr

24 JUN 05

"All good work is done the way ants do things: little by little."
      - Lafcadio Hearn

25 JUN 05

" Hard work pays off in the future, Laziness pays off now."
      - Steven Wright

27 JUN 05

" Be true to your work, your word, and your friend."
      - Henry David Thoreau

28 JUN 05

"Let your work brag for you."
      - Unknown

29 JUN 05

"Hold yourself to a higher standard than anybody expects of you. Never excuse yourself."
  - Henry Ward Beecher

30 JUN 05

"It is the character of the brave and resolute man not to be ruffled by adversity and not to desert his post."
  - Cicero

1 JUL 05

"Courage is not the absence of fear, but rather the judgment that something else is more important than fear."
  - Ambrose Redmoon

2 JUL 05

"If you fall down seven times, get up eight."
  - Chinese Proverb

04 JUL 05

There is a wonderful mythical law of nature that the three things we crave most in life – happiness, freedom, and peace of mind – are always attained by giving them to someone else.
  - Peyton Conway March

05 JUL 05

"I am convinced that life is 10% what happens to me and 90% how I react to it. And so it is with you... we are in charge of our attitudes."
- Charles Swindoll

06 JUL 05

"I swore never to be silent whenever human beings endure suffering and humiliation. We must always take sides. Neutrality helps the oppressor, never the victim. Silence encourages the tormentor, never the tormented."
- Elie Wiesel

07 JUL 05

"A rock pile ceases to be a rock pile the moment a single man contemplates it, bearing within him the image of a cathedral."
- Antoine de Saint-Exupery

08 JUL 05

"In order to be walked on, you have to be lying down."
- Brian Weir

09 JUL 05

Picture this: Half time pep talk from the coach. "There were some out there that thought we would not even make it this far. We are proving them wrong. I'm proud of ya!! You are doing great, but this thing is not over. We have to keep our heads in the game. Get out there and show them what you're made of. GO TEAM (HOOAAH)."

14 JUL 05

"What you really value is what you miss not what you have."
          - Jorge Luis Borges

15 JUL 05

"A person should never be ashamed to own that they were wrong, which is but saying…that they are wiser today than they were yesterday."
          - Alexander Pope

16 JUL 05

"Real valor consists not in being insensible to danger; but in being prompt to confront and disarm it."
          - Sir Walter Scott

20 JUL 05

"If the going is real easy, beware, you may be headed down hill."
          -Unknown

21 JUL 05

"A smooth sea never made a skillful mariner."
          -Unknown

28 JUL 05

"The secret of joy in work is contained in one word – excellence. To know how to do something well is to enjoy it."
                    -Pearl Buck

29 JUL 05

"You can only protect your liberties in this world by protecting the other person's freedom. You can only be free if I am free."
                    - Clarence Darrow

1 AUG 05

"Much of the stress that people feel doesn't come from having too much to do, it comes from not finishing what they started."
                    - David Allen

4 AUG 05

"I think the person who has had more experience of hardships can stand more firmly in the face of problems than the person who has never experienced suffering. From this angle then, some suffering can be a good lesson for life."
                    - The Dalai Lama

CFLCC ROE CARD

1. On order, enemy military and paramilitary forces are declared hostile and may be attacked subject to the following instructions:

    a. Positive Identification (PID) is required prior to engagement. PID is a reasonable certainty that the proposed target is a legitimate military target. If no PID, contact your next higher commander for decision.

    b. Do not engage anyone who has surrendered or is out of battle due to sickness or wounds.

    c. Do not target or strike any of the following except in self-defense to protect yourself, your unit, friendly forces, and designated persons or property under your control:

        * Civilians
        * Hospitals, mosques, churches, shrines, schools, museums, national monuments, and any other historical and cultural sites

    d. Do not fire into civilian populated areas or buildings unless the enemy is using them for military purposes or if necessary for your self-defense. Minimize collateral damage.

    e. Do not target enemy Infrastructure (public works, commercial communication facilities, dams), Lines of Communication (roads, highways, tunnels, bridges, railways) and Economic Objects (commercial storage facilities, pipelines) unless necessary for self-defense or if ordered by your commander. If you must fire on these objects to engage a hostile force, disable and disrupt but avoid destruction of these objects, if possible.

2. The use of force, including deadly force, is authorized to protect the following:

        * Yourself, your unit, and friendly forces
        * Enemy Prisoners of War

* Civilians from crimes that are likely to cause death or serious bodily harm, such as murder or rape
* Designated civilians and/or property, such as personnel of the Red Cross/Crescent, UN, and US/UN supported organizations.

3. Treat all civilians and their property with respect and dignity. Do not seize civilian property, including vehicles, unless you have the permission of a company level commander and you give a receipt to the property's owner.

4. Detain civilians if they interfere with mission accomplishment or if required for self-defense.

5. CENTCOM General Order No. 1A remains in effect. Looting and the taking of war trophies are prohibited.

REMEMBER

* Attack enemy forces and military targets.
* Spare civilians and civilian property, if possible.
* Conduct yourself with dignity and honor.
* Comply with the Law of War. If you see a violation, report it.

These ROE will remain in effect until your commander orders you to transition to post-hostilities ROE.

AS OF 311330Z JAN 03

Appendix E – Press Clippings

Priest heading for Iraq duty

By Randi Weiner
THE JOURNAL NEWS
(Original publication: September 24, 2004)
Reprinted with permission from The Journal News.

When he's in his Army fatigues, only the small cross on his lapel and the fact that he doesn't carry a weapon indicate that the Rev. Robert Repenning is a military chaplain. You can't tell from a distance that Repenning is a Catholic priest, which can be an advantage in Iraq, where Repenning is heading within the next few days. Threats to noncombatants are common, and the low profile may save his life. But while Repenning is apprehensive about his first deployment to a war zone, his sense of mission is clear.

"The principle of being a chaplain is ensuring the religious needs of the soldiers are met," the 31-year-old New City native said. "I'm also a reminder of the obligation to keep the standards of law. I become a conscience to my commander and my soldiers. I'm living out my role as a religious leader by being there and being present with the soldiers."

Repenning grew up hearing the war stories of his grandfather, Marion J. Wyatt, who served in World War II, Korea and Vietnam. The two had a close relationship - Repenning called his grandfather "one of the great presences in my life" - and that bond included numerous trips to West Point. He remembers watching the cadets marching and the thrill their drills gave him.

"When I was in high school, I thought about entering West Point, but I realized God was calling me to a different life. But I always kept in mind that, if God wants this in my life, it will happen," Repenning said.

Encouraged by a military chaplain who stopped by to talk with young seminarians about enlisting, Repenning joined the New York Army Reserves in 1998 and took some core classes to become a chaplain. Before the course was over, he was assigned to St. Mary's in Wappingers Falls. At St. Mary's, he made the acquaintance of an Episcopal priest who convinced him to switch his service to the National Guard if he wanted to serve the active military.

Repenning served as a chaplain candidate with the 156th Field Artillery while leading St. Mary's from 2001 until May, when he was called by the state office of military chaplains and told he was being deployed.

Although Pope John Paul II has publicly spoken against the U.S. presence in Iraq, Repenning received approval from the Archdiocese of New York to serve.

Repenning knows he's heading to the northeast quadrant of Iraq, but not Baghdad; he'll be one of two Catholic chaplains on the division level. In addition to his ministry work, he'll be the liaison with chaplains of other faiths and will function as the local expert on religious affairs. He's expected to pinpoint mosques, holy sites, churches and synagogues and make sure everyone understands the local religious customs.

"For instance, you never walk in front of someone facing Mecca and praying. The bottom of the (shoe) sole can never face anyone, that's an insult. There are certain hand gestures," he said. "It's really interesting."

Repenning is getting trained to operate a Humvee, because he will drive one in Iraq. In peacetime, he would have a driver. In wartime, the chaplain drives while his assistant rides point.

Both of his parents are worried, Repenning said. His mother, Christel Repenning, lives in New City. His father, the Rev. David Repenning, a Methodist minister, lives in Milford, Pa. But Repenning said he was honor-bound to serve in Iraq with those who are now there. "They don't have the freedom to say, 'I don't want to go to this particular war.' They are honoring their commitment," he said. "I'm to see that their relationship with God and their family is kept strong.

Repenning said he could bemoan his deployment, but that would belittle other soldiers' sacrifices. "I think of all the people over there who are like me," he said, "regular Americans who for one reason or another joined the military and are now in harm's way. "Whether I agree with the war or not isn't important," he continued. "There are people over there, and however I can bring care and comfort to them and make their lives easier, that's what I'm there for. "My job is to lift them up, to be a presence of reassurance and joy. It's what I did at St. Mary's. I'm just taking the show on the road."

Local priest to serve as part of the National Guard

By Michelle J. Lee
POUGHKEEPSIE JOURNAL
(Original publication:)
Reprinted by permission from the Poughkeepsie (NY) Journal.

WAPPINGERS FALLS -- For three years, the Rev. Robert Repenning attended to the spiritual needs of followers at St. Mary's Church. During the school year, Repenning taught adult and children religion classes and read stories at St. Mary's Catholic School. Every March, Repenning dressed up as St. Patrick in the village's annual parade. He would bless motorcycles for The Ground Hog, a nearby coffee house and motorcycle company. Lately, he is answering a different calling by serving in the New York Army National Guard.

Repenning, 31, is enrolled in the U.S. Army Chaplain Center and School in Fort Jackson, South Carolina. He will graduate in September, after which he expects orders for deployment, which could send him to Iraq anytime between November and February with the Army National Guard 42nd Infantry Division. "It's a baptism by fire, going there. This will be my first major assignment," Repenning said about his first call to duty.

As part of his job, Repenning said he would act as a confidant to the soldiers, in addition to holding services. Raised in New City, Rockland County, Repenning said he made the choice to become a priest early on while watching the monsignor and priests in his local parish, St. Augustine's Church.

But it was the childhood trips to the U.S. Military Academy at West Point with his grandfather, Marion Wyatt, a World War II and Vietnam War veteran, that solidified his decision to sign up for the Army. In 1998, Repenning signed up for the U.S. Army Reserves while attending St. Joseph's Seminary in Yonkers, and later transferred to the Army National Guard.

Repenning was appointed to serve St. Mary's Church after he was ordained, in June 2001, and quickly adopted the village as his new home. "I absolutely loved it. It was a friendly atmosphere and a welcoming people," he said. Mary Ellen LaRose, principal of St. Mary's Catholic School, said Repenning would visit the classrooms every day. He taught students the different aspects of his job and the church, such as the symbolism behind his vestments and Mass. "He gave something to the school while he was here that was unique and no one else could have given us," LaRose said.

Mike Kocan, owner of a local business, called Repenning "a permanent fixture" and said Repenning frequently walked up and down the streets with a cup of coffee in his hand.

"Everybody's kind of sad he had to go," Kocan said. "I was in this line - - the Marine Corps. I understand why he would do something like this, to be a part of helping to defend this country."

Monsignor Francis Bellew said Repenning's personality would benefit the Army. "He's not shy. He's very outgoing, loves to talk, loves people," he said. "He'll do well."

Repenning said he plans to stay in touch with village residents via e-mail and will set up a Web site to record his experiences.

"I want to give a nod of thanks and gratitude. They helped me learn about myself and my gifts. ... I learned to put joy in what I do and I hope to bring that same joy to the soldiers in Iraq," he said.

NEIGHBOR

ROBERT REPENNING
Age: 31.
Home: New City, Rockland County.
Hobbies: Writing, music, motorcycling, movies and cats.
Web site: www.livejournal.com/~raqnrevrep

Appendix F - Task Force Liberty Honor Roll.

Honoring those who have died is one of the chief responsibilities of an Army Chaplain. Therefore, I can think of no more fitting way to conclude this volume than by recounting the names of those of Task Force Liberty, who died during our tenure in Iraq. The motto of the 42nd I.D. is "Never Forget!" The names, lives and service of these men and women must never be forgotten. Please, remember their families and offer a prayer for them.

Task Force Liberty Honor Roll
Operation Iraqi Freedom III

SSG Todd Olson, Tikrit, 27 DEC 04
SFC Mark Warren, Kirkuk, 31 JAN 05
SSG Steven Bayow, Bayji, 04 FEB 05
SGT Daniel Torres, Bayji, 04 FEB 05
PFC David Brangman, Samarra, 13 FEB 05
SPC Dakotah Gooding, Balad, 13 FEB 05
SGT Rene Knox, Balad, 13 FEB 05
SGT Chad Lake, Balad, 13 FEB 05
SFC David Salie, Baqubah, 14 FEB 05
SPC Justin Carter, Samarra, 16 FEB 05
SPC Jacob Palmatier, Muqdadiyah, 24 FEB 05
SPC Adriana Salem, Tikrit, 04 MAR 05
SGT Paul Thomason III, Kirkuk, 20 MAR 05
SFC Robbie D. McNary, Hawijah, 31 MAR 05
SFC Stephen C. Kennedy, Balad Ruz, 04 APR 05
SSG Kevin D. Davis, Balad, 08 APR 05
SPC Aleina Ramirez-Gonzalez, Tikrit, 15 APR 05
PFC Steven F. Sirko, Muqdadiyah, 17 APR 05
SPC David Rice, Balad, 26 APR 05
SGT Timothy Kiser, Kirkuk, 28 APR 05
SGT Gary Eckert, Balad, 08 MAY 05
SPC Steven R. Givens, Balad, 08 MAY 05
SGT Andrew Jodon, Samarra, 12 MAY 05
PFC Travis Anderson, Bayji, 13 MAY 05
PV2 Wesley Riggs, Tikrit, 17 MAY 05

SGT Carl Morgain, Balad, 22 MAY 05
SGT John Ogburn, Kirkuk, 22 MAY 05
SPC Alfred Siler, Tuz, 25 MAY 05
CW3 Matthew Lourey, Buhriz, 27 MAY 05
CW2 Joshua Scott, Buhriz, 27 MAY 05
SGT Manny Hornedo, Tikrit, 28 MAY 05
SFC Virgil Case, Kirkuk, 01 JUN 05
SPC Carrie L. French, Kirkuk, 05 JUN 05
CPL Randall Preusse, U.S., 05 JUN 05
1LT Louis E. Allen, Tikrit, 08 JUN 05
CPT Philip T. Esposito, Tikrit, 08 JUN 05
1LT Michael Fasnacht, Tikrit, 08 JUN 05
SSG Mark O. Edwards, Tuz, 09 JUN 05
1LT Noah Harris, Baqubah, 18 JUN 05
CPL William A. Long, Baqubah, 18 JUN 05
SPC Charles Kaufman, Baghdad, 26 JUN 05
SPC Robert Hall, Ad Dujayl, 28 JUN 05
SPC Christopher W. Dickison, Baqubah, 05 JUL 05
SFC Ronald T. Wood, Kirkuk, 16 JUL 05
SSG Frank Tiai, Baghdad, 17 JUL 05
SSG Christopher J. Taylor, Balad, 24 JUL 05
SPC Adam Harting, Samarra, 25 JUL 05
SPC Edward L. Meyers, Samarra, 27 JUL 05
PFC Jason D. Scheuerman, Muqdadiyah, 30 JUL 05
SGT Brahim J. Jeffcoat, Balad, 06 AUG 05
SPC Kurt E. Krout, Balad, 06 AUG 05
SPC John Kulick, Bayji, 09 AUG 05
PFC Nathaniel E. Detample, Bayji, 09 AUG 05
SPC Gennaro Pellegrini, Jr., Bayji, 09 AUG 05
SGT Francis J. Straub, Bayji, 09 AUG 05
1LT David L. Giaimo, Tikrit, 12 AUG 05
SSG Asbury F. Hawn II, Tuz, 14 AUG 05
SPC Gary L. Reese, Jr., Tuz, 14 AUG 05
SGT Shannon D. Taylor, Tuz, 14 AUG 05
SGT Nathan K. Bouchard, Samarra, 18 AUG 05
SSG Jeremy W. Doyle, Samarra, 18 AUG 05
SPC Ray M. Fuhrmann II, Samarra, 18 AUG 05
PFC Timothy J. Seamans, Samarra, 18 AUG 05
SGT Joseph D. Hunt, Samarra, 22 AUG 05

SSG Victoir P. Lieurance, Samarra, 22 AUG 05
SSG Jeffrey Rayner, U.S., 30 AUG 05
SGT Monta S. Ruth, Samarra, 31 AUG 05
SGT Matthew C. Bohling, Ramadi, 05 SEP 05
SGT Travis R. Neil, U.S. 09 SEP 05
SGT Dale M. Hardiman, U.S., 10 SEP 05
SPC Kurtis D.K. Arcala, Tikrit, 11 SEP 05
SPC Donnie S. Hamilton II, U.S., 19 SEP 05
SPC Joshua J. Kynoch, Bayji, 01 OCT 05
SSG Jens E. Schelbert, Ar Ramadi, 01 OCT 05
SPC Robert W. Tucker, Ad Dujayl, 13 OCT 13
SPC Kendall K. Frederick, Tikrit, 19 OCT 05
SSG George T. Alexander, U.S., 22 OCT 05
SGT Michael T. Robertson, U.S., 25 OCT 05
SPC Kenny D. Rojas, Bayji, 29 OCT 05

"Rainbow! Never Forget!

Whereof what's past is prologue, what to come,
In yours and my discharge.

WILLIAM SHAKESPEARE,
The Tempest, <u>act II, scene i</u>, lines 253–5